Go-To-Market Strategist

Everything You Need to Reach Product-Market Fit

MAJA VOJE

GO-TO-MARKET STRATEGIST

Everything You Need to Reach Product-Market Fit

Copyright © 2023 by Maja Voje

All rights reserved

This book is protected by copyright. No part of this book may be reproduced or transmitted in any form or by any means, electronic or mechanical, including photocopying, recording, or any information storage and retrieval system, without prior written permission from the author or the publisher, except for brief quotations embodied in critical articles and reviews.

The scanning, uploading, and distribution of this book via the internet or any other means without the permission of the author is illegal and punishable by law. Please purchase only authorized electronic editions, and do not participate in or encourage electronic piracy of copyrighted materials. Your support of the author's rights is appreciated.

Inquiries: grow@majavoje.com

Written by: Maja Voje

Editor: Laura Kluz
Design: Domen Klinc
Illustrations: Domen Klinc, Zala Reberc
Print layout: Aero Print d.o.o.

Disclaimer:

The information provided in this book is intended for general guidance and is not intended **to constitute financial or legal advice. The author is not responsible for any decisions made** by readers based on the information in this book, nor for any costs, expenses, or outcomes resulting from such decisions.

TABLE OF CONTENTS

Go-to-Market Strategy (GTM) 1
   Think and Act like Special Ops 8
      6 Principles of Special Ops 9
   Goals and Objectives are Your GTM Compass 15
      Find your North Star 17
      Monitor and Manage with OKRs 21
   The Good and the Bad GTM Strategy 26

Market 37
   Plan to Win 43
      Generate Good Intelligence 46
         Market Research: Know the Terrain 49
         Who Else is Playing to Win? 54
      Playing On Your Strengths and The Enemy's Weaknesses 60
      Innovate to Build a Competitive Edge 64
   Choosing the Market Segment 69
      From Overwhelmed to Hyper-Focused 73

Early Customer Profile 81
   Make ECP Decisions Confidently 85
      Map your ECP Assumptions 90
      ECP Validation Toolkit 93
         Experimentation: Learning by Doing 102
   Early Customer Profile (ECP) 106
      Early Customer Profile vs. Ideal Customer Profile 107
      Multiple-Player ECPs 110
      ECP Framework 112

Product 119
   Why Should Customers Care? 123
      Communicating and Testing your UVP 129
   Deliver Value 132
      Minimum Viable Product (MVP) 135
      Metrics and Analytics 140
      Choose the Right Metrics to Track 141
      Connecting Your Business Model to Your Data 144
   Aiming for Product-Market Fit (PMF) 150
      Measuring PMF 151

    Life After PMF 157
Pricing 163
    What Influences Pricing? 169
        Added Value: What Are They Paying For?................................169
        WTP: How Much Will They Pay? 172
        Competition and Alternatives: How Much Are They Currently Paying? 175
        What Do You Want and Need Them to Pay? 177
    Pricing Strategies 180
        Optimize for Adoption First 181
        Optimize for Profit First 183
    Pricing Models: How to Charge for Your Product? 185
        Packaging: How to Package Your Product? 188
    Behavior and Psychological Aspects of Pricing 190
    Pricing Work is Never Really Finished...196
    How to Run Monetization Experiments 198
Positioning 205
    Positioning: Be in Control of the Narrative 210
        Positioning Process 213
        Positioning Steps 214
        Positioning Special Ops..221
    Messaging: How Do You Tell It? 225
        Messaging Tailored to Your Target Audience 231
        Messaging in Action 234
    Branding: Express Yourself..237
        GTM Friendly Branding Process 238
        Branding Special Ops...244
            Rebranding 245
            Brand Architecture..246
Growth 253
    Traction Channels 257
    Generating or Capturing Demand? 262
    7 Growth Channels for GTM Companies 265
        Inbound: Give Before You Ask 268
        Paid Digital: Pay to Play 270
        Outbound: Proactively Reaching Out 275
        Account-Based Marketing (ABM): Market of One 279
        Community: Build a Tribe of Raving Fans................................283

Partners: Together, We Stand Stronger	288
Product-Led Growth (PLG)	293
Growth Loops	298
5 Archetypes of Growth Loops	301

GTM System 305

Prepare the Grounds	308
Your GTM Execution Backpack: Pack What You Can Carry	310
Timeline: When Will You Make it or Break it?	311
Your Special Ops Team	312
Organization: The Way You Work	314
Tools: A Lean GTM Tech Stack	317
Budget	320
GTM Experimentation Process	323
Experimentation Loop	324
Experimentation in Practice	327
Your Turn to Go-to-Market	331

Glossary 336
Acknowledgments 343

CHAPTER 1
Go-to-Market Strategy (GTM)

"A go-to-market strategy is the difference between a hope and a plan."

J.P. Eggers,
Associate Professor at NYU Stern School of Business

Unknown unknowns are the biggest hurdle to navigate in business.

You will face an uphill battle when introducing a new product or service. It's both exciting and stressful. You have so many important decisions to make that have the gravity to lift or sink the business.

Sadly, over 95% of businesses fail in their first three years of existence[1]. Competition is rising because of rapid technology innovation and lower barriers to entering new markets. Customers are now more demanding than ever and well-informed about alternatives.

Securing your chances to win has become mission-critical.

A **go-to-market strategy (GTM)** refers to a company's plan and approach to bring its product or service to market and reach its target customers. It outlines choices, steps, and activities that need to be taken to introduce and sell a product or service effectively. A well-designed GTM strategy leads the company **to cross "the chasm"** and reach the Growth phase.[2]

When you launch a new innovation to the market, it's important to consider that:

- **2.5% of the market are Innovators**. They are tech enthusiasts genuinely interested in trying new technologies and ideas. While not that difficult to convince to take a new solution for a spin, there are too few of these users to build a sustainable business around. On top of that, they're not necessarily interested in your long-term success because there might be another shiny solution around the corner.

- **13.5% of the market are Early Adopters**. They are willing to embrace new ideas and innovations but need solid proof they deliver value. As customers, they are eager to build cases and co-create solutions that will make them look good for being innovative. They also consider your best interests, so they will make a couple of compromises.

---

[1] Christensen, C.M. (2011). The Innovator's Dilemma: The Revolutionary Book That Will Change the Way You Do Business. HarperBusiness.
[2] Moore, A. G. (2014). Crossing the Chasm, 3rd Edition: Marketing and Selling Disruptive Products to Mainstream Customers. Collins Business Essentials.

- **34% of the market are Pragmatists, Early Majority buyers.** They will not compromise and do not take much risk. They want solid evidence that the solution works before ever considering it.

- **34% are Conservatives, Late Majority.** They do not like change and would rather compromise on the old way of solving their challenges and buying from the market leader. In their world, consistency outweighs the benefits.

- **16% of the market are Laggards**. They are skeptics in innovation who will only adopt if there is no other way but to do it.

In GTM, it is essential to win **Innovators** and **Early Adopters** to create a critical mass of adoption so you can start to win an early majority in the next evolution of your business – the Growth stage in which you scale upon proven **Product-Market Fit** (PMF). In simple words, PMF refers to the fact that there is sufficient proof the market wants your product.

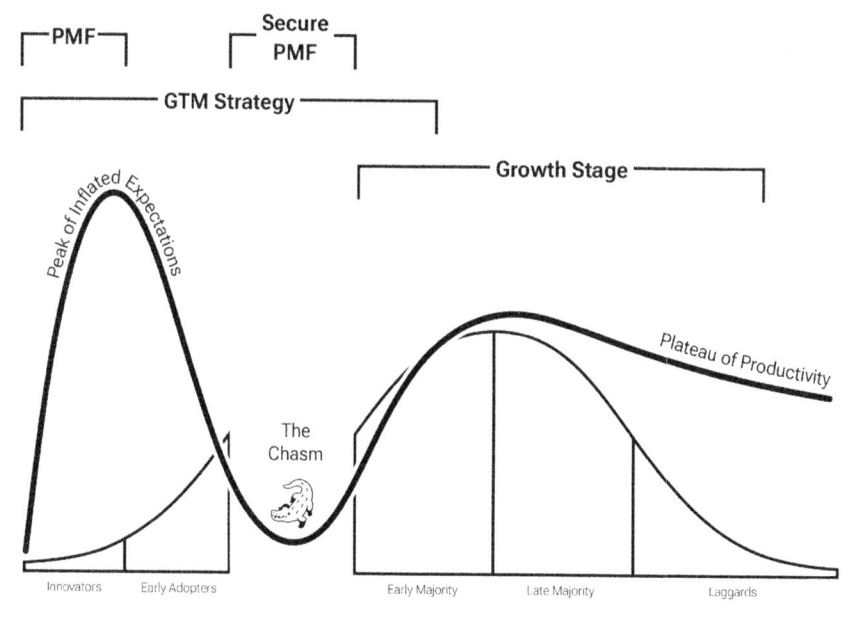

Adjusted from Crossing the Chasm: Marketing and Selling Disruptive Products to Mainstream Customers by Geoffrey A Moore

You need PMF to grow. Period.

But there is no clear direction on how to get there. Most advice out there is given from Silicon Valley well-funded startups. What they did 10 years ago will unlikely help you win in business. The world needs a better and more holistic GTM playbook. And that is the mission of this book.

This is an email from a founder who is preparing to go-to-market. His name is Jasper, and he is a technical founder who is trying to launch an onboarding SaaS. He works with other developers and designers and thinks they must prepare for a launch *after* the product is finished.

To: **Maja Voje** (grow@majavoje.com)

Subject: **Question about our project**

Dear Maja!

How are you? The workshop was great last week. I have some follow-up questions, and hopefully, you can help me out here.

My team and I are working on this cool software that will help people make no-code onboarding to their product and improve activation globally.

Here are my questions:

- We have a limited runway, and investors said that we need some traction before they would consider us seriously. Any thoughts on which channels we should use?
- I have no idea how to price the software. What do you think about $10 or $50 subscriptions per month? That is approximately where the competition seems to be, and we will go in a bit cheaper to win more customers.
- Oh, btw, do you think we should give a higher price to big companies, or does it not matter at this stage? We believe that our solution could help everybody and we don't want to lose some interest by going too narrow.

Thanks so much for all of the insights and knowledge that you share with us. Have a great day & let's talk soon!

Jasper

Of course, confidence, purpose, and commitment are needed to win, but after seeing hundreds of strategists from startups to Fortune 500 companies begin their GTM journey, here are the mission-critical decisions to make that separate winning teams from those who tried very hard, but could not make it:

1. **Market: Carefully choose the terrain on which you want to win.** Want it or not, the market and timing matter. Carefully choosing the GTM terrain and being present with the right offer at the right time will be your key to success. When ChatGPT proved an instant success and many people were wondering how this tool could help their business, clever entrepreneurs started mass-selling prompts to better leverage the use of ChatGPT.

2. **Early Customers: Niche down and serve the selected audience first.** While "there can be only one" seems scary initially, the intercept of an excellent GTM strategy happens when you have the solution that perfectly captures the target market's needs. Niching down and solving the target audience's specific pain points and problems makes a huge difference. The narrower you can be, the more you can tailor your offer to them and charge a premium for it.

3. **Product: Craft a product, an offer, and a business model that the target market cannot refuse.** You test and iterate on it to prove that you have product-market fit (PMF) and a sustainable business model that will fuel future growth.

4. **Pricing: Capture this value with value-based pricing or a proxy of it.** Imagine price as a currency of value exchange. Most GTM companies can range 20 to 30% above or below the existing competition's pricing. Pricing should support a healthy business model in the short to mid-term period.

5. **Positioning: Learn how to communicate your solution for users to understand and fall in love with it.** Users are mainly interested in what is in it for them. They are unlikely to purchase a solution if they don't understand its value or how it can solve their problem. Remember, users will shop around. So, you need to create differentiated positioning to communicate a competitive edge.

6. **Growth: Select channels that are actually relevant to your target audience and add fuel to it with Growth Loops.** Some marketing channels play well with your business model. Others, not so much. When building

a growth engine for your product, the winning combination consists of customer preferences, competition, and strong points in execution. But there are so many channels to choose from. Focusing on 1 to 3 and testing them before moving on to the next shiny opportunity is a wise decision to create a critical mass of users and build a predictable funnel for your business.

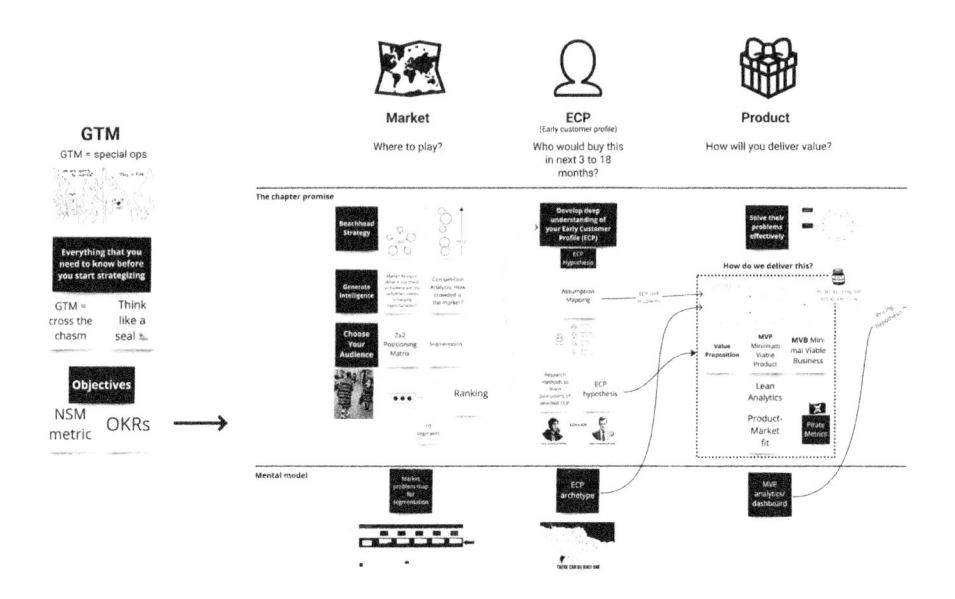

Overall, these are the main decisions you need to make to craft a holistic GTM plan:

- What market opportunity should you pursue?
- Who is your target audience?
- What is your value proposition and product?
- How should you price the product?
- How do you present it in a unique and compelling manner?
- Which channels work best for your product, and how do you scale them?

The hard part is putting it into practice.

You can refine your strategy to drive better results for your business, thanks to testing your GTM assumptions against market realities. After each iteration, you'll get a bit smarter, better, and closer to your goal of crossing the chasm. In the meantime, it's best if you develop a resilient mindset.

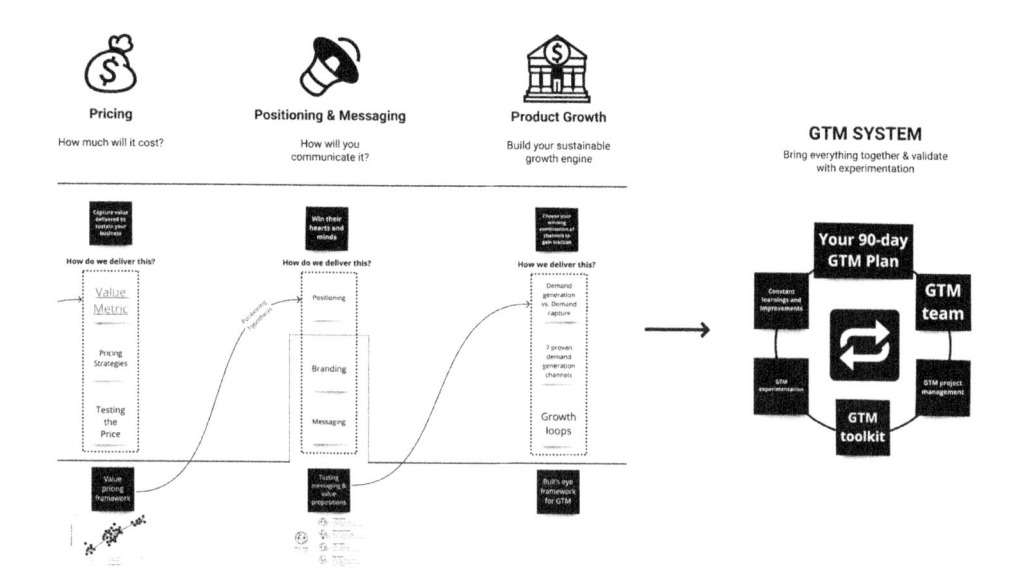

GTM STRATEGIST

Think and Act like Special Ops

"Success consists of going from failure to failure without loss of enthusiasm."

*Sir Winston Churchill,
UK prime minister and world-celebrated leader*

GTM is unlike anything you will ever do in your career. There are more unknowns than you know.

You are under pressure to make decisions that can have huge consequences and usually operate with scarce resources on a lifeline of 3 to 18 months. The stakes are high. You'll feel stressed, and what makes it worse is that you are usually competing against a much stronger competitor that's defending its existing market share.

It's often a David vs. Goliath situation. And you need a clever plan of how you can win if the stakes are against you. In business lingo, we call that a strategy.

As a GTM strategist, you are under pressure to deliver under extreme circumstances and don't have the luxury of spending six months defining purpose and drawing pyramids of a company's values with a senior consultant. You need to secure results – fast. Sometimes, against all odds.

More than 95% of innovation-to-market efforts traditionally fail. Those 5% who succeed change the business arena and users' lives. Your mission is to secure healthy traction for the innovation you go-to-market with and build a sustainable business out of it.

Winning strategies are always made to play on your strong points – and your competitor's weak ones.

You are David. You can be swift, clever, subversive, hungry to win, and more agile. But the odds are against you at first glance. The opposition is Goliath. They can fiercely respond if they see you coming. Still, since they are a larger force and move like tanks, it usually takes them longer to detect what you are doing, take you seriously, and prepare the defense. Goliaths have the size, scope, resources, strength, and longevity. Davids have drive and speed.

After studying strategy literature, I came to the conclusion there are more similarities between GTM and military strategy than a usual business strategy and GTM. That makes so much sense since all strategy is rooted in military strategy.

I discovered a subfield of military literature that tremendously resembles GTM: **special operations (special ops)**. The area studies the extreme cases of how much smaller and weaker forces beat an enemy. Special ops are extremely organized, well-trained, committed, laser-focused on the mission, and extremely swift. Just like you should be in GTM.

6 Principles of Special Ops

"A simple plan, carefully concealed, repeatedly rehearsed and executed with surprise, speed, and purpose."
Willian H. McRaven, United States Navy four-star admiral

The **principles of special ops' planning, preparations, and execution** jointly empower a smaller force to win[3]. Some of them are extreme, but they apply to GTM businesses. To prove this, I will briefly explain and provide an example of how my team applied them to our GTM strategy for this book.

---

3 McRaven, W.H. (1996). Spec Ops: Case Studies in Special Operations Warfare: Theory and Practice. Presidio Press.

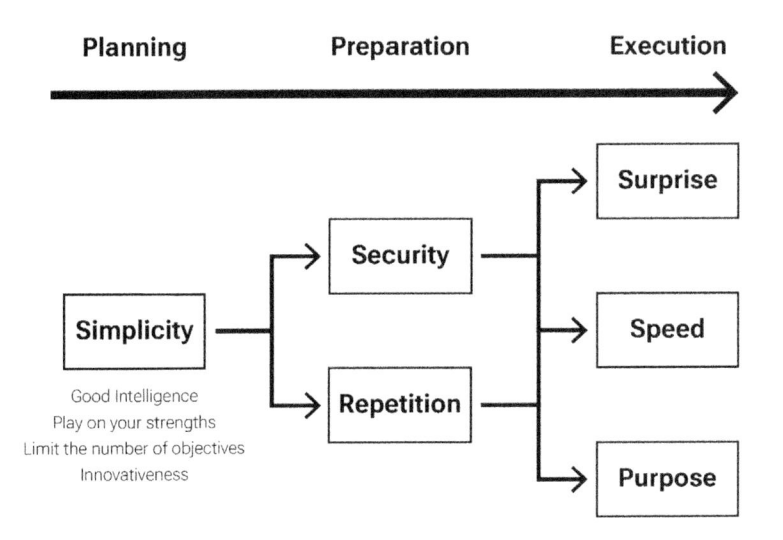

```
Planning          Preparation          Execution
───────────────────────────────────────────────▶
```

Diagram:
- Simplicity → Security → Surprise
- Simplicity → Repetition → Speed
- Repetition → Purpose
- Security → (Surprise)

Under Simplicity:
- Good Intelligence
- Play on your strengths
- Limit the number of objectives
- Innovativeness

A simple plan, carefully concealed, repeatedly rehearsed, and executed with surprise, speed, and purpose.

Adjusted from Spec Ops: Case Studies in Special Operations by William H. McRaven

Stage 1: Planning

Simplicity is the most crucial and difficult principle to follow in planning. A lot of thinking and research can go into crafting a plan, but a simple plan has to check these boxes:

- **Limit the number of objectives.** A special ops unit cannot rescue a hostage from a guarded house, burn a bridge, and generate critical intelligence on a single mission. Having too many objectives at once scatters your already limited resources and decreases your chances of success. In GTM, you focus all your efforts on what is mission-critical and say "no" more often than "yes".

For this book, it is mission-critical to sell 2,000 copies by the end of the year. We will achieve that by generating a waitlist of 5,000 with content marketing – LinkedIn, conferences, podcasts, etc. Later on, we will launch the book on Amazon and run ads.

- **Good intelligence.** This refers to developing a plan by reducing the unknown factors and the number of variables that must be considered. If a special ops team is planning how to rescue a hostage from a guarded house, they observe when the guards are changing shifts. They will study any unguarded or weak entry points before deciding on the optimal time and place. When it comes to GTM, many strategists vaguely pay attention to competitors and instead rely on their own subversiveness and uniqueness. But ignoring the competition is short-sided and dangerous. If nothing else, users will be comparing your solution with existing alternatives. Months of research without execution is not a luxury, given the short timeline of a GTM. Yet, it is reasonable to expect a strategist to make decisions based on empirical evidence to confidently make choices.

On the journey to launch this book, I had accountability partnerships with five multiple time authors, I observed and analyzed 10 different launches, I hired an editor with two business bestsellers in her portfolio (kudos, Laura Kluz), and I launched three digital products to learn the specifics of selling lower-priced products.

- **Play on your strengths.** After generating good intelligence as a pillar of understanding competitors' weaknesses and seeking windows of opportunities, consider your strengths. What are the resources, skills, proprietary knowledge, or information you can use to build a winning GTM strategy? What could give you a competitive edge?

After pitching the book concept to more than 50 people, I understand the strengths of our GTM approach are that it's developed for bootstrapped companies, makes sense even to very technical people, and is die-hard pragmatic. As I "compete" with other experts, my strengths are building communities, doing partnerships, and conceptualizing really quickly. My weaknesses are that English is not my native language, and I do not have a publisher because I want to maintain control of sales and marketing.

- **Innovation.** This contributes to simplicity by helping to avoid or eliminate obstacles that would otherwise compromise surprise or complicate rapid execution. Innovation can come from new technology or innovative, unconventional tactics.

This book offers made-for-you Miro templates and Google Docs that are ready to plug and play in your GTM strategy. I aim to make an interactive playbook for your GTM, not a "read it and forget it" dust-magnet. I also interviewed world-class experts for the book, who shared their hands-on knowledge and will hopefully support the promotion of this book and remain open for joint consulting opportunities.

Stage 2: Preparation

- **Security** is done to prevent the opposite party from gaining an advantage through the foreknowledge of your plan. It is unwise to think that "the opposite party," such as your competitor, is unprepared. Same as you, they are playing to win. Tight security prevents them from gaining an unexpected advantage and prepares them well for your actions. In special ops, it can happen when locals are spying for the enemy. The tactical plans of missions are kept at a top-secret level and shared on a need-to-know basis with clearances. While this is a bit much for business, security is undervalued in GTM. In the spirit of "open knowledge sharing" and "building in public," the information is widely democratized, and sharing it is almost perceived as a virtue. You have to protect not only your tactical plans but also your intellectual property. Security in the forms of NDAs, IP protection, cyber security, and legal paperwork can make a difference. Think about non-formal protection as well: keep responsibilities and knowledge separate, and be sure to distribute plans through more than one person. Make it clear to team members what is confidential and what is okay to share publicly. Hoping for the best is a daydream in GTM. Expect the unexpected. Be prepared for that.

One of the advisors from my past career, John Keogh, who served in the Irish Army, UN, and Canadian Police Reserve unit, taught me to "Think like a criminal." What could go wrong, and what is the probability of it? Protect your operation against these risks. I signed NDAs with and gained written permission from all participants to approve the final content. You cannot "cease and desist a book" – that would literally mean a product recall. It must be rock solid.

- **Repetition** is indispensable in eliminating the barriers to success. Routines hone tactical skills to the degree that allows quick and desirable reactions to threats. Recreating the natural circumstances in which the threat might appear is vital. Special ops have at least one or two full dress rehearsals before the mission. Do the same. Your development team might perform a stress test of your technical infrastructure. Repetition hones individual and team skills, while "full dress rehearsals" unmask weaknesses in the plan.

I had a stiff morning routine and a social media diet while writing this book. For 4 to 5 hours every day, I wrote. My key to consistency was never breaking the chain. We completed several usability tests and bug hunts before releasing our first chapter. Then we had a test launch for the waiting list and did a retrospective of what to improve for the main book launch.

Stage 3: Execution

- **Surprise** is the ability to strike at a time or place or in a manner for which the opposition is unprepared. You will unlikely catch them completely off-guard, but predicting when they are less prepared or occupied elsewhere is possible. In special ops, this is achieved through deception, timing, and taking advantage of their blind spots. Deception, when it works, delays a response long enough for success to be gained at the crucial moment. Timing is critical. Stay in the shadows, but when you strike, go all in. You need to be ready for any surprise and be able to react to those unexpected events. As a GTM company, you sometimes have to be 10x more valuable for a customer than someone who already has their business. Focus your efforts on a single point and fiercely strike when they don't see you coming – a Beachhead Strategy.

No, I was not very good at this. I was building the book in public. An element of surprise was building the ecosystem around the book by secretly working with great partners and experts. Maybe most of my audience also anticipated me to write a growth hacking book, so the overall subject was a shocker for some.

- **Speed** means getting to your objective as fast as possible. Any delay will expand your area of vulnerability and decrease your opportunity to win. Special ops are generally small and lightly armed to gain surprise and speed. Therefore, they are vulnerable to long, intense opposite pressures. Agile methodologies, rapid interaction, and the whole notion of using the scientific method in business clearly support that speed is of the essence. Tanks move slowly and with great force. Mobile units can be elsewhere in a matter of minutes without friction. The renaissance of agile methodologies and work modes has left a lasting impact on your work. GTM strategies are more of a wartime leader than a peacetime leader. While soft elements matter, the ability to create pressure at the focal point of a competitor's weakness and deliver the solution that fixes it is of vital importance. Fight, flight, or freeze are our natural responses to danger. Most people freeze. If you do it quickly, you can thrive (or at least get out of the situation).

My office turned into a war room. I was on calls non-stop to support team members to help them prioritize what is mission-critical and what the dependencies are between tasks. You don't want to read a "good enough" book. But it has to be "perfect enough" within the shortest time possible. It took me a year to write it. Some authors take 2 to 3 years for a well-researched book.

- **Purpose** is understanding and executing the mission's prime objective regardless of emerging obstacles and opportunities. The mission must clearly define the purpose: rescue somebody, destroy the bridge, or gain a specific piece of intelligence. It is critical that your mission statement is crafted to ensure every individual understands the primary objective. The best way to test if that is the case is to ask the team members to state the mission. Apart from knowing it, there needs to be a buy-in of the mission. Everyone, without exception, should develop a sense of personal alignment that drives the team toward victory. No exception.

The moment I knew my team had a shared purpose was when I didn't hear from my designer during the hours leading up to the launch of our sample chapter. I was worried sick. When he picked up the phone, he said: "Maja, you know I would never do that. I just had my phone in airplane mode to focus." And "mission-critical" was probably the word I repeated most at team meetings.

Thinking like special ops begins with knowing what the mission is. Let's continue our learning path by defending the objective of your mission. What does your GTM success look like?

Goals and Objectives are Your GTM Compass

"If you do not know where you are going, how will you know that you are there?"
Peter Drucker, a US professor and management expert

Strategy is a plan of action designed to achieve a goal. Without a goal, there is no strategy.

Yet, many teams do not set goals or cannot clearly state what their goal is. They describe it vaguely as "building something and introducing it to the market to make money." If the goals are the essence of any strategy, why do many fail to set them up or stick to them?

If a mission is a journey, a goal is a milestone on that journey. It has to contain a number (how to measure it); otherwise, you cannot surely know that you achieved this milestone on your mission. Here is an example of the thinking and validation process in GTM.

My business partner Tim Berce and I aimed **to enable 100 solo businesses in 2023**. This is aspiring, but we had to develop intermediate objectives to get us there.

- Background: We ran an 8-week cohort for $1,000, limited to 22 students. This was to empower their businesses. From a single post in a Facebook group, 50 people applied in a day. Based on this traction, we validated that the market embraced the program. It was not a difficult sell.

- Plan: Since the cohort was such a success, we wanted to validate if the value delivery could be done at scale. Running live cohorts is a huge commitment in terms of time and effort. Tim and I recorded an online course and weekly office hours and sold it for $279.

- Outcome: It took us one month to get 50 students enrolled in the program at a lower price point. The commitment and time pressure of the previous offer converted much better. Now, we are building a funnel (testing webinars, ads, and free content for lead gen) to scale the online course. Due to time constraints, we cannot run another cohort, even if it would sell much easier.

This example clearly demonstrates what you already suspected. GTM is simply too volatile to stick to one long-term goal alone. The intermediate target is dynamic and moves in an unpredictable way. We need a different type of compass to guide us on the journey to consistently deliver and capture value to the target market.

Two frameworks embrace the dynamic nature of GTM:

- **North Star Metric** is the stable element of goal setting in GTM. It is a measurement of the overall value that a business delivers. An example of this for our online course is sales, created by students.

- **OKR** (a system of objectives and key results) helps to break down the broader goals into smaller, manageable steps that can be measured in between to guide behavior and decision-making.

    Example: The objective is to empower 100 entrepreneurs to kick off their businesses.

    - Key result 1: 22 attendees of the cohort.
    - Key result 2: 78 sales of the online course.

I recommend you use both concepts in GTM. Your North Star Metric will clearly indicate how the value you provide moves and evolves. It is an important starting point for value-based pricing and signals early product-market fit. Oppositely, OKRs are very hands-on and will help you plan and lead your GTM orientation. In my experience, they are one of the most valuable management and leadership tools for GTM strategists.

Let's meet both concepts and start implementing them into your GTM.

Find your North Star

"I'm here to build something for the long term. Anything else is a distraction."
Mark Zuckerberg, Founder of Facebook

In GTM, we often have to deliver 10x as much value as established solutions to get a foot in the door. Many are skeptical about new solutions and would rather see them in action elsewhere before considering taking it for a spin. Old habits die hard, so why fix something when it's not broken? You must become incredibly effective in delivering value to users and learn how to measure this transaction of such value to keep our business in good shape.

Key performance indicators (KPIs) are widely used in business. They are metrics that a company agrees to use to measure progress against important strategic objectives. They are often set up for a department and role to measure success and performance.

Sometimes, deciding on which KPIs to choose can be tricky. If you work on a GTM strategy for a social media network, for example, you would naturally like to increase the user base. Yet, if you focus too much on rapidly increasing registrations of new users, it can happen that you end up reducing value added to users, not increasing it. Server and support overloads come to mind first, but the user experience for others can also be compromised. Remember how happy you were when your aunties and grandparents joined Facebook? The value you receive from the platform is never the same.

Most GTM companies would naturally lean towards revenue and profit metrics when selecting KPIs. That makes sense business-wise, but if revenue and profit are value-captured metrics, how could you determine the value delivered as a base to build a healthy business model? In GTM, measuring value delivered is one of the single most important metrics to predict success in the market.

North Star Metric, as defined by Sean Ellis, is a core measurement of how much value added you are delivering to your target market.[4] Your North Star Metric (NSM) is not just any metric.

---
4 Ellis, S. (2017). What is a North Star Metric? Growth Hackers. https://blog.growthhackers.com/what-is-a-north-star-metric-b31a8512923f

If improved, it is the one metric that will have the greatest impact on your business.

The criteria for selecting a good NSM are the following:

1. Leads to revenue (but does not have to be revenue per se).
2. Reflects value creation for customers.
3. Measures progress as a result of value creation.

How do you select it? In the case of our previously discussed program to train freelancers, our objective was clear: to empower 100 entrepreneurs. But how do you measure empowerment? Empower is a self-reported metric. We agreed that an empowered student of a freelancing course will manage to win at least one customer in the first three months of running their business. The NSM, for us, became the number of empowered students.

We measure our NSM by interviewing and surveying attendees. If they are doing well in business after finishing our course (and more than 80% do), they will happily refer it to others and support the program's growth.

Here is another more advanced example for Amplitude. Amplitude is a product analytics and event tracking platform trusted by Hubspot, Intuit, Paypal, Atlassian, Notion, and many others. The product is as good as the value that users derive from it. After extensive research and data analysis, Amplitude's team agreed on the NSM of Weekly Learning Users (WLU). A WLU is a user who is active and shares a learning that has been consumed by at least two other people in the previous seven days.

But why does deciding on an NSM really matter? After introducing the new NSM to help guide product and growth decision-making at Amplitude, the team saw a 50% increase in the number of WLUs per active organization, which ultimately led to better business results.[5]

An NSM includes both:
- The solution vision element of the company.
- Key metrics that indicate how the solution delivers value to its users.

---

5 Bauer, J. (2019). We're Evolving Our Product's North Star Metric. Here's Why. Amplitude. https://amplitude.com/blog/evolving-the-product-north-star-metric#benefits-of-this-change

Based on Amplitude's research of more than 11,000 companies and 3 trillion user actions, they have learned that **all digital products** are playing one of three possible games:

1. The Attention Game: How much of your customers' time can you capture in your product?

2. The Transaction Game: How many commercial transactions does your user make on your platform?

3. The Productivity Game: How many high-value digital tasks can your customer perform in your product?

Here are some examples:

Game	Companies	Candidates for NSM
Attention	Facebook and Instagram Netflix Spotify	Daily active users (DAU). Medium view hours per month. Time spent listening to music.
Transaction	Amazon Uber Walmart Airbnb	Purchases per Prime subscriber. Number of rides. Purchases per customer per session/visit. Nights booked.
Productivity	ChatGPT Salesforce Miro Adobe	Weekly active users. Average records created per account. Number of collaborative boards within a business. Number of engaged cloud subscribers.

A company normally has one NSM, but if you operate with different product lines, there could be multiple product NSMs, but they should still align with the overall company's NSM.[6]

---

6 Hegde, S. (2018). Every Product Needs a North Star Metric: Here's How to Find Yours. Amplitude. https://amplitude.com/blog/product-north-star-metric

For example, if Amplitude decided to introduce user onboarding software in addition to their analytical software, they would have to find a new NSM.

After understanding the core principles, it is time to find your NSM. These steps will help you get started.

1. **What game are you playing?** Is it an attention, transactional, or productivity game? Review some well-known examples and create a shortlist of your NSM candidates.

2. **Identify your core value proposition.** What is the core value that your product or service provides to customers?

3. **Determine the key actions that drive your business.** What are the key actions that customers need to take to receive the core value of your solution?

4. **Identify the metric that best represents the key action.** Once you've determined the key action that drives your business, identify the metric that best represents that action. This will be your NSM, which:

    - Measures the moment that a customer finds value in your product.
    - Represents the core of your current product strategy.
    - It is a leading (not lagging) indicator of a future business outcome your company cares about.

   It is important to avoid vanity metrics. For example, the number of followers of your page on social media might look good to you, but without a clear strategy on how they contribute to your revenue, it's probably not a good NSM. Your NSM should apply to your entire business and be easy to track, measure, communicate, and influence your business actions.

5. **Act on your NSM.** It is a moving target. To observe and optimize the results, follow these tips:

- Make your NSM visible. Your team should be able to see your NSM on a regular basis. This will help keep everyone focused on the ultimate goal of the business. It is best to include it on your main business dashboard and revise it daily or at least weekly.

- Set targets for your NSM. Set ambitious but achievable targets for them. This helps your team understand what success looks like and motivates them to work towards that goal. It is best to shape them on a monthly or quarterly basis.

- Align your team around your NSM. It should be the focal point of your team's efforts. Ensure everyone understands how their work can improve the NSM. All KPIs for teams and team members should be aligned to support it.

- Experiment to find ways to improve your NSM. Try different approaches to improving it. Experiment with marketing strategies, product features, or customer experiences to see what works best. Do not simply state that revenue or number of units sold could be the only NSM. Think harder.

You can keep the team focused on what matters most by identifying one metric. Once you have it and measure it continuously, it is your compass in the wild waters of GTM.

Monitor and Manage with OKRs

> "Shoot for the moon. Even if you miss, you'll land among the stars."
> Norman Vincent Peale

OKRs are a collaborative goal-setting methodology used by teams and individuals to set ambitious goals with measurable results. With OKRs, you track progress, create alignment between teams, and encourage joint efforts around measurable goals.

OKRs were born and raised in technology. They were first coined by Andy Grove, who worked in Intel in the 1970s but experienced true glory in the past two decades when an author, John Doerr, published his book Measure What Matters. Companies such as Google, LinkedIn, Google, Netflix, Dell, Amazon, Slack, and others adopted a quarterly OKR system and tightened their performance reviews around them.

An OKR model consists of two components that can be applied to multiple levels in the organization:

- **Objectives (O):** An objective means what is to be achieved. Objectives can be:
    - **Commitments:** Action-oriented; what needs to be done.
    - **Inspirational**: What companies aspire to achieve.
    - **Learning**: Specific to GTM, they have to be ambitious. The difference between the learning type and the other two is that it is okay to fail with a learning objective as long as you actually learn!

    Ideally, you use both types at a company level. When properly designed and deployed, they are the glue of alignment in the organization and prevent ineffective execution. The objective must be bold, ambitious, and usually does not include a number.

- **Key Results (KR):** This is how you reach the objective. Effective KRs are specific, time-bound, and aggressive yet realistic. A team regularly checks the KRs and grades them at the end of the designated period, typically each quarter.

Where an objective can be long-lived, rolled out for a year or longer, KRs evolve as the work progresses.
Let's review some GTM OKR examples to make this clear.

A GTM company called SalesWhale (I'm keeping the real name a secret because they are a client) developed a SaaS solution that sources companies' company data via the Google Maps API. The software is intended to help marketers, salespeople, and business developers find contact data of prospects who are not present or active on LinkedIn.

Suppose a company wants to build a list of all "injection molding" companies in the Frankfurt area. In that case, SalesWhale will find emails, addresses, and phone numbers.

They gained initial traction by running some queries themselves and sending out cold emails to them (eat your own dog food style). The contacts converted better than those found with alternative tools. After tweaking the program a bit more, they posted in a local Facebook group inviting sales and marketing with 9,000 members to test their beta. With that post alone, they got 131 testers in the product, which was an early indication of interest. The team observed the testers by analyzing their data and interviewing them about the most value added.

Based on the analysis of usage and retention data of these beta users, they hypothesized that the tool is useful for IT agencies with up to 100 employees who are searching for clients abroad. They also found another interesting segment: larger companies from traditional industries such as steel, plastic, automotive parts, etc., who also expressed interest but are not yet at scale.

Here are the OKRs the team set up for the next quarter:

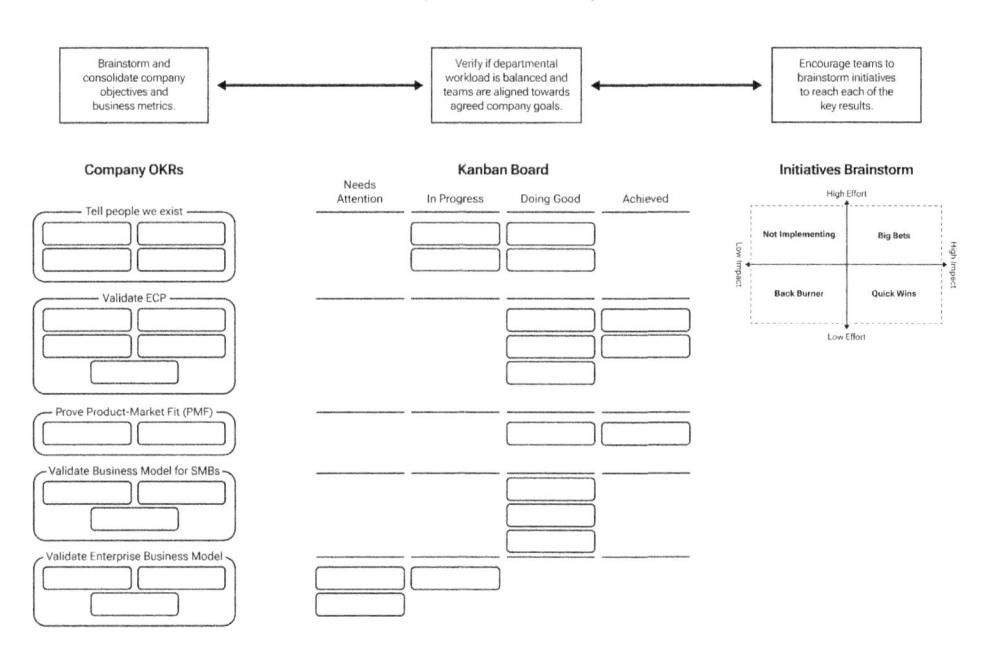

While setting up OKRs is an art and a science, it is worth tackling because they can become a valuable tool for leading and managing your entire company.

Doerr, who contributed significantly to the popularization of OKRs, provides helpful guidance if you are crafting OKRs for the first time: "First OKRs will not be great, and KRs will need to be replaced, changed, and challenged. It is important to learn from the KRs, even if you discard them. Understanding what made them good, bad, or unachievable is a strong driving force."

Here is how you start setting up OKRs:

- Consider reviewing examples from similar companies in the space, but the ground logic can be grasped quickly.

- Start from the top down. Best GTM OKRs are aligned with the company's OKRs and co-created with the team. First, align the company-level OKRs. What is the most important goal for everyone? Second, set OKRs for your teams that support company OKRs. Last but not least, each individual should create personal OKRs for themselves. These OKRs have to contribute to the team and to the company OKRs.

- It is best if teams do OKRs at a workshop and present their proposals to get buy-in and understand how OKRs can help all colleagues.

- Always first determine the objective and then attach the KR to it. If you see that achieving KR brings you closer to your objective, it's a good one. If it doesn't really contribute, replace the KR. This is also a main difference compared to KPIs. With KPIs, we don't make a direct connection to the objective. But in OKRs, KRs are linked directly to the objective.

- How many OKRs can an individual or a team have? Having three to five objectives per individual is recommended, and each of those should have up to five KRs. Don't obsess yourself too much with benchmarks of what is an ideal number of objectives and key results. Make them work for you. One is better than nothing, but how many are too many for you to achieve in the given timeframe? The OKR system should motivate, not overwhelm.

- Display OKRs in a visible place and refer to them often so they become the compass and glue of your company's joint efforts.

Of course, it adds value if you do it with a professional specialized in strategic planning and goal setting, but take it for a spin first. The DIY approach should cut to the chase after you have failed and learned on your OKR journey. The experts can provide a framework and warnings, but the numbers are always your responsibility.

Then comes the time to review your progress. Mature companies usually evaluate OKRs at the end of the quarter. In GTM, it is better to do it monthly to get faster feedback loops and room for adjustments if needed. Whichever path you take, make sure to have an agreement before you start with the check-ins.

You always only measure KRs, as objectives are not directly measurable since they are not specific enough. When you're ready, you'll assess the success of KRs on a scale of 0.0 to 1.0, where 0.0 is an absolute miss, and 1.0 is a KR achieved. If your KR was to get 10,000 followers and you got 5,000, your score of the KR is 0.5.

To grade an objective, take the average of all KR grades. The aim is to achieve an average of 1.0 for commitment objectives, while aspirational objectives are considered successful if the average KR is between 0.4 and 0.7.

For learning objectives, any mean grade is acceptable. If your average grade is below 0.5, you should probably continue with a different assumption. If you scored above 0.5, you are on the right path.

This may sound daunting, but remember that OKRs are a compass. Use them whenever you see fit. They exist to send you to unlock the "learning by failing" mentality. Failing is okay as long as you learn from it. Feedback when evaluating OKRs is as essential as it is to achieve objectives in GTM. As a best-selling author, leadership coach, and entrepreneur, Anne Morriss suggests: "Move fast and fix things."

The Good and the Bad GTM Strategy

"Great products without great go-to-market strategies often die in obscurity."
Marc Andreessen

By now, you realize that a strong GTM strategy is critical for a company's success, as it helps ensure that its solutions are developed, marketed, and sold to the right audience at the right price to build a sustainable business.

This section will teach you what makes a good and bad GTM strategy — both with examples from bootstrapped SaaS companies. The good GTM strategist did the heavy lifting of making tough calls. The bad GTM strategist was operating from a scarcity mindset and rushing to launch the product.

Let's start with the bad first.

Bad GTM strategy *(with commentary)*

This company develops solutions for engaging remote teams to nurture employee engagement. The team uses an outsourced development agency for development. The business and product sit in different countries. The development agency has several other clients. They co-invest in the development for a small fee in addition to having a stake in the company. Developers work on the product whenever they have time to do it.

Market: Due to cultural proximity, the business part of the team went ahead and stuck to the local market to run business development meetings in person. Since one of the founders had traction in the technology sector and remote work is pretty common in the tech field, they addressed that segment first.

The team talked to zero customers and didn't complete market research before investing in this "joint venture" product development. They went with whatever felt comfortable instead of checking who had the biggest pain point in the area. While tech is not a bad vertical to be in, based on its value proposition, the team did not narrow down the target segments it would serve in GTM. Therefore, they ended up with confusing messaging and a list of references that the solution can "help everybody," which is a very weak positioning.

Early Customer Profile (ECP): Naturally, the solution can help everyone who has remote workers and uses online tools for communication. Whoever needs a better culture could be a client.

If you are serving everybody, you are not doing a fantastic job for anybody. References matter; early traction matters. You go much faster and further in your GTM by focusing your resources on a specific niche. Here, you'll also want to consider the company's size and whether they have an HR department or if it's the founder who makes decisions. What company size and vertical you will be targeting cannot be decided by reverse engineering the results of 50 beta users who did not even commit. It was too small of a sample.

Product: They invited 50 companies to beta. These companies took it for a spin, and 47 of them did not retain the product for a week. Three companies that could self-onboard themselves somehow came back with additional feature requirements before considering upgrading to a paid plan.

Facepalm. If the batch of companies responded poorly to the value proposition, it is probably the wrong target audience or the solution simply is not good enough to serve them. There is no product-market fit. Ideally, you would have customer insights before launching beta to ensure it suits their needs. Still, since that is not the case here, finding an audience that will respond well to the solution or go back to development is mission-critical.

Pricing: Most of their target customers use Slack and Microsoft Teams for internal communication. The team felt it was a great idea to sell licenses for their product at a similar price range but made it a bit cheaper to "win more customers."

Ouch. There can only be one cheapest player on the market. How are the customers solving this pain right now? Well, probably with some team-building and culture-binding rituals that HR developed. The price of team building for, let's say, 100 people is $20,000, more if the company brings in employees from several companies. The problem you are solving (hopefully effectively) is worth much more if you communicate it correctly. The cost of onboarding a new employee in tech are 6x their monthly wage. This means that if a person leaves after their onboarding period, the company's damage is $30,000. If their revenue model is to sell affordable subscriptions, they need mass adoption with their selected pricing strategy.

Positioning: The solution helps companies with a remote workforce foster employee engagement and increase employee retention and loyalty (hypothetically).

Yawn. What if I send the team a gift basket every 14 days, and we have a company meetup on Zoom? Would that not be more fun than adding another software to our stack and motivating employees to use it? Why should a user choose you over an alternative? Does the team have evidence that your solution is 10x to solve my problem?

Growth: Since the founder did not want to do sales, they hired a business developer who was paid based on a small fee and commission. In addition to that, they tried to penetrate local HR meetups and social media groups and win some PR. At this point, meeting prospects at events and organizing demos worked best for them.

Okay, where to start? Basically, they have no idea whom they are targeting, how much it will cost, and how they will communicate it. But marketing has to be done, right? Keeping it safe and comfortable leads to nowhere. In GTM, it is all about pushing the boundaries and building something proprietary and special. Channel selection is determined by the target audience and is unfortunately impossible to hit right from the get-go if you have no idea who will buy from you.

Systems: While the team raised an investment 14 months ago, they have not yet validated a business model to sustain their expenses. Their current Monthly Recurring Revenue (MRR) is below $15,000, which does not even cover the costs of wages. The development partner lost interest in a project since it was not profitable. The company is in the "survival bias" mode, taking on new tenders and small investments to get by. They have not yet gained international traction; unfortunately, they struggle to keep the lights on.

What can you learn from understanding the bad strategy?

Based on a global survey of 481 executives conducted by Harvard Business Review Analytic Services in 2022, only 29% of respondents think their organization believes they are doing a good job of implementing its GTM strategy.[7] Yet, more than half (55%) of the respondents plan to increase their GTM budgets in the next 18 months.

---

[7] 2022. Unlocking Go-To-Market Success with Insight into Strategic Initiative. Harvard Business Review https://hbr.org/sponsored/2022/10/unlocking-go-to-market-success-with-insight-into-strategic-initiatives

What are the remaining 71% of companies struggling with? Most companies struggle to create an effective GTM due to the following:

1. **Misalignment with the company's core strategy:** The GTM strategy must align with the company's overall goals, resources, and capabilities while also effectively meeting the target customers' needs. GTM will most likely fail if it is not aligned with the core business strategy.

2. **Lack of market research.** Without a thorough understanding of the target audience and competitive landscape, developing a strategy that resonates with potential customers and differentiates the company from its competitors can be a needle in a haystack.

3. **Poor alignment between departments.** Silos are toxic. They can appear within a company or between agencies and freelancers who are serving the same account. A successful GTM strategy requires alignment between different departments within a company, such as marketing, sales, product, design, user experience, customer support and development, and all the stakeholders.

4. **Unclear goals and objectives.** If a company doesn't understand what it wants to achieve with its GTM, developing a plan that effectively supports those goals can be challenging.

5. **Very tight resources:** All resources are limited, but sometimes GTM requires a significant investment, which can be challenging for companies with limited budgets and bandwidth and on a short lifeline with their founding. When panicking, people usually do not make the best decisions possible.

6. **Resistance to change:** Implementing a GTM requires changes to existing processes and systems, which can be met with resistance from employees accustomed to working in a certain way. GTM work should be seen as an opportunity to advance the company and grow, not as a chore and additional workload on the team's shoulders. Planning and committing enough resources will help you get there.

7. **Lack of leadership:** Without strong leadership and a clear vision, it can be difficult to develop a GTM strategy. It starts from the top down. GTM must also be reviewed regularly to ensure it's still relevant and effective. It is not a "set it and forget it" document. It should evolve with the learnings in your business.

8. **Loss of enthusiasm:** GTM is a game of delayed gratification. You can work for months before seeing any signs of tangible progress. Therefore, working on a clear timeline, celebrating milestones, and creating a working process with frequent feedback loops from testing is important. Engineer these elements to your GTM plan to keep the team excited to do it. Celebrate small wins.

GTM is not all about launching something. As a trained marketer and growth strategist, I was astonished by how much broader the GTM field is. My reality before I went onto the structured GTM journey was that you create the product and have audacious goals such as "let's get it in front of 1,000 users in the first week."

While I was always selective of what projects I took on, I never fully had a say in how the product would be developed. My experience is not an outlier. The silos between product and marketing are real.

The best teams I have worked with had a strong product management culture, with leaders who understood business models and promotion and were diligent in their research. The same applies to founders. Spending heavily on product development before it's seen in the real world is a dangerous path that often leads to oblivion.

Now, let's look at what happens with a winning GTM.

Good GTM strategy *(with commentary)*

Context: The company sells software for designing labels in an internationally compliant manner that makes distribution easier. Their label builder was initially sold in a package with other features the company offers customers. However, due to extremely high engagement with this feature, the company determined that it could serve as an acquisition ramp for low-market customers who would not need the entire set of labeling solutions. This could help them reach new prospects and customers earlier on their journey. Since the partner channel is so important, the product and sales team agreed not to promote the solution of markets that are breadwinners for the company. It would be tested on markets with which the company has not built solid traction yet so as not to cannibalize the channel.

The company was definitely building on its proven strengths and made sure that there was an alignment between the new venture. The GTM and business strategies are aligned, and stakeholders are prepared for the new venture and working together to make it happen.

Market: They determined it would be UK and US small packaged goods producers. The company has a lot of partners that work well within continental Europe. Still, there is an ambition to build traction elsewhere and test a new business model of product-led growth instead of only being invested in one channel of selling through partnerships. If the market validates to be profitable for the company, they will gladly extend their proven business model there as well, but not before they see early signs of adoption and product market fit.

The market selection was made based on real data so as not to jeopardize the main business model. The company will be testing a new offer on a new audience. The market was proven to be big enough for this model to work and lacked holistic labeling solutions.

Early Customer Profile (ECP): A direct-to-consumer (D2C) brand in the UK and US, such as cosmetics or food, that is doing labeling and currently uses Canva or a free online tool to label the products. The direct decision maker is the founder. Usually, such companies make less than $2 million a year and have limited expertise in labeling their products to be compliant. They cannot afford specialized designers to do the job for them because they are tight on budget or may not be familiar with all the regulations.

This ECP is specific and will be more refined in the future after the company gains more data. First, they must test if their ECP assumptions were right; otherwise, they will pivot to a different audience. While the ECP could be further defined, it is a good start to test GTM assumptions.

Product: The company will launch a free-of-charge label builder for small companies that are expected to bring in new leads. The registration will be simple, and after monitoring product analytics, the company will try to upsell users the premium version of the product after they have designed five or more labels or if they need more advanced features such as multilingual descriptions.

Since it is the first time the company is testing direct value delivery, the best decision was to invest in product analytics early on and do customer research based on interviews and analyzing their clients' and partners' existing data. The company has a strong product management culture, which will lead the GTM for this product diligently.

Pricing: The product is intended to be freemium – up to five labels are available to everyone, and whoever needs more or wants advanced features can invest $19 a month to gain access to their labeling wizard. Compared with hiring a specialized designer, this is a fraction of the cost, and for those who need labels at volume, the product delivers fantastic value.

Definitely do more testing on willingness to purchase. But overall, it is a good start to be more expensive than Canva, which is not a specialized product for making labels. The business model should be observed and adjusted once real business traction data come in.

Growth: The company will first send an email to churned customers who found their flagship solution to be too expensive. Later on, they will double down on SEO and content marketing efforts and invest $10,000 in Google ads since there is a lot of search volume for label making.

Sounds good. There are no further comments apart from the importance of building templates and galleries of designs that enable future users to discover their products based on their specific use cases.

Systems: The company successfully opened a new market and delivered its first product-led solution. They gained 11,000 users in the first quarter after launching the solution. They are considering investing more in growth and marketing and expanding acquisition to Spanish-speaking countries. All content is planned to be localized there, but they will first validate the market with digital channels before they invest in building a team there.

Now that you've seen these two contrasting examples in action, let's walk through what great GTM strategies have in common.

1. **Do it as an interdisciplinary team.** Forget the division of "product builds it, marketing sells it." We are on the same ship, on a mission to build a strong business. Non-product people can participate by supporting your research and serving additional insights and points of view. This levers the chances of your GTM success. The sooner you include them in your GTM, the stronger bond and commitment you build between teams. Make them think. Include them ASAP.

2. **A clear sense of direction.** The glue of your GTM operation is team alignment and buy-in. A clear goal, strong leadership, and sufficient resources are key to success. When planning for GTM, make budgets and get commitments on how many people will work on a project and the timeline and milestones.

3. **Create a critical mass.** Following the special ops principles, your best chances at winning GTM are to place intense efforts on a single focal point and swiftly encounter the opposite party with all your force. That can never happen if you work on 20 projects simultaneously because you simply do not have the strength to make a difference. Choose your battlefield and go all before choosing the next one.

4. **Iterate fast**. In GTM, you mainly operate with assumptions that should be tested on the field. The sooner you validate them, the faster you learn and grow a better GTM operation. Speed is the name of the game. Embrace it as your new superpower.

5. **Implement adjustments.** GTM strategy will inevitably change. Insights should leave to the improvements. Diligently adapt your GTM strategy to your learnings from the field. Evolving the strategy to reflect new learnings nurtures a competitive edge.

As you can see from examples of good and bad strategy, oftentimes, GTM is not (only) about finding brilliant cutting-edge solutions but doing simple tasks that make sense in a strategic order – consistently.

Remember the special ops lesson? The best plans are simple and understandable to everybody on the team. Your GTM does not have to be a 50-page document filled with fancy frameworks. It can be a slide, a one-pager, a spreadsheet, a Gantt chart, or any other diagram or project-management tool you prefer. Feel free to shape your strategy to suit your unique style and needs. The best strategy is one that you feel confident executing.

Rome was not built in a day. You aim to build a thriving business. Your GTM strategy must undergo multiple iterations and adapt to the changing environment, opportunities, and insights. But you need a starting point. In the next chapter, you start building it.

Buckle up. It will be quite a journey!

Here is a small reminder of what you have learned from this chapter and your suggested to-do list.

Key Takeaways:

- GTM is a very wide area. It is hard to master all of the elements (market research, target audience selection, product and value proposition development, pricing, positioning, and growth) by yourself. While having some knowledge of these areas definitely helps, most successful GTM strategies are planned and executed as an interdisciplinary team effort and lead with your vision, mission, and goals.

- GTM has a lifespan of three to 18 months, and you are operating with multiple unknowns with very limited resources. It is important to build a simple yet holistic plan with a small interdisciplinary team that will execute it.

- Your best chance of winning early adopters and the early majority to cross the chasm is to act like special ops.

- Leverage your strengths and enter all your efforts around a single objective. What is the value that you are ultimately bringing to the market? You can measure it with your North Star Metric.

- Most technology companies agree that OKRs are the most recommended method of goal-setting for GTM companies because they are done for a shorter period of time and can be revised and adjusted quickly. It is important to co-create them with a team to get the ultimate buy-in.

- There will always be new opportunities, distractions, potential partnerships, and other shiny objects. In GTM, you have to be extremely careful to resist them and commit your limited attention and resources to the mission that you have already committed to. Do not scatter yourself too thin. Center your efforts on a single point, then move forward. Be proactive instead of reactive.

- Best GTM strategies are simple yet proprietary. Simply coping with similar companies' GTM strategies will only get you that far. Build your winning GTM strategy by finding your best assumptions in the key areas presented in the GTM model and testing them first. Quickly adjust them if they will not be proven right. Welcome to the experimentation loops, where the magic of GTM happens.

To-Do List:

☐ Define your North Star Metric (NSM).

☐ Use OKRs as a goal-setting technique to develop a clear understanding and create KRs that will ultimately lead you to achieve your objective.

☐ Start thinking about your GTM model using this framework. Who would you need in a GTM team to make the best bets on all these elements?

> Find all the worksheets, frameworks, and models mentioned in this chapter at *https://gtmstrategist.com/resources*. **They are free and yours to benefit from.**
>
> If you're unsure of terminology, skip to the GLOSSARY at the end of this book.

CHAPTER 2

Market

"No plan of operations extends with certainty beyond the first encounter with the enemy's main strength."

*Elder Moltke,
German field marshal and strategist in Prussian times*

Focus is hard.

Rationally, while you well know that you cannot spread your finite resources too thin, the decision to focus carries a large weight. The consequences of niching down to the wrong market entry segments can be scary. It is really hard to make a good decision with a limited understanding of the market in the early stages of GTM. This is why the mission of this chapter is to help you choose the best terrain to win.

If your thought process is similar to this email from Jasper, a technical founder who is developing an onboarding SaaS solution, this chapter will take you from being overwhelmed to hyper-focused. Buckle up.

To: **Maja Voje** (grow@majavoje.com)

Subject: **Should we go for indie, corpo, or SMBs?**

Hey Maja!

Something has been puzzling my team.

We launched an invite for our beta on private social media and got over 250 applications from various people.

Initially, we believed our user onboarding solutions would be an excellent fit for indie developers. That was our vision from the get-go.

Yes, there were some, but based on beta applications, we found three additional segments that responded positively to our invite:

- **Many B2B SMBs**
- Even **larger SaaS** companies
- **Ecommerce companies** also applied, and we were stunned.

Now we are in doubt. You always say that we need to focus on a single or be very limited about our ICPs. But how? Many different groups are interested in the tool.

Thanks for sharing your knowledge, as always!

Jasper

The special ops plan discussed in the previous chapter focuses your GTM efforts on a **single focal point (the market)** that you will conquer first. By focusing all your forces here, you increase your chances of winning. You also strengthen your company's capacity and resources to conquer other markets later on. This is called the **Beachhead Strategy.**

The Beachhead Strategy was named after one of the most pivotal battles in World War Two. The Allies struck strongly at the beaches of Normandy and created a critical breakthrough that was the turning point in the war. Crafted and led by Supreme Commander of the Allied Expeditionary Force Dwight D. Eisenhower, the plan was to establish a beachhead by taking one beach after another. The rest is history.

In business, the Beachhead Strategy is all about focusing on a small market segment first to increase your odds of winning. It is called the **Beachhead Segment**, and choosing the right one can be pivotal for your GTM.

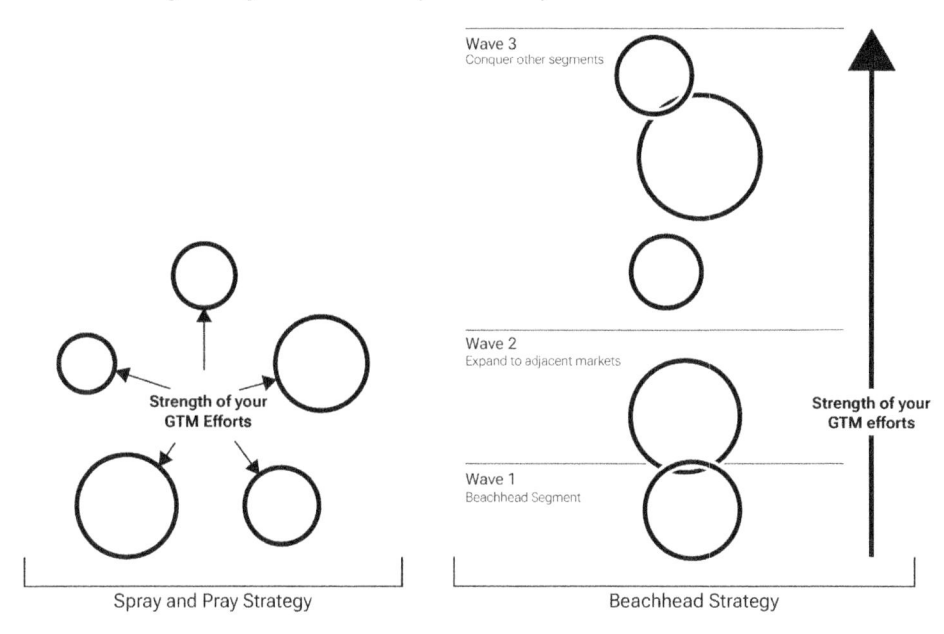

Spray and Pray Strategy

Beachhead Strategy

After creating significant traction with your selected Beachhead Segment, a company is in much better shape to start expanding to adjacent markets. Preferably those that have some intercept with your Beachhead Segment will give you a competitive edge. There are numerous examples of unicorn companies that used a Beachhead Strategy for gradual expansion:

- Facebook was first available exclusively for Harvard University students, then for other Ivy League and Boston-area universities, then gradually other American universities and high schools, and then finally, the general public.
- Uber started to expand city-by-city in California.
- Figma first targeted game designer studios.
- Amplitude became a trusted ally for product managers by organizing conferences for them.
- Tinder started by organizing parties at fraternities and sororities.

The selection of the Beachhead Segment has a huge impact on your GTM. It will determine other aspects of it: the product, messaging, pricing, branding, marketing and sales channels, etc. Remember Jasper's email? If their Beachhead Segment is **indie developers**, they will probably:

- Create a bunch of commits (pushing the code to GitHub) and create docs on GitHub.
- Invest in developing a strong community.
- Use content marketing, which is very education-oriented.
- Pricing will remain accessible because there is only so much they would spare so they would need a lot of users.
- Have an ungated demo version of the product available (a try it before you buy it approach, also known as product-led growth).

Oppositely, if Jasper's team selects **ecommerce companies** as the Beachhead Segment, their GTM will look entirely different:

- Launch some pilot projects with early customers to prove results.
- The solution will probably have to integrate easily with popular ecommerce platforms such as WooCommerce and Shopify. Since it's hard to develop all integrations at once, they'll first have to limit to one underlying technology and narrow down the market to their users.
- Mainly communicate conversion uplifts and revenue increases by using a solution. Case studies will become their next best friend.
- Price-wise, they could charge a higher fee or even sell consulting services in addition to subscriptions based on complex integrations.
- Channel-wise, there are podcasts, social media groups, and technology marketplaces such as the Shopify store, WooCommerce plugins, etc.

- Since many teams do not have in-house development, get ready for some hands-on work with teams or vendors, which calls for partnership programs.

These are two entirely different companies.

Jasper might be facing another problem. It can be psychologically hard to accept many trade-offs of implementing a Beachhead Strategy. There are mental barriers to cross, such as:

1. **My solution can help everybody.** And you probably built it with this grand vision in mind, right? Even though you've got the enthusiasm, try to make peace knowing that one of the most secure paths to success in GTM is to win one segment after another. This decision is made to derisk your business. And remember this:

   YOU CAN'T MAKE EVERYONE HAPPY YOU'RE NOT A NUTELLA JAR

2. **What if I am leaving money on the table?** A Beachhead Strategy will strengthen your business by focusing on the terrain you can most likely win, while protecting you against spreading yourself too thin. In GTM, you need to create a critical mass of validation. That is usually more likely to be achieved with a smaller selected target market than "go big or go home." Some of you might be shaking heads here. You have different plans: grow fast and exponentially across a big market. Fair. A Beachhead Strategy is not the only option. There are other GTM strategies. Yet, the Beachhead Strategy is one of the most applicable for bootstrapped companies and ones that are still on their route to verify pre-product-market fit.

3. **Shiny object syndrome.** There are so many opportunities out there. New technologies emerge, and you might be presented with an interesting new business opportunity. Most practitioners leave some lever for "moonshot projects," and up to 20% of available resources can be used to explore such opportunities. However, 80% or more must be invested into the original GTM plan to create a critical mass of activities for success. You will not come a very long way if you keep on changing directions. Focus on validating the opportunity at hand before moving to the next big thing.

Beginnings can be very humble. But one year and a half from now, others will look at your traction and say: "Wow, they have become the #1 choice for ecommerce onboarding. We should check them out!" Your punching power in business increases with GTM traction. You have more insights with each segment you win. Once you achieve your objectives there, you win other segments with greater confidence because you already have existing traction. Ideally, these segments are slightly interconnected, so they serve as a great reference to each other.

Deciding whom to target is a serious strategic choice since it can make or break the business. Yet, sometimes, making that choice seems like playing battleship: guessing where to start and hoping not to sink. There must be a better way. Let's learn how to analyze the market to select the terrain that will most likely make your go-to-market triumphant.

Plan to Win

> *"If everybody else seems to be doing it one way, there might be more opportunities the other way."*
> Andrew Scheuermann, industrial IoT and AI entrepreneur

GTM values speed, intensity, and action. But action could be placed in the wrong direction.

Since you now understand how important the selection of your Beachhead Segment is, you will stop the fast-paced and turbulent reality of a GTM ride and do some planning. Planning in GTM is not limited to desk research and reading reports. You need proprietary information since you're taking on the unknown unknowns.

But if you are in a new market with a new solution, how much planning can you or should you really do? Enough to ensure that your Beachhead Segment matches the following criteria:

- **You can win it over in the next 18 months or less.** Entrepreneur and GTM expert Rishi Chowdhury shares a convenient rule of thumb rule for selecting your Beachhead Segment: "In B2B, the focus can be as narrow as choosing a Beachhead Segment of 100 companies and consider it a win if you can win 30 to 50% of that segment in a year and a half. At Incube Space, we selected UK universities as our Beachhead Segment for CubeOS, which maximizes commercial real estate energy efficiency. Part of why is because universities occupy their own business, whereas, in an office building, you have to convince the building manager and tenants, which would take longer."[8]

- **A high pain point for the solution you are bringing to market.** Your solution should be a painkiller, not a vitamin to your Beachhead Segment. A well-chosen Beachhead Segment has to be aware they have a problem. When you pitch them, they should reply with more of a "shut up and take my money" than an "interesting, we are budgeting in November, maybe let's follow up then." If you developed software to identify vulnerabilities in code, clients from industries that process highly sensitive data, such as

---

8 Voje, M. (2023). Rishi Chowdhury: Beachhead Strategy. GTM Strategist Podcast. https://open.spotify.com/episode/44JumI4h8ADANXYU3QEuF

banks, hospitals, and insurance, would be more likely to care about solving this problem than small ecommerce companies that are tweaking their WooCommerce stores with 30 plugins.

- **Adequate willingness to pay for the solution.** Do budgets for solving this problem already exist? If so, what is the money they can spend with you? I had this issue once in an online course. Usually, my B2C products are priced at up to $99 a product. No complaints. But when we launched a B2C online program for $297 (+VAT), users started asking if they could buy it in three installments. The challenge was that it was targeting people who were still employed and wanted to start their own businesses. The price of the product was nearly 1/3 of monthly earnings for some. In retrospect, I should have crafted the program towards experienced professionals who already run successful side or main service businesses. For them, if they got one client by implementing the knowledge, the return on investment is already 10x.

- **The market is seizable and healthy enough to support your future growth.** While the Beachhead Segment can be very small, the total market you choose should be in good shape – preferably low in competition, open to embrace innovation, and with manageable market barriers. I mentored a company that developed software for recruitment and candidate selection. Their selected Beachhead Segment was hotel chains. Unfortunately, they entered the market in 2020, just before the COVID-19 lockdowns. For nearly two years, they had to pivot to other industries and rely on much smaller businesses that remained open. Once the pandemic settled, the market went crazy for hiring. It looked great, but at the same time, hotels wanted recruiting services, not software to evaluate candidates. That team had quite a ride. I am very proud they endured. But I cannot help but wonder if they had chosen another market, such as small IT development agencies, that their life would have been much easier.

A Beachhead Strategy in GTM leads you to identify the minimum viable segment (**MVS**) that your minimum viable product (**MVP**) can serve better than anything else. This is how you win markets.[9] Entrepreneurship, at its heart, is all about

---

9 Skok, M. J. (2023). | Startup Secrets: Go to Market StrategiesHarvard i-lab. Harvard Innovation Lab. https://www.youtube.com/watch?v=rqi-n0hA4uo

creating solutions to solve problems, finding target audiences that appreciate this value the most, and capturing a proportion of the value added as an exchange in the foreseeable future.

Another reality strikes for bootstrapped GTM companies here. Not only will they love it – but are they prepared to pay for it? If you need to monetize soon, you will have to test product-market fit and business model simultaneously.

A winning strategy is the following:

- Your customers recognize you for delivering a unique value-added solution and are willing to pay for it.
- The solution is valuable to the target audience and differentiated from your competitors' offers.
- It is hard to copy in a short period of time.

Your Sweet Spot
Smaller Segment = Easier to Cover

Adjusted from Startup Secrets: Go to Market Strategies by Michael J. Skok

Planning in GTM is all about doing sanity checks that you are not on a bad terrain and generating proprietary knowledge and insights that will lead to creating a truly differentiated and hard-to-copy GTM strategy. Remember the special ops lesson. The kernel of the GTM strategy is to create a **simple plan** which consists of:

1. Limiting the number of objectives (done with OKRs).
2. Having good intelligence.

3. Playing on your strengths and the enemy's weaknesses.
4. Innovating to build a competitive edge.

You already limited the number of objectives with OKRs to focus your GTM mission. Now, it's time to start developing a proprietary plan to win. By researching the market and crafting your GTM strategy based on high-quality intelligence, the fit between MVS and MVP can be found more reliably and quickly.

Generate Good Intelligence

> "Intelligence is quickness in seeing things as they are."
> George Santayana, Spanish-American philosopher, essayist, poet, and novelist

In GTM, the research part is far from boring. You seek proprietary information that will drive a competitive edge and make you different, better than others, and ready to win. In special ops, one of the greatest ways to generate great intelligence is to infiltrate enemy camps, engage spies, get information from locals, and secretly observe enemy territory without them knowing.

The best research is generated in the field and used swiftly to create an advantage.

I launch anywhere from five to 10 products each year. This includes online courses, workshops, frameworks, and cohorts. The inception process is so optimized by now that I spend up to two hours putting the idea together. The rest is research and validation. For each new product, I structure a one-pager that answers six questions:

1. **What is the core idea of the product?** Let's say I want to build a LinkedIn content creation system to help experienced professionals unlock new business opportunities by sharing knowledge without becoming "crying CTOs" and "copywriting wizards." The mission here is: let's make LinkedIn a more intelligent place to learn from experts who are walking the talk.

2. **For whom is this product the best fit?** Product managers, consultants, technology experts, and communication professionals who identify as introverts and believe they (may) have imposter syndrome, but in reality, they have 10+ years of experience being a world-class professional, and have a ton of knowledge and examples to share.

3. **What are the problems the product is solving?** These professionals love processes and structure. Vague advice such as, "Just write whatever is on your mind," will never land. The other issue is that LinkedIn will definitely not be their part-time job. They work elsewhere and may invest two to three hours a week on LinkedIn. We have to make the system work for them. Last but not least, certain formats and messages are just a no for them. They might not be open to sharing about their personal life and don't want to shoot videos or design their posts. The system has to accommodate their preferences.

4. **Who am I competing against? What is their offer, traction, and price?** Some experts price their one-on-one LinkedIn programs at $600 a month or more. Online courses are available in the range from free to $300, mostly gravitating towards $99. Cohorts are available for monthly fees of $79 to $500.

5. **What is your MVP and business model that you would like to test?** Courses enable scale. The problem with online courses is that only up to 6% of participants finish them, and I would not even want to guess the percentage of participants who actually apply the knowledge. Personal consultations take a lot of time and resources to deliver but provide better results regarding transformation. Cohorts work well if they are managed as communities of a finite number of attendees on a mission to deliver results in a finite time. In terms of value delivery and exchange, we believe that our best bet is an 8-week cohort for professionals on how to develop and grow personal brands on LinkedIn. We'll measure their success by the number of new followers, opportunities, reach, and engagement they receive during the program. We will mostly focus on North America and Western Europe at first since the class will be in English and priced within the $450 to $1,000 range and limit each cohort to 30 to 50 attendees.

6. **What is the customer transformation? How can I validate this product in the next 2 weeks?**
    - Write a Google Doc with the idea and offer.
    - Test the doc with five to 20 representatives of the selected target group and discover who immediately resonates with the idea. Is there a sub-group who is already eager to buy the program? If so, sell it to them.
    - If not, it's best to revamp the offer and incorporate their feedback before sending it out into the wild.
    - Send out a batch of emails, or post in a social media group that's identified to be relevant to the target audience. Ask them to either already buy or give feedback.
    - Run a pilot.
    - See what happens and elaborate. Choose a new channel, do it in partnership with an accelerator instead of yourself, improve the document, and learn from the previous iterations.

Points 2, 4, and 6 are specifically interesting. It's a very light version, but almost any research is better than no research when you are starting out. I didn't spend months on it; it was done in a week. I did not secretly infiltrate all of my competitors for months; I read their reviews and asked colleagues who had experience with their program.

That example was fairly straightforward. Let's move on to a more complex case.

Simon Belak is a data scientist, CTO, Growth expert, and one of the smartest people I have ever met. He built state-of-the-art solutions and algorithms to support GoOpti, Metabase, and Zebra BI. Here is an example from his practice.

GoOpti is a shuttle that gets passengers from one city to a more prominent airport in Europe, where they can continue their journey at a lower cost than if they flew from a smaller city. The value proposition is to "save up to 50 euros per hour." When Simon was a CTO there, one of his core interests was to build a data model to help the company decide which city to enter next.

What would happen if you were willing to drive four hours to another airport? Would you get a better deal that would still cover that ride? Simon realized that understanding value propositions and scraping flight data for all European airports are connected.

What is the average price, the best traveling option, and the best connection?

By assuming that passengers are keen on making rational choices, Simon could calculate a difference in what would happen if people drove to other airports. Eventually, the GoOpti team determined how much value they could bring to a certain town and calculated potential savings. They did it for all the towns in the EU with a population between 150,000 and 800,000 and clustered the findings to create heatmaps of town-to-town dependencies that helped inform their GTM strategy.

Ultimately, it all came down to identifying the value proposition and determining how much value they could bring at a certain time. This insight gave them a prioritized list of interesting markets to enter. The result of this study was a virtual map of which town in Europe they should enter.

Fascinating, isn't it? You can generate intelligence without having the product ready to launch and buying fancy industry reports that your competitors have at their fingertips. Now let's dive into the competitive research world.

Market Research: Know the Terrain

"If we knew what we were doing, it wouldn't be called research."
Albert Einstein, theoretical physicist, one of the most influential scientists of all time

In GTM, market research is done to prove there is a sizable opportunity for the company to build a sustainable business. Even if you select a Beachhead Strategy – a radical focus on growing segment per segment – you should ensure you're not serving a market "of too few" where you could not build enough traction to move to other market segments.

The TAM, SAM, and SOM model (I'll define these acronyms below) is the most widely used model based on which companies prove their selected markets offer attractive growth prospects. The ground logic is to start in a niche and expand towards areas with great TAM to secure further growth potential.

Let's visit this using an example of a genetic testing provider.

- **Total Addressable Market (TAM)** was estimated at $7.4 billion USD in 2022. According to Grand View Research, the global market size is projected to reach $35 billion USD in 2030,[10] at a compound annual growth rate (CAGR) of 21.4% during the forecast period (2022 - 2030).

- **Serviceable Addressable Market (SAM)** is calculated by the market growth and the number of companies in the vertical (heritage testing). By calculating the market growth and considering the number of companies in the vertical, the SAM was estimated at $1.6 billion USD in 2022, which is the total market for heritage genetic tests in North America and Europe.

- **Serviceable Obtainable Market (SOM)** is the portion of SAM you can capture in the short to medium term, usually within the next few years. The team sees some strong competitors already in the field, which is also a sign of existing demand and awareness in the market. Based on projections, the portion of the market they can obtain is $190 million USD a year.

- **Early adopters** are those early customers who are very important in GTM. Remember Roger's bell curve from the previous chapter? These will be the early adopters you need to win before daydreaming about what is around the corner. In the lifespan of GTM, this genetic testing provider has to start somewhere. Based on market research, they decided to launch their solution in the European market and target individuals who have been adopted and wanted to learn more about their biological families. Based on their strong points and the market characteristics, the company can project that it's realistic to earn $10 million a year after two years in business. Right now, they are seeking to achieve $200,000 in monthly recurring revenue to get started.

If you are preparing a pitch deck for investors, TAM/SAM/SOM is an important slide to present the size of the market opportunity. This is how you can present it:

---

10 This data is usually sourced from external reports created by market intelligence companies, consulting companies or independent analysts.

Market definition (category)	Genetic testing
Market size	$7.4 billion USD in 2022
Market growth	CAGR of 21.4%, $35 billion USD by 2030
Main product applications	Ancestry and ethnicity, traits screening, genetic disease carrier status, health and wellness predispositions.
Key market players	Illumina, Thermo Fisher Scientific, PacBio, Oxford Nanopore Technologies
Key market trends	• Growing awareness about a personalized approach to training and nutrition. • Increasing adoption of direct-to-consumer (DTC) testing. • Integration of AI for data analysis and interpretation. • Next-generation sequencing (NGS) technologies enable high-throughput, cost-effective sequencing. • Growing availability of genomic data for large-scale analysis. • Expanded scope of genetic testing. • Integration of genomics in clinical practice.
Closest competitors	AncestryDNA, MyHeritage, MyDNA
Customer type (individual/ business)	• Individual (B2C, DTC) • Physically active people who are interested in their health. • People interested in longevity.
Customer geographical location	North America, Europe

Source: *https://www.grandviewresearch.com/industry-analysis/genetic-testing-market-report*

So where do you get this data from? An independent research firm might have an excellent industry report available to buy, such as "Genetic Testing Market Report 2025-2030." But it costs $8,000 to download. Should you invest in this purchase? Of course you can, but most of us would rather first do a sanity check using free or inexpensive sources and, whenever possible, go directly to the source: to industry experts and prospective customers.

While not everyone has access to market research reports done by Big 4 consulting firms or Gartner, nowadays, data is hugely democratized, and there are more ways to learn about markets and their prosperities, many of them free. You can source from government and statistics office websites, academic research papers, publications, and tools from private data providers or use paid data collection.

You can do the market analysis yourself or rely on external sources. There is much more useful information on how to do research in the next chapter, but for now, let's focus on how GTM combines insight from secondary and primary sources.

Here are three examples of how different companies conduct valuable market research:

- **Social monitoring.** An entrepreneur was developing anti-hangover shots – a supplement a person takes before and after a lively night out. He checked the search volume for the category and found some brands abroad that are already crushing it. To find the best ingredients for his product, he spent months analyzing and engaging in Reddit discussions where people with alcohol addiction or problems talked about their go-to anti-hangover solution. He got a lot of great insights for product development and continued to study professional articles of the industry to get a formulation. Later, he developed a prototype and took it to popular party places in his town. He was chatting with people about their challenges after a night out. These conversations gave him valuable messaging for marketing, and he later offered them a sample shot. Their positive feedback gave him social proof, tons of recommendations, and provided valid proof that he was on the right track with his development.

- **Marketing test with advertising.** A well-known hardware company was researching the market potential for gaming gear for women. They studied Discord, Facebook, and Twitch groups to see how many female players have unfulfilled wants about their gaming gear and setup. They analyzed market data and learned what popular games female players played, along with the most popular groups and influencers they trusted. Before diving into an expensive R&D process, they launched a survey and promoted it via their newsletter and to a specific ad set: females only, on social media groups. The response rates were suboptimal. It proved the female gamer segment included a large proportion of mobile gaming. For that, you don't need computer hardware and accessories. It also took them a lot of effort and advertising dollars to even get responses. Therefore, the company decided to shut down the project because there were better opportunities to pursue based on the core competencies and audiences the company had already successfully marketed to.

- **User interviews and usability tests.** A team wanted to develop a Slack and Microsoft Teams integration to help employees connect and nurture their culture while working remotely. In the post-pandemic world, many employees did not wish to return to the office. Based on external research of public data available and by analyzing the discussions in HRM Facebook groups, they realized that technology companies have the most widespread organizations of remote work and are relatively easy and friendly to test new technologies. One of the founders organized 25 customer discovery interviews from a selected vertical in which she learned more about the existing solutions companies were using, what they lacked with current solutions, and what their ideal solution would look like. This research provided valuable insights for product development, and she was happy to learn that many of the companies interviewed actually signed up for the service later on.

We could go on and on with these cases. Almost every company has it, but here is what we can learn from them:

- Use at least some external data to inform your decision-making.
- Test assumptions you made using primary research methods.
- Enrich findings and decide if you want to pursue this assumption.
- Nurture relationships with people participating in your research because they might make excellent early adopters and ambassadors of your innovation.

Now, let's double down on learning who you compete against in your "playing to win" GTM strategy.

Who Else is Playing to Win?

> "I'm not in competition with anybody but myself. My goal is to beat my last performance."
> Celine Dion, Canadian singer and "Queen of Power Ballads"

Business is never done in isolation. Other businesses are playing to win, too. If you enter a new market, it's nothing but a good signal that some competition exists. That means there is an existing demand for it, and your job will be to find a market segment with an unfulfilled need that you can serve as your first focus.

There are two vastly different views explaining whether or not you should pay attention to competitors in the first place:

1. **Do not reinvent the wheel.** Those who believe there is value in learning from the established players and replicating some of their selected good practices.

2. **"Steve Jobs and Henry Ford" tribe:** Those who believe there is little value in competitor research because the team knows best and should innovate to their best capacities.

If you invent something radically different and new, you might have an opportunity to rewrite the game's rules and educate a new market. But even in this case, can you really completely ignore your surroundings? Your target market probably has an alternative to solving a problem.

Competition comes in many different shapes and forms. Consider these four types of competitors:

1. **Direct competitors** are companies you compete against neck-to-neck. They target the same customers with a similar type of offer at a similar price point. Think iPhone vs. Android, Intercom vs. Drift, or Shopify vs. WooCommerce. Usually, they are direct substitutes. Not many customers use them together.

2. **Indirect competitors** cater to the same audience at similar prices with your differentiated offers. This might be a DIY workflow with an Excel sheet. Consider all of the existing alternatives by which customers satisfy the need for a solution. You can learn that by analyzing social media groups, surveying, or interviewing clients or prospects.

3. **Replacement competitors** are sometimes also called phantom competitors. You do not see them coming. They sell a solution different from yours to different customers, but consumers would still choose to spend their money with them. If customers manually create social media content using a copywriter and designer, an AI platform that provides social media materials to companies is a replacement competitor. Such competitors can threaten the category's existence. But usually, these changes do not happen overnight, and there is plenty of room for differentiation.

4. **Aspirational competitors** are companies that you admire and can learn from. They have developed brilliant marketing and sales strategies, stunning designs, superior products, and stellar customer care. They can inspire your marketing and sales efforts even if you work in another industry. The usual suspects of such companies are Apple, Patagonia, Gymshark, Hubspot, and Tesla. Many GTM experts hold a swipe file or a mood board of examples from awesome companies who are not in direct competition but are more of an inspiration to them.

By now, you might be thinking, wait, do I have 50 competitors? It is impossible to analyze and monitor them all. And you are right. Overanalyzing competition in a 200-page competition report makes limited sense. Your team is unlikely to read it all. To select the best rivals' you are competing with, consider the following:

- **Your target customers know them and consider them as replacements for you in the purchasing decision.** You can learn this very quickly by simply asking your customers what other options they considered before signing with you. Another way would be to observe the discussions in online groups where customers are searching for advice. Whom do others recommend? The answers can be upsetting because you might disagree with them (perhaps you even define the competition differently), but they can be eye-opening.

- **Comparable size and resources to your company**. Industry whales can be a source of inspiration for ideas, but most companies are much tighter with their resources. Choosing competitors that are up to 10x bigger than you are now is wiser. It is more realistic and actionable.

Limit your scope of competitors for analysis to a reasonable number of competitors. Up to 10 will do, but if you learn that your target market has only two to three competitors, that is enough to start with. For the selected batch of competitors you want to analyze, consider using the following competition research methods:

1. **DIY customer research.** Asking or interviewing customers or prospects and learning what the relevant set of competitors they were comparing when they made a purchasing decision is extremely insightful.

2. **Analyzing competitors' online presence.** If you compete against a bigger brand, they might publish yearly reports, roadmaps, and case studies. That is a goldmine of information. Do a teardown of competitors' websites and capture notes on their messaging, pricing, sales funnels, number of offers, etc. Multiple online tools can help you provide better data. It is also great to analyze competitors with tools such as SimilarWeb and BuiltWith, which provide insights into their tech stack and traffic on the website.

3. **Analyzing competitors' marketing and sales activities**. Find the best players in the game and create a swipe file with their examples. It is great to start with SEO tools such as Ahrefs, and Semrush, social media monitoring services such as Brand24 or BuzzSumo, and ad spy tools such as SpyFu, Google Ads, and Meta Ad Library. You can also set up Google Alerts or similar notification tools to get alerts when a competitor has an important announcement.

4. **Hands-on experience with the competitor.** A sales call or an online purchase from competitors will provide invaluable insights. If you are not in a position to make the purchase yourself, you can ask a colleague or a team member to do it on your behalf or hire a mystery shopper who will conduct the purchase and report on it. Stay ethical while you are doing this.

5. **Netnography.** Online user groups and review sites are a threshold of great opportunities and understanding the upsides and downsides of current offers on the market. If you discover that certain reviews and remarks are repeated, you might have an opportunity to fill that gap in the market. You can find reviews on websites like G2, Software Advice, TrustRadius, Capettera, and Clutch for B2B. In B2C, we find them on sales channels such as Amazon, app stores, TrustPilot, forums, Facebook, online stores, and independent review sites. Be careful with the interpretation because many companies incentivize their customers to post reviews. Try to find honest reviews. Those that describe what was missing in the experience are especially useful.

Once you have identified relevant competitors and analyzed them, it's time to compare them.

You'll want to start by selecting criteria to make competitor comparisons. When doing this, it's best to include the criteria that actually influence a buyer's decision-making. Common criteria such as the number of employees, yearly revenue, number of followers on social media, and alleged monthly website visits may or may not be relevant. Do some customer research and determine comparison criteria yourself. You might be surprised that "free trial," "sustainability," or "quality of customer care" may be perceived as the most important. You can select better signals for your industry that will serve as an excellent platform for future differentiation, positioning, messaging, and other elements of GTM strategy.

In the spreadsheets below, there are multiple dimensions where you can run a competitive comparison. It's best to choose ones that are of strategic interest to you and compare them based on the same criteria that are relevant to the customer. To keep the workload manageable, analyze 3 to 10 direct competitors based on 5 to 10 criteria. Below is a simple competitive comparison table for a B2B company. The company works in the HRM process automation space and aims to improve the hiring experience; it's a CRM for candidates who are applying for jobs.

You can run this research again and again. It has the potential to become a living, breathing working tool that you can return to every quarter (at least twice a year) or whenever a new company appears in your competition arena. This overview will give you a snapshot of the current state of the market. But with an evolving landscape, how comprehensive should this analysis be each time?

	My company	**Competitor 1**
Target Audience	Development agencies with minimum of 100 people in the product who are building projects for their clients.	"Everyone" – all SMBs could potentially benefit from it (poor positioning).
Delivery of Service	SaaS – monthly payments.	SaaS – monthly payments.
Case Studies and Reviews	None (Pilot to be launched soon, 5 prospects).	Some – mostly MSEs appear to use it.
Number of Customers	0	50,000
Pricing	MRR per team license: Up to 10 seats = $200 10 to 50 seats = $400 +50 seats = enterprise deal	Free version of a product – one job to fill + $50 to 200 a month, depending on the number of jobs
Top marketing channels	- Key account management - Sales - Social media	- Product-led growth - Referrals - Paid ads
Messaging	"Developers are hard to find. Never lose a candidate due to system flops."	"HRM does not have to be expensive; this is Trello for hiring."

If the insights start to repeat themselves, stop. If you run an analysis of another competitor, the new insights are marginal. There are two extremes when it comes to running this analysis:

- Some companies deprioritize research, customer discovery, or market analysis. Remember, there are always more urgent tasks to complete.

Competitor 2	Competitor 3	Notes
Corporates	Users of Microsoft Projects (limiting!)	We appear to be the only vertically specialized company – niche down.
Integration – yearly contract.	Integration – yearly contract, product-led	Product-led growth for more affordable products.
Plenty – 20 Fortune 500 company logos in their portfolio.	They are in Microsoft accelerator, and will be pushed through by their partner.	Partnerships and acceleration with a corporate seems like a good way in.
800	50	We have not launched yet, but expect to onboard 50 prospects to beta.
$50,000 a year – license payment in advance (they do not communicate it).	$12,000 a year license.	Will multiple people buy licenses or share them? Should we consider pushing a yearly limit per number of seats?
- Enterprise sales - Content marketing - User education	- Partnerships (Microsoft) - Cold outreach - Product-led growth	Should we add a free version of the product, at least a demo, video to get our foot in the door?
"Remove the hassle of application. Let AI help you nurture relationships."	"You do not need another tool. Bring it to your Microsoft project system and make it work.	It appears that we are the only company specializing in developers and preventing getting rid of work.

GTM STRATEGIST

- Other experts are simply obsessed with their competitors to the extent that when a rival sends out a newsletter, they send it to the company's Slack channel within five minutes: "@everyone, why are we not doing this? Calling in a red meeting to get it done asap." Being obsessed with competition is neither healthy for your or your team's well-being. It brings a company to a reactive state. You cannot win your GTM if you merely manically respond to whatever your competitor is doing.

Market and competition analyses are merely reports if you don't put them into action. It is time to bring all the insights together and come one step closer to winning GTM.

Playing On Your Strengths and The Enemy's Weaknesses

"If you don't have a competitive advantage, don't compete."
Jack Welch, US business executive, chemical engineer, and writer

Analyzing market and competition takes time and work, but it is doable. In the wild waters of GTM, you rarely find time and mind space to reflect on the strengths of your team and the company. Some things are so obvious that you take them for granted.

This is why a **SWOT** analysis (Strengths, Weaknesses, Opportunities, Threats) can be so insightful for GTM teams. In addition to market and competition insights, this oldie goldie from the 1960s provides a wonderful inception for your strategy work. It is still widely used in business. Why fix something that's not broken?

To help you get started with your SWOT analysis, here are some questions to think about.

1. **Strengths**
   - What is compelling about the company? (IP, patents, networks, data, process, technology, business model.)
   - What do competitors or even customers acknowledge you do really well?

- Do you have strong brand awareness?
- What is compelling about the clients?
- What is compelling about the partners, such as supplier, distributors, and influencers relationships?
- What proprietary or unique assets do you have?
- What skills do you have that the competition lacks?
- How do your profit margins compare to the industry average? Are they higher?
- Do you operate with strong capital? Can you outlive the competition?

2. **Weaknesses**

- What are the downfalls that your company has?
- What do the customers and partners frequently complain about?
- Where can you improve based on the feedback from the market?
- Which objections before the sale are to be addressed?
- Are you a new company that still has to earn trust and a good reputation?
- Do you happen to have outdated resources or equipment?
- Are there any limitations to your distribution or market access?
- Are you lacking staff or core competencies to deliver your value?
- Are you struggling with cash flow? Do you carry debt?
- Are your profit margins below the industry average?

Now let's bring the market and competition environment into the mix to get the full perspective.

3. **Opportunities**

- What unique opportunities derive from the environment that you operate in?
- Do your competitors have any weaknesses that you could benefit from?
- Is the target market growing or shifting in your favor?
- Is there a breakthrough in solution and science that you can utilize faster and/or better than anyone?
- Is there an untapped pain point or niche market that you could win?
- Are there upcoming events you could benefit from?
- Are there geographical expansion opportunities?

- Are there potentially strong sources or financing available?
- Industry or economic trends that you could benefit from?
- Social or political trends that could play to your advantage?

4. **Threats**

    - What is going on in the environment that will change the business pace and modus operandi in your company?
    - Is there a threat of new competitors entering the industry or an expansion of existing ones?
    - Is your target market shrinking or shifting?
    - Could indirect competitors become your direct competitors by using innovation or targeting market segments that are relevant to you?
    - Industry in economic trends that could work against you?
    - Social or political trends that could bring you a disadvantage?
    - Any new technology that could work against you?

After identifying these elements, you are ready to derive different strategies for each matrix quadrant. A SWOT analysis does not end by identifying and listing elements. Its main value is to combine elements into possible strategic directions. Here is an example of a SWOT analysis for an email marketing automation software:

	Opportunities	**Threats**
	- Growing demand for email marketing automation in B2B industries. - Expansion into non-English speaking markets with language support. - Integration with emerging technologies such as AI and machine learning. - Partnership opportunities with other B2B software providers.	- Intense competition from established players in the email marketing industry. - Constant changes to email provider algorithms and spam filters impacting deliverability rates. - Increasing privacy regulations such as GDPR[11] and CCPA[12] impacting email marketing practices. - Economic downturns are impacting marketing budgets and demand for email marketing services
Strengths - Advanced email marketing features, including A/B testing, segmentation, and automation. - Easy integration with third-party software such as CRMs and website builders. - User-friendly interface and customizable templates. - Strong customer support and training resources. - Competitive pricing compared to industry leaders.	SO Strategies (strengths and opportunities): - Leverage the software's strengths to take advantage of opportunities in the market, such as expanding to new markets, targeting specific niches, or offering new features. - Develop partnerships with other companies or platforms that complement the software's strengths and can help to reach new customers or markets.	ST Strategies (strengths and threats): - Mitigate potential threats that could impact the software's strengths, such as increased competition or changing regulations, continuously improving the software, and offering exceptional customer support. - Develop strategic marketing campaigns to highlight and differentiate the software's strengths from competitors.

11 GDPR stands for the General Data Protection Regulation. It is a regulation in EU law on data protection and privacy in the EU and the European Economic Area.
12 The California Consumer Privacy Act (CCPA) is a state statute intended to enhance privacy rights and consumer protection for residents of California.

Weaknesses	WO Strategies (weaknesses and opportunities):	WT Strategies (weaknesses and threats):
• Limited social media marketing features. compared to some competitors. • No built-in landing page builder. • May not be suitable for businesses with very large email lists. • Limited language support for non-English speaking countries. • Relies heavily on email deliverability rates, which can be impacted by changes to email providers' algorithms and spam filters.	• Address the identified weaknesses of the software by investing in research and development, improving user experience, or offering additional training and support to customers. • Exploit opportunities in the market by leveraging the strengths of the software and addressing its weaknesses, such as targeting new markets or customer segments.	• Mitigate potential threats that could impact the weaknesses of the software by continuously improving the software and addressing customer complaints and concerns. • Develop partnerships with other companies or platforms that can help mitigate the identified weaknesses of the software and reach new markets or customers.

You'll want to do a sanity check of all strategy candidates that fit your GTM lifespan of 3 to 18 months. While the SWOT matrix can provide some excellent grounds for your strategy work, you have more deep thinking to do. What would make your GTM strategy distinctive? Maybe it's not a straightforward comparison with a competitor. Maybe you can source more inspiration from your previous experiences or aspirational companies from other industries. Seek strategies that would make the most difference to your GTM business. Let's bring another layer to your winning GTM strategy – subversive thinking.

Innovate to Build a Competitive Edge

"Don't try to serve everyone, or you will end up serving no one."
Serena Carcasole, entrepreneur and author

No winning strategy was ever done by copying others. This is what followers do, not winners. It is time to think subversively and add spice to your strategy.

You start this thinking process by identifying where you want to play and what the rules of the game there are. What is the beach you want to conquer first?

A useful tool to find your best terrain to win is the **2x2 positioning matrix**. By visualizing the competitive landscape, it is easier to see where there are potential gaps you could fill in. In its simplest form, it provides an insightful visual representation of how different competitors rank based on two selected criteria. In most cases, this is price and perceived quality. This will help you determine whether to pursue a **Penetration Strategy,** where you win a big market share fast, or a **Differentiation Strategy**, where you create a unique added value and have the opportunity to charge a higher price.

Below is a simple 2x2 positioning matrix for mainstream cars. The question marks indicate potential market entry options for a new brand in this simplified arena. I completed this matrix based on technical performance (I hope), while others would do it based on safety, image, design, and brand reputation, or most likely, a combination of all these factors.

Here are some best practices to consider when making the positioning matrix:

- **Choose dimensions (axes) that are actually relevant for customer decision-making in the category.** What you put on these axes makes a huge difference. It's best if you have done some customer discovery research to determine what characteristics customers really value.

- **Scale realistically.** Put all of the data down in a spreadsheet first to find the relevant scales for the axes you have selected. You can do it based on your gut feeling, but it is nowhere as insightful as if you operate with real data.

- **Represent the market share.** Make the "competitor bubbles" different in size according to their market share. This helps you greatly understand the dynamic of power in the market and helps you reconsider some choices.

This matrix will give you first inceptions of where there are potential gaps in the market that you could fill in better than anyone else. Depending on where you have found the gap, you will pursue it differently. If you have high operation costs and low funding, a Penetration Strategy might be a risky move. Most GTM strategists would lean more toward the Differentiation Strategy.

Even if you decide on a Differentiation Strategy, there are multiple opportunities to differentiate. Think of this Tesla example. Tesla found there are no high-end cars that are technologically advanced. They went into the market with something that was missing in luxury cars and was valued by customers – a car that has a lot of high-tech gadgets in it. Nobody before them considered putting a 32-inch tablet in front of the driver. Tesla successfully competes because there is a market gap that users care about.

	Comfort	Luxury	Quality	Reliability	Tech
Audi	9	7	5	4	3
Porsche	7	9	6	5	2
BMW	7	7	8	7	3
Lexus	8	8	8	8	4
Tesla	5	2	2	2	9

By now, you have ideas of where you could potentially win and what card to play. Let's learn how to narrow them down to a couple of opportunities that are the most feasible for you to explore.

What makes you special? How can you create a competitive edge?

The mission of this chapter is to find a couple of entry points to the market segment where you can deliver high value. Customers buy solutions to solve their problems, serve their needs, and advance their lives and businesses. It is all about "**getting the job done**" better than competitors for a selected segment.

When it comes to the innovativeness of your GTM strategy, there are multiple opportunities to stand out. It is not easy to explain how to craft innovative strategies, but these examples may inspire you:

- **Product innovation:** A team I mentored mainly consisted of developers who love sports. They centered their sports activity dashboard GTM around a Chrome plugin and launched on Product Hunt. Instead of playing the app competition game with Strava, Fitbit, Garmin, and other products, they build a Chrome background to inspire users to remain physically active while they are working on their computers.

- **Marketing innovation:** Another team I mentored was on a mission to launch a marketplace and collaboration platform between verified freelancers and small-to-medium companies who would like to develop web apps but do not have the internal resources to manage such projects. Since it's a marketplace, the company had to attract both freelancers and companies at the same time. The company acquisition was done the old-school way – through personal outreach and sales. To increase the awareness of the platform among freelancers, the team organized a contest for 30 days of free rent and a coworking space in their lively city for digital nomads. They promoted it in social media groups. Users started to nominate each other. The campaign went viral and attracted a lot of attention.

- **Pricing innovation:** Two of the biggest concerns direct-to-consumer (DTC) small businesses have when choosing website vendors is if the final price is much higher than their budget. Are there hidden costs? Will the project be delayed? To solve this problem, Jim Huffman and his team launched One Day Design, a productized service that delivers a landing page for a flat fee of $1,300 within a day. The service generated more than $100,000 in a couple of months without big marketing investments. They launched on Product Hunt and in Indie Hackers. They had a preexisting email list, a mini-podcast tour, and posted into some smaller groups on social media just to let them know the offer exists. The offer almost sold itself.

There are many more examples of the GTM "edge" in strategy. Remember strengths from the SWOT matrix; they can be technological, connected to skill, access to a channel, knowledge to solve a very specific problem, etc. But all the winning edges have one element in common: they add value to your selected target market. Therefore building "the edge" to the strategy begins with the target audience.

Choosing the Market Segment

> *"The aim of marketing is to know and understand the customer so well the product or service fits him and sells itself."-*
> *Peter Drucker, US professor and management expert*

The process of slicing and dicing markets is called **segmentation**. A **segment** refers to a group of individuals or organizations that share a common trait and have similar characteristics, needs, preferences, or behaviors. By dividing a market into segments, you can better understand and target specific customer groups, compare them by ranking, and ultimately select your Beachhead Segment and its adjacent segments.

There are two schools of thought here:

1. **Some GTM strategists and founders swear by empirically testing first and reverse engineering the ideal segment later on** by analyzing data from the early traction of the solution. The underlying premise is "do not assume, test." Once the teams learn from the data what works well for them, they strategize how to find more people like this. "Throw it against the wall and see what sticks" works if your TAM is relatively large and the risk in decision-making is quite low. In other words, even if you mess around at first a little, no one will seriously mind or remember.

2. **Others prefer to do a lot of research before going to market.** They rely on research methods such as customer interviews, surveys, and social media analysis (which you will learn more about in the next chapter), to find signals about who the early audience can be. Later on, they tailor the messaging, communication, value proposition, and all the other elements of GTM to cater specifically to them. This approach works well when customers are extremely involved in the purchasing decisions and when the GTM stakes are high.

Whatever your situation may be, you will benefit from some customer segmentation to test who interacts best with your value proposition before aiming your communication cannons at the market.

But how to find the "common trait" that is shared by a segment? In business school, they say there are different bases for segmentation you can choose from:

- **Demographic segmentation** involves identifying consumers based on their inherent characteristics, such as age, gender, education, occupation, and income. It is one of the most common segmentation methods in B2C because it is easy to target in advertising.

- **Firmographic segmentation** is the practice of segmenting business markets based on specific characteristics and traits of the target companies. It is particularly relevant for B2B. Its criteria include industry, ownership status, legal status, number of employees, profits, etc. It helps in understanding the demographics of businesses, just as demographics are used to understand individuals.

- **Geographic segmentation** involves dividing people into segments based on their residential, work, or travel locations. It can either be done on the regional, country, city, or neighborhood level. While geographic traits may be less significant for companies selling technology online, they become crucial for businesses targeting local markets, as knowing the exact location of customers helps effectively reach them. For some businesses, it makes sense the customers are close together. Consider Uber; it makes sense to do a city-by-city expansion because they need a critical mass of passengers and drivers to succeed in a given geographical area.

- **Psychographic segmentation** is the practice of dividing people into groups based on unobservable aspects of their psychology, such as personalities, lifestyles, habits, social status, activities, interests, opinions, and attitudes. It involves categorizing customers based on how they think, perceive themselves, and what they aspire their lives to be like. Psychographic segmentation can be used in B2B too.

- **Behavioral segmentation** analyzes consumers' behaviors throughout their purchasing journey, including their desires, problems, motivations, sought-after benefits, engagement level, and methods of meeting their needs. It is done by analyzing customer research or product usage data.

Sounds great in theory, but in GTM, we have very limited resources for market research. We are short on time and aim to do what is mission-critical as soon as possible. That's why we lean away from standard frameworks.

Word of advice from the field:

While it is appealing to use demographic and firmographics describe segments because that makes it easy to target them in advertising on social media platforms, it can also be limiting and short-sided. Dr. Else van der Berg, interim product lead/ product advisor specializing in working with B2B SaaS, has a strong point of view when it comes to using B2B:

To her point, oftentimes companies narrow down their markets too soon by strictly using demographic or firmographic data. If you have small, medium and large companies using the same product and getting value for it - doing segmentation based on the company size is suboptimal. The common nominator of your audience is something else. Therefore...

Only use demographics if it's strictly relevant.

Dr. Else van der Berg suggests using these segmentation bases instead of the standard ones when a "shared characteristic does not compute" or customer data is not yet in abundance:

- **Jobs to be Done** helps teams to understand why customers choose a product and what outcomes they seek. It focuses on identifying desired outcomes and problems rather than features and solutions.

- **Pain points** are the reasons consumers buy a product.

- **Alternatives** that they are using now (or considering using).

- **Values and fears** are psychological segmentation, which can also be used in B2B. [13]

No matter which segmentation base you end up using, it is essential that you describe the segment in detail to make it actionable for marketing and sales messaging. Vague definitions are our enemy in GTM. We need clarity and a shared understanding of what is mission-critical.

Segment	Top-of-mind segment description	Better definition (demographic and firmographic)	Jobs to be done (JTBD) definition
We are selling pre-cooked healthy meals to "Busy moms."	Married women with children.	A female 30-35 with an annual income of at least $140,000 who is a founder and has children in the age group of 2 to 6.	To feed the family with high-quality food that does not take long to prepare.
Compliance automation software for GDPR to "Corporates."	Companies that have more than 2500 employees.	A compliance manager in big pharma who is in charge of internal audits for a region that makes at least $4.5 billion a year.	To protect the company against legal risks in privacy.
We would like to see CRM to "Startups."	Startups with VC money.	EU-based startups that have raised at least $1,000,000 pre-seed capital in AR/VR space.	To ultimately achieve better sales by organizing the pipeline.

---

13 Van der Berg, E. (2023). Creating a Differentiated Product Strategy. Sonderhouse https://www.linkedin.com/feed/update/urn:li:activity:7100864562463166464?updateEntityUrn=urn%3Ali%3Afs_feedUpdate%3A%28V2%2Curn%3Ali%3Aactivity%3A7100864562463166464%29

By running a segmentation process, you can end up with multiple potential segments that you could be serving. But if you're following the Beachhead Strategy, you cannot focus on them all at once. Your next job is to narrow them down to find your best candidates.

From Overwhelmed to Hyper-Focused

"Do or do not. There is no try."
Master Yoda, a fictional character from Star Wars

For many GTM teams, there are many segment options, and it is hard to decide what the ultimate Beachhead Segment should be. If your list of Beachhead Segment candidates consists of more than five segments, it will be challenging to do additional research.

Resist making this decision solely based on the "gut feeling." You might choose the non-optimal segment and end up failing or leaving a bunch of money on the table. According to Dr. Else van der Berg, the sweet spot in GTM is to compare 3 to 5 possible segments and research them further to find "the one."

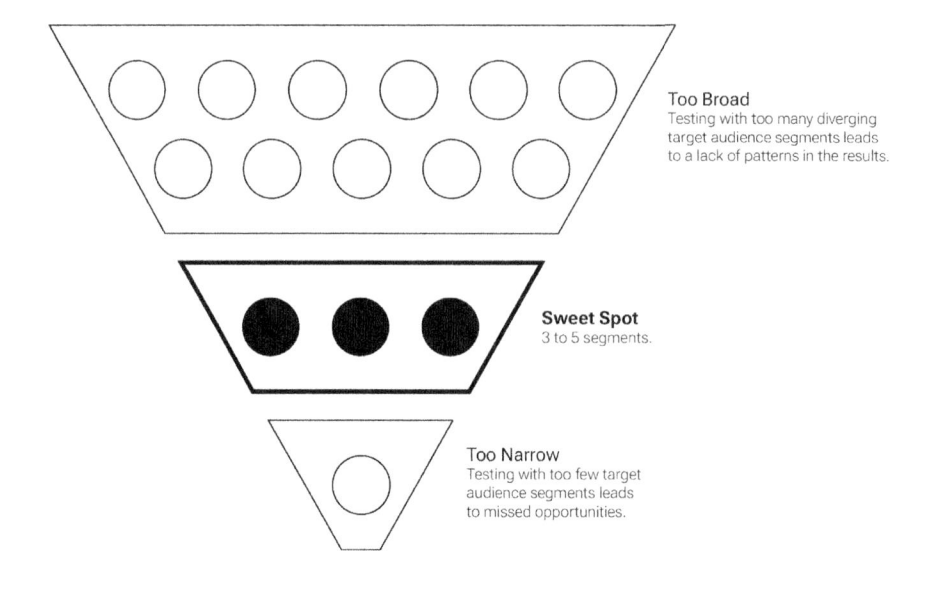

Too Broad
Testing with too many diverging target audience segments leads to a lack of patterns in the results.

Sweet Spot
3 to 5 segments.

Too Narrow
Testing with too few target audience segments leads to missed opportunities.

To narrow down to 3 to 5 segments, you can use a segment ranking table. This can help reduce the number of segments to a manageable selection you will research further.

Put all your segment hypotheses in a spreadsheet and start ranking them from 1 to 5 based on the Beachhead Segment must-haves. Here's an example of such a spreadsheet:

	FAIR CHANCE	PAIN	PAY	MARKET SIZE	GROWTH POTENTIAL	SCORE
1: IT dev agencies with up to 20 employees	4	4	3	4	3	3.6
2: Marketing agencies up to $2 million a year	3	3	3	4	2	3
3: Freelancers and solopreneurs in digital space	2	5	1	5	4	3.4
4: B2B companies with new products in tech	4	4	3	3	2	3.2
5: Accelerators in Europe	3	5	4	2	3	3.4
6: Product Managers	3	4	5	3	5	4
7: Second time technical founders	4	3	3	4	5	3.8
8: D2C ecommerce companies	2	4	3	3	3	3
9: Innovation centers of large companies	1	2	5	2	1	2.2
	How likely can you win this segment in the next 3 to 18 months? (Think access and competition.)	How strong is the painpoint you are solving for the segment? (Are they motivated to solve it now?)	What is the segment's willingness to pay? (Also think overall lifetime value if it can be a repeated purchase.)	Are there many more such users?	Does this market grow rapidly? (Does the future look good?)	

Next, you want to create a **Market-Problem Map**. This was originally crafted by Simon Belak, a former mad scientist at Metabase, now CTO at Zebra BI. More than 1,000 individuals and teams have gained valuable insights from this exercise. In 2023, it won the Strategy and Planning award at Miroverse, a gallery of templates for collaboration.

A Market-Problem Map is the process of identifying the most pressing problems your customer is facing that you can solve. It helps you decide which segment is most likely going to be a good candidate for centering your GTM market strategy around. At its core, the model has two dimensions:

- 2 to 5 potential segments you could be serving and the problems you could solve for these target audiences.

- Problems that your solution could be solving.

Once you have your segments and problems listed out, focus on the inner fields of the model. How would each segment describe the problem? In their own words, what would they say? Remember, customer interviews are a gold mine here.

Under each problem statement in the inner section, you score them based on the following:

- **Pain level:** How relevant is this problem in your customer's view? If your customer has bleeding pain, they are much more motivated to find a solution. But if they know the solution exists but don't act upon it, the desired change is less likely to happen.

- **Ease of sale:** Do you have access to this segment? Is the sales cycle short and relatively cheap and easy? That would be a high-ease score. Oppositely, if it will take you 12 meetings and 14 months to seal the deal, that would be a low ease level.

- **Ease of implementation:** How easy is it to implement the solution for the segment? It's also relevant if adjustments must be made to serve this segment well. If the segment is easy to please with existing solutions, the ease of implementation effort would be high. There are no worries whatsoever. Whereas if it requires product tweaking, extensive user education, or even a custom solution, the ease of implementation would be on the lower part of the spectrum. If you do not have a developed product yet, feel free to leave this criteria out. The model will serve you without it.

The suggested scoring for this system is from 1 to 10. Once you finish the scoring, sum up all the scores. Segments with the highest scores are most likely to be your best target market to focus on right now.

This model will serve you beautifully to narrow down your thinking and confidently find the focus for the optimal Beachhead Segment.

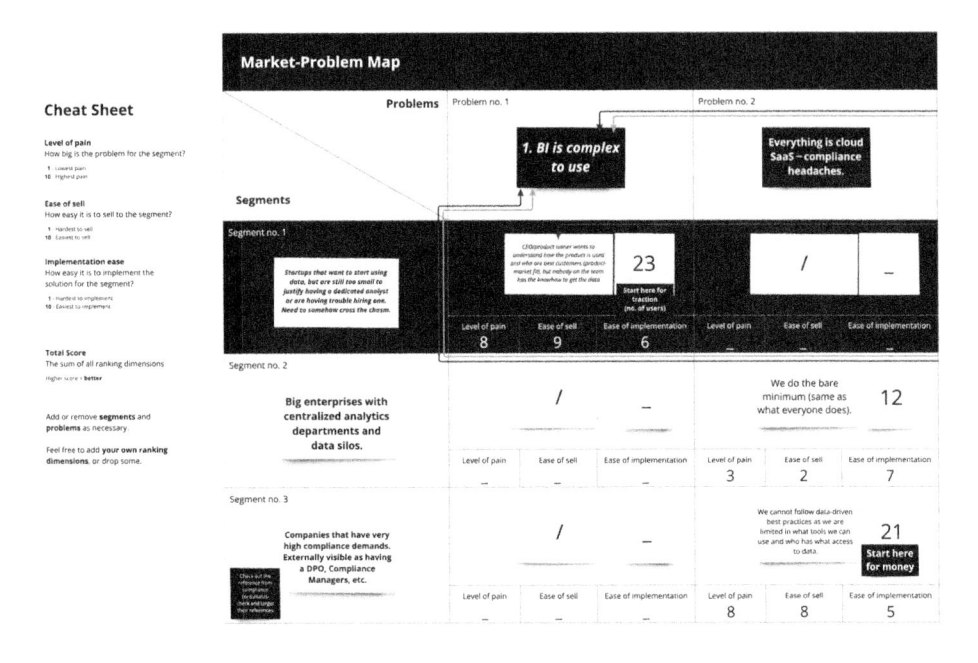

Market-Problem Map

Cheat Sheet

Level of pain
How big is the problem for the segment?
1 - Lowest pain
10 - Highest pain

Ease of sell
How easy it is to sell to the segment?
1 - Hardest to sell
10 - Easiest to sell

Implementation ease
How easy it is to implement the solution for the segment?
1 - Hardest to implement
10 - Easiest to implement

Total Score
The sum of all ranking dimensions
Higher score = better

Add or remove **segments** and **problems** as necessary.

Feel free to add **your own ranking dimensions**, or drop some.

Segments	Problem no. 1 — 1. BI is complex to use			Problem no. 2 — Everything is cloud SaaS – compliance headaches.		
	Level of pain	Ease of sell	Ease of implementation	Level of pain	Ease of sell	Ease of implementation
Segment no. 1 — Startups that want to start using data, but are still too small to justify having a dedicated analyst or are having trouble hiring one. Need to somehow cross the chasm.	8	9	6 (CEO/product owner wants to understand how the product is used and who are best customers (product-market fit), but nobody on the team has the knowhow to get the data. **Start here for traction** (no. of users)) **23**	/	–	
Segment no. 2 — Big enterprises with centralized analytics departments and data silos.	/	–	–	3	2	7 (We do the bare minimum (same as what everyone does)). **12**
Segment no. 3 — Companies that have very high compliance demands. Externally visible as having a DPO, Compliance Managers, etc. (Check out the reference from [illegible] check and target their references)	/	–	–	8	8	5 (We cannot follow data-driven best practices as we are limited in what tools we can use and who has what access to data. **Start here for money**) **21**

Congratulations, you made it! By now, you have a much better understanding of where you should be playing to win, and you have selected promising market segment candidates with whom you can target your GTM strategy. Now, let's dive deeper into understanding who exactly is "the one" to target in your GTM by conducting some really cool customer research in the next chapter.

Key Takeaways:

- For most GTM companies, a Beachhead Strategy – winning one segment after another by focusing all the resources to get the job done – is the key to success.

- Your Beachhead Segment should be carefully selected since it strongly determines all other GTM elements: price, brand, messaging, sales, and marketing channels, and even the product.

- You have more insights with each segment you win. Once you achieve your mission there, you win other segments with greater confidence because you already have existing traction.

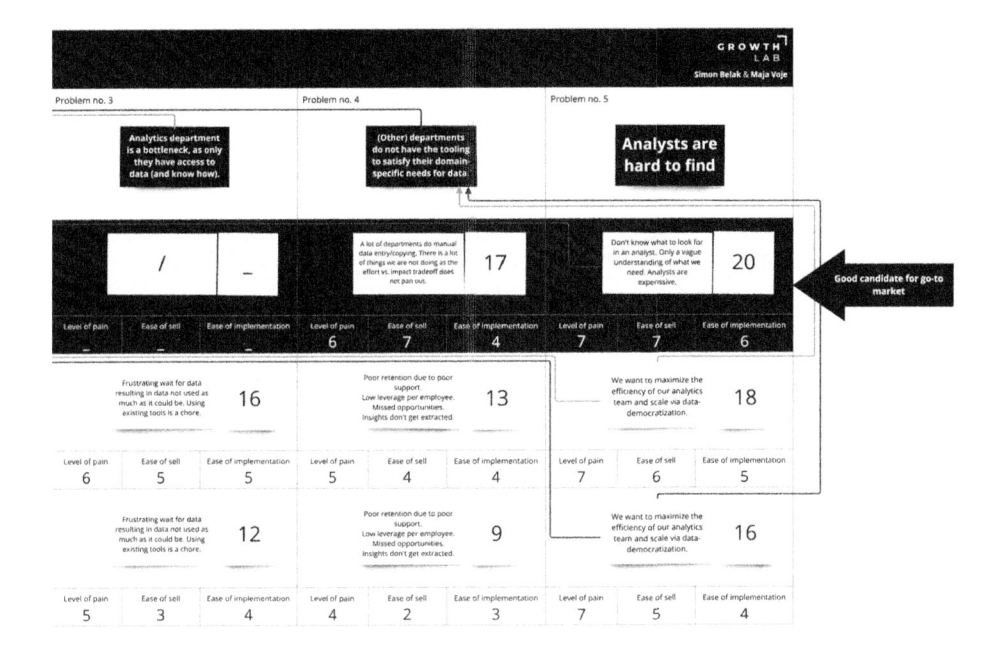

- Ideally, these segments are slightly interconnected, so they serve as a great reference to each other.

- In GTM, you aim to find a winning intercept between the needs of the target audience (called a minimum viable segment, or MVS) and your solution (called a minimum viable product, or MVP). You have to solve your target customer's problem better than anyone else. Sometimes, 10x more added value needs to be created by a GTM company.

- In GTM, it is essential to choose market segments that you can create significant traction on in 3 to 18 months. Early adopters and early majority consumers play an especially important role in GTM.

- 90% of success correlates with having the correct data. The remaining 10% could be a lucky coincidence.

- The first sanity check happens with market research. Is there a market out there that you can grow your business? Combine multiple primary and secondary research methods to gain a holistic understanding of the space.

- Since you are not the only player who plays to win in that market, there will always be some competition present. Make sure to study them, analyze their strengths and weaknesses, and compare them to yours.

- To win, you need to determine your competitive edge and specific space on the market that is currently being underserved or neglected by market leaders.

- The choice is very important because niche specialization and differentiation strategy are the best chances to win. Most GTM companies cannot solely compete on low prices in the long term.

- There are multiple bases on which you can do segmentation, but for most GTM companies, it is recommended to start with problem statements or jobs to be done.

- After identifying multiple market segments, it is important to compare them. Ranking based on selected criteria will help you narrow this range to a manageable selection of 3 to 5 segments that you can best cater to.

- A Market-Problem Map is a tool that helps you better understand selected segments' pain points and rank them based on pain levels, ease of sale, and ease of implementation.

To-Do List:

☐ Conduct market research and present key characteristics of the market and its trends in a spreadsheet.

☐ Prepare a competition comparison spreadsheet.
  ☐ Optional: Create a swipe file in which you can collect the most interesting competitor's resources that are relevant to watches.

☐ Create a SWOT matrix for your solution.
  ☐ Optional: Craft a 2x2 positioning map.

☐ Do the segmentation and rank segments with the segments ranking spreadsheet to find the best GTM candidates.

☐ Refine problem statements with a Market-Problem Map to find the best market entry opportunities.

Find all the worksheets, frameworks, and models mentioned in this chapter at *https://gtmstrategist.com/resources*. They are free and yours to benefit from.

CHAPTER 3

Early Customer Profile

"It's impossible to be everything to everyone, so by identifying and understanding the needs of your ideal customer, you can create a product or service that speaks directly to them."

Sir Richard Branson,
British entrepreneur (Virgin Group), investor, and philanthropist

Winning Beachhead Strategies are built around your selected **Early Customer Profile (ECP)**. We are dealing with a period of up to 18 months in GTM. Customers who will trust you with their business in the GTM stage will usually be different from customers whom you will target five years in business. That is why luring an "ideal customer" in the GTM stage is not always possible. We work with what we have. Your product, offer, marketing, communication, channels, messaging, and price points should suit the needs and preferences of **Early Adopters.** It will help you bridge the gap to the **Early Majority.**

Ideally, you will do this job so well that when an early customer meets you, they're wowed by your offer and believe it was created only for people like them. In GTM, the promised land looks like this:

But how do you find these people? Can you sit down with your team and craft a persona – an archetypal visual representation of your ideal clients? Do you sit down with your team and let your imagination run wild?

> To: **Maja Voje** (grow@majavoje.com)
>
> Subject: **Investor told me to build personas. Who should I hire?**
>
> Hey Maja!
>
> Thanks for all of your help with narrowing down the target segment. After some research and ranking, we decided to go with non-technical founders in the UK who outsource development to lower-cost countries. Developing their own onboarding would cost them a lot and delay the launch.
>
> We are quite happy with that. Thanks again for your help.
>
> Now we are talking with an investment fund, and one of their folks was shocked that we do not have personas made.
>
> To be honest, personas are bullshit, but who am I to object to "the money." :)
>
> Do you have a useful template or know someone who would help us get something done, so we can proceed with real work in customer acquisition?
>
> By no chance will we do a tedious workshop. No, no.
>
> Our developers have other work to do, and they do not like such sessions.
>
> Thanks so much for your guidance.
>
> Looking forward to seeing where this road takes us.
>
> Jasper

Not quite.

If you have followed the book's process, you should have three to five potential Beachhead Segments by now. Next, your job is to collect empirical evidence that you are making the right call in selecting "the one" to focus on. In this chapter, you will learn how to collect these insights using research methods. After that, you can present your findings using the **Early Customer Profile (ECP) Framework** to create what is known to be a "persona" – a customer archetype that we use to understand our customers better.

Why should you bother doing that? Evolving your strategy around a customer definitely pays dividends. According to Paddle's research, companies in the SaaS space with personas achieve 9.16% higher growth rates than other organizations.[14] Moreso, companies that have done some research to make their

---

14 Patric Campbell's presentations Pricing in a Downturn https://paddle-7.wistia.com/medias/mk9ecwpgy2

personas rank 22.51% higher in their growth rates than others. The data shows a correlation between having personas, lowering customer acquisition costs (CAC), and having a higher Net Promoter Score (NPS). Researched personas scored 26.45% lower in CAC, whereas the willingness to recommend the product was a whopping 41.80% higher. Convinced?

To wrap up, great customer archetypes are research-driven, proprietary to the company, and constantly evolving with new insights. ECPs should become a useful compass for your GTM, not a poster of "John Smith from Nashville, Texas, 37, who likes to grill, drives a Buick, has two children, and happens to be a decision-maker in an accounting software company." Sadly, most personas I have seen in my line of work are "John Smith." Let's do it better so they will be really useful.

Make ECP Decisions Confidently

"Research is what I'm doing when I don't know what I'm doing."
Wernher von Braun,
German-American aerospace engineer & father of space travel

Everyone told you you should get to know your customers and listen to them before rolling out a full-blown product, but In practice, many teams still build their products in isolation from the target audience.

Sara Stojanovski, a Senior Product Lead at Glofox, a fitness software platform and passionate believer in customer development research, explains: "At Glofox, product works with marketing on the GTM plan, defining the success metrics, problem overview, messaging proposals, user segment pain points, product value, use cases, etc., followed by a detailed marketing plan. Whoever is responsible for GTM should already be involved in the very early stages of product development. They should be pivotal in setting success metrics instead of being delegated to execute some unrealistic goals. That starts with understanding the problem space, participating in customer development, and creating a value proposition."

Sara and I discussed reasons why such collaborations are more of an exception than a rule in organizations:

- **Know it all**. Some decision-makers, especially founders, believe they know best. They operate as if they serve a market of one (themselves), and customers will get it.

- **Loss of enthusiasm**. At the beginning of every project, the sky is the limit, and motivation is at an all-time high. As time passes, motivation fades, and executing is far less effective. Eventually, it can also die off. Do not rely on motivation and enthusiasm alone. Set up processes, goals, and timelines to support the project.

- **Confusion.** Customer discovery research is sometimes difficult to do, and it takes additional effort to interpret the insights. Learning it is a valuable skill, but some do not even know that they should do it or where to start.

- **Analysis paralysis**. Sometimes, there can simply be too much information. It is vital to implement findings as the insights are discovered and repeat themselves. You can never collect perfect information. Imperfect information paired with fast execution works much better.

- **Laziness.** "Get out of the building" is not a famous mantra. Sitting in an office and daydreaming about what customers might want is cozier.

- **Ego hits.** Psychological barriers, such as fear of rejection and learning the market does not appreciate the innovation as much as the team, make customer discovery challenging to implement in practice.

- **Do it when there is time.** With huge backlogs of tasks to complete, many companies fail to prioritize customer discovery. It should become the backbone, not the backburner of development.

- **Time spent not "working" is a waste of time**. What is your definition of working? Is it coding, designing wireframes, or writing? In GTM, thinking, research, and testing are essential work. Try to internalize this. It takes effort but intense intention in GTM.

In recent decades there has been a drastic shift from "a leader should make decisions and tell the team what they should be doing" towards empowering team members to co-decide by participating and challenging different assumptions. There are usually more unknowns than knowns in GTM. When you know and have evidence to support the decision, you know. When you assume, you validate before making a final decision.

But where to start? You probably have certain ideas about whom you can help most with your product coming from your vision and which problems to solve. But how do you make such an important decision with confidence?

Another military strategy comes into play. The **OODA Loop** is a mental model created by the U.S. Air Force Colonel John Boyd.[15] It's a practical concept and the basis for logical thinking in complex or chaotic circumstances. It consists of four

---

15 OODA loop inspired one of the most well known books for startups: Steve Blank's best-seller The Four Steps of Epiphany.

stages: Observe, Orient, Decide, and Act, collectively known as the OODA loop.

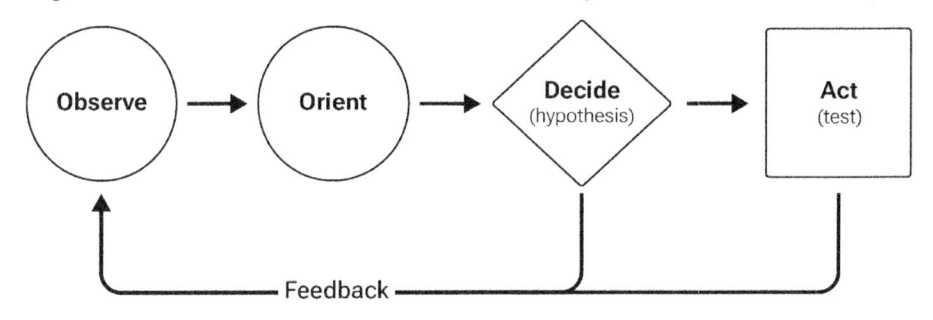

```
Observe → Orient → Decide (hypothesis) → Act (test)
                                              ↓
         ← ← ← ← ← Feedback ← ← ← ← ← ← ← ←
```

Adjusted from OODA Loop by John Boyd

I'll explain this using an example from Jim Huffman, CEO of GrowthHit, co-founder of One Day Design, and CEO of Handsome Chaos. He used these principles to validate the demand for his brand of men's dry shampoo, Handsome Chaos:

- **Observe**: By conducting research and observing customer behavior, this phase aims to validate the problem you're solving. You learn who responds to your solution and how to most favorably solve it. Here's how Jim went through this exercise: *"I am a man with longer hair. My hair gets oily. I've been stealing my wife's dry shampoo. I hate putting powdered sugar on my hair. There has to be something better for a guy like me. I want a product that won't make my hair look oily. There's a problem on the market. My next question is: do other people have this problem?"*

- **Orient:** By doing customer research and collecting insights and feedback, you'll learn more about the problem and test if the proposed solution resonates with the market. But with whom? For Jim, he ran a poll through a survey tool: *"I invested $1,200 to talk to 1,000 people over a certain age and income level to learn if this problem exists elsewhere. Over 70% of people agreed it's a problem and were willing to pay money to solve it. That encouraged us to keep on testing the idea."*

- **Decide:** Based on research findings, a team formulates a hypothesis and continues validation using an experimentation process with methods that provide higher confidence for decision-making. Jim and his team went for a pilot sale: *"The team ran ads to a website with a rendered product image to see if we could sell it. We sold over 50 products at a very good cost per acquisition. That was another signal that we have a problem-solution fit. Later on, we built a waitlist of 1,000 people. That was enough to invest in making the product."

- **Act:** By successfully validating the problem, solution, and customer segment, a team is in much better shape to develop a winning GTM. Jim explained: *"After 14 iterations, we found something I use daily, and the team was also satisfied with the results. Now, we can finally start talking about the go-to-market strategy for the product. We analyzed the market and learned that two things are important to succeed:*

  1. *We should first target customers who are informed buyers in GTM – those who are problem and solution-aware. They will be switching from their existing solution or have done solid research in the field of interest.*

  2. *Develop an irresistible offer and give them a reason to act now."*[16]

Jim and his team did a great job in researching the market before investing in a formulation. They wanted to sanity check if the market had that problem, and if so, they are actively looking for a solution. This journey gave them many insights on who responds best to their offer – their ECP.

Let's look at another great example of how to kick off customer research, and this one is in B2B. During the COVID-19 lockdown in 2020, senior growth expert and author Anuj Adhiya led growth and GTM at the AR reality startup Sophya.[17] Here's how he describes their process of discovering their ECP:

"The team made an assumption that remote and hybrid teams feel disconnected from each other. At customer discovery interviews, we kept hearing that people had Zoom fatigue and did not want to look at a bunch of talking heads anymore. They missed in-person connections. The initial assumption was that a virtual workspace could solve that disconnection people were experiencing.

---

16 Recommended further reading Alex Hormozi's book $100M Offers: How To Make Offers So Good People Feel Stupid Saying No (2021).
17 A solution is now called SoWork and combines virtual spaces with AI - "Sophya bot" into a smart office.

It was our big hypothesis to prove. If it was not true, people might still feel disconnected from their colleagues.

Once we discussed the need for a virtual workspace for teams, multiple other assumptions were nested within it:

- What kinds of teams need that?
- Are these teams of 10 or fewer members, 10 to 50 members, or 50 to 100 members?
- Are these only the teams that need to collaborate a lot?
- Is it marketing teams, HR teams, or any kind of team?
- And if they feel disconnected, what are they feeling disconnected about? Do they just want to chit-chat, or do they want to work?

We needed to research and run experiments to answer all of these questions before moving on. Our selected methods were customer discovery interviews, user testing, and usability tests in the platform's beta version. We wanted to know if we could build a viable business."

This case is similar to hundreds of teams I have worked with. It comes down to three critical steps:

1. **Map and rank your assumptions**. Not all assumptions you test will move the business. This is why it is wise to list the assumptions and select those that are mission-critical for your GTM to succeed.

2. **Choose two to five research methods that are stage-appropriate**. A wide variety of research methods are available to teams, but most narrow down the selection based on their confidence level for validation. While nearly everyone can do 10 to 20 customer discovery interviews, not all teams have the means to conduct a valid A/B test.

3. **Build a system of experimentation for constant learning and improvement**. Testing hypotheses are relevant throughout your GTM journey. Start building a testing methodology as soon as possible and create a shared database of learnings that will transform your company into a lean GTM machine.

Let's dive into these three steps and learn how to apply them to your business.

Map your ECP Assumptions

"Assumption is the mother of all mistakes."
Eugene Lewis Fordsworthe, Political Scientist

Instead of acting upon leap-of-faith assumptions and serendipitous moments of good luck, let's build the foundations of how you can test your ECP assumption that you generated with the Market-Problem Map.

An **Assumption Map** is a mental model that will help you list and prioritize assumptions that you should test first.[18] In this model, the focus is on identifying and examining the assumptions that are driving the current thinking around a particular problem or opportunity. The goal is to surface hidden assumptions and validate if they are reliable.

The first step in the process is listing your assumptions. Remember Jasper's case? He wanted to validate the Beachhead Segment of non-technical founders in the UK for his easy-to-use onboarding tool. This was his core assumption. To validate these assumptions, Jasper sat down with his team and brainstormed the following assumptions:

1. What problem does our customer want to solve in the first place?
2. Why can't our customers solve this problem today?
3. What is the outcome - what does our customer want to achieve?

---

18 Bland, D. J., & Osterwalder, A. (2020). Testing Business Ideas. Wiley.

Brainstorming Assumptions

1. What is the problem that our customer wants to solve in the first place?
2. Why can't our customers solve this problem today?
3. What does out customer want to achieve?

Prioritizing Assumptions

High risk assumptions—if proven wrong—could mean that our initiative fails. Unknown assumptions are those that we don't currently have much information about. How would we prioritize our assumptions along these axes?

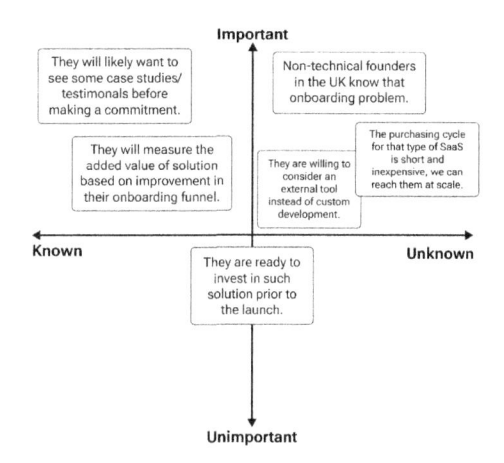

Brainstorming board:

- Non-technical founders in the UK are a Beachhead for a simple onboarding SaaS.
- Non-technical founders in the UK know that they have an onboarding problem.
- They are willing to consider an external tool instead of custom development.
- They are ready to invest in such solution prior to the launch.
- They will measure the added value of solution based on improvement in their onboarding funnel.
- The purchasing cycle for that type of SaaS is short and inexpensive, and we can reach them at scale.
- They will likely want to see some case studies/testimonials before making a commitment.

Prioritization matrix (Important/Unimportant × Known/Unknown):

- Important / Known: They will likely want to see some case studies/testimonals before making a commitment.
- Important / Unknown: Non-technical founders in the UK know that onboarding problem.
- Important (mid): They will measure the added value of solution based on improvement in their onboarding funnel. They are willing to consider an external tool instead of custom development.
- Important (mid-Unknown): The purchasing cycle for that type of SaaS is short and inexpensive, we can reach them at scale.
- Unimportant / mid: They are ready to invest in such solution prior to the launch.

Adjusted from Peter Osmenda's Assumptions & Experiments

The team came up with multiple assumptions. It does not make sense to validate them all at once; therefore, they prioritized their assumption in the matrix consisting of two dimensions:

- **Known - Unknown**: Do you have any tangible or even anecdotal evidence that the assumption could be true?
- **Important - Unimportant.** What is the actual business impact that assumption could have? How dangerous would it be if these assumptions proved wrong?

Their unknown, high risk assumption should be tested first. Their assumption is that non-technical founders in the UK are aware of their onboarding problem and are ready to act upon it now.

How can Jasper and his team test this assumption? Should they just roll out the product and see what happens? Do a couple of interviews with potential customers? A survey on social media groups?

Let's figure that out in the next section. For those who would like to dive into assumption mapping further, I added an advanced tip on how to use the model beyond validating the ECP assumptions. The original model has much broader implications but has the same principles:

1. List down the assumptions.
2. Prioritize them, and find those that are critical to validate.
3. Start validating.

Now, let's start validating!

> **Advanced tip:** Assumption mapping model originally consists of three types of assumptions- desirability, viability and feasibility. It was simplified for this section of the book to work on ECP, but if you want to apply it holistically, here is the recommended method to do it:
>
> **Desirability assumptions** - Do they want this? (orange post-its)
> Who are the target customers for our solution?
> What problem do our customers want to solve?
> How do our customers solve this problem today?
> Why can't our customers solve this problem today?
> What is the outcome our customers want to achieve?
> Why will our customers stop using their current solution?
>
> **Feasibility assumptions** - Can we do this? (blue post-its)
> What are our biggest technical or engineering challenges?
> What are our biggest legal or regulatory risks?
> What are our internal governance or policy hurdles?
> Why does our leadership team support this solution?
> Where does our funding for this solution come from?
> Why is our team uniquely positioned to win?
>
> **Viability assumptions** - Should we do this? (green post-its)
> What are our main acquisition channels for obtaining new customers?
> How will our customers repeatedly use our solution?
> Why will our customers refer us to new customers? How does this solution support our company vision?
> Who are the primary competitors to our solution?

How will our solution generate revenue?

1. Do they want this?
Write each answer on *orange* stickies.

- Who are the target customers for our solution?
- Why can't our customers solve this problem today?
- What problem do our customers want to solve?
- What is the outcome our customers wants to achieve?
- How do our customers solve this problem today?
- Why will our customers stop using their current solution?

2. Can we do this?
Write each answer on *blue* stickies.

- What are our biggest technical or engineering challenges?
- Why does our leadership team support this solution?
- What are our biggest legal or regulatory risk
- Where does our funding for this solution come from?
- What are our internal governance or policy hurdles?
- Why our team is uniquely positioned to win?

3. Should we do this?
Write each answer on *green* stickies.

- What are our main acquisition channels for obtaining customers?
- How does this solution support our company vision?
- How will our customers repeatedly use our solution?
- Who are our primary competitors to our solution?
- Why will our customers refer us to new customers?
- How will our solution generate revenue?

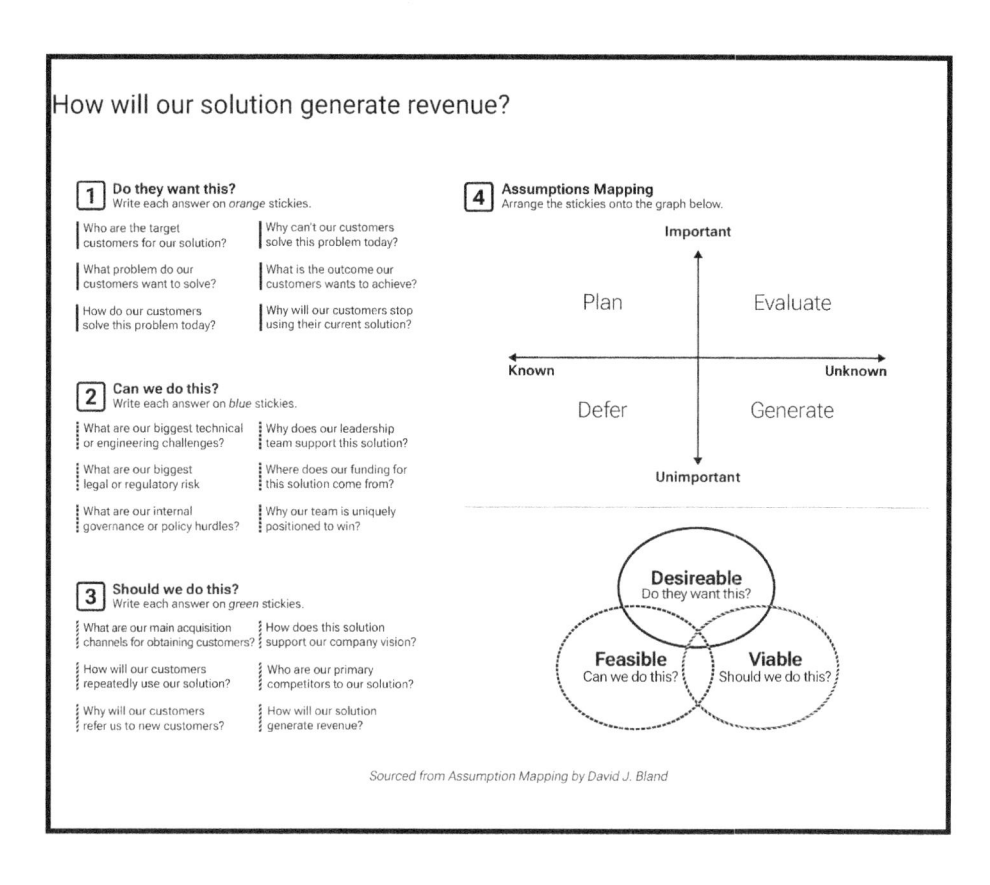

4. Assumptions Mapping
Arrange the stickies onto the graph below.

	Known	Unknown
Important	Plan	Evaluate
Unimportant	Defer	Generate

- **Desireable** — Do they want this?
- **Feasible** — Can we do this?
- **Viable** — Should we do this?

Sourced from Assumption Mapping by David J. Bland

ECP Validation Toolkit

> "One of the things that make any company successful was that we understood and catered to the customer. If it didn't sell, it didn't make a difference what we thought or our research told us. They told us if it was successful by buying it or not."
>
> Bernard Marcus, Co-Founder of Home Depot

In GTM, we lean on research methods to do the validation. When it comes to customer research, it is a bit similar to flossing teeth. Many know they should be doing it, but they don't. I get it. Research can be overwhelming, and it can feel like it's non-mission-critical. Merely the selection of a research method can be confusing. So, let's break it down into manageable chunks to find your two to five appropriate research methods and find insights that will inspire your hypothesis for experimentation later on.

There are two types of research methods. In professional jargon, we often refer to them as qual and quant.

Qualitative methods (Qual) such as user interviews, focus or user groups, usability tests, etc., where you deal with fewer participants but get deep insights from them. Qual methods are used from the early stages. Later on, your assumptions can be tested more reliably on a more significant sample, if needed.

Quantitative methods (Quant) include surveys, MVP tests, A/B testing, multivariate testing, etc. The samples should be big enough to achieve statistical significance and read patterns from the numbers instead of deep-diving into a single research participant. The samples of hundreds or thousands of responses are generated and interpreted together. Quant methods often require a certain level of product maturity and large enough traffic volume before you can use them reliably. Doing quant of a sample that is too small can lead to non-optimal decision-making in GTM.

Combined, qual and quant research methods can create powerful intelligence for any company. But which one should you start with? Is it enough to do 12 interviews, or do you need to run ads to attract thousands of people to do a full-blown A/B test to validate the assumption? Your decision will mainly depend on two factors: **the state of product development** that you can work with and the level of **confidence** that you want to create for your decision-making.

While the product development stage is more or less a given, confidence refers to the strength of evidence you aim to get. As indicated above, common advice is to aim for a 95% confidence interval when using quant methods. However, according to Dr. Else van der Berg, many GTM companies settle to operate within a range of 70 to 80%. When discussing confidence, "people do" always triumphs, "people say." If someone says they are interested in buying a solution, the confidence is lower than if they have already bought your product.

Dr. Else van der Berg and I joined forces to create a framework that will help you select the optimal research method for you at the moment. Given the product development stage and the required level of confidence, you can easily narrow down the validation methods that make the most sense for you.

Else and I created the framework from our experiences of working with more than 600 GTM companies and shortlisted the validation methods we have seen working very well repeatedly. Some are ongoing, such as interviews, since you can always learn plenty from talking to a customer. Others are state-of-product dependent, such as MVP testing and presale. No matter where you are on the spectrum of product maturity, you can use these methods to make GTM decisions with more confidence.

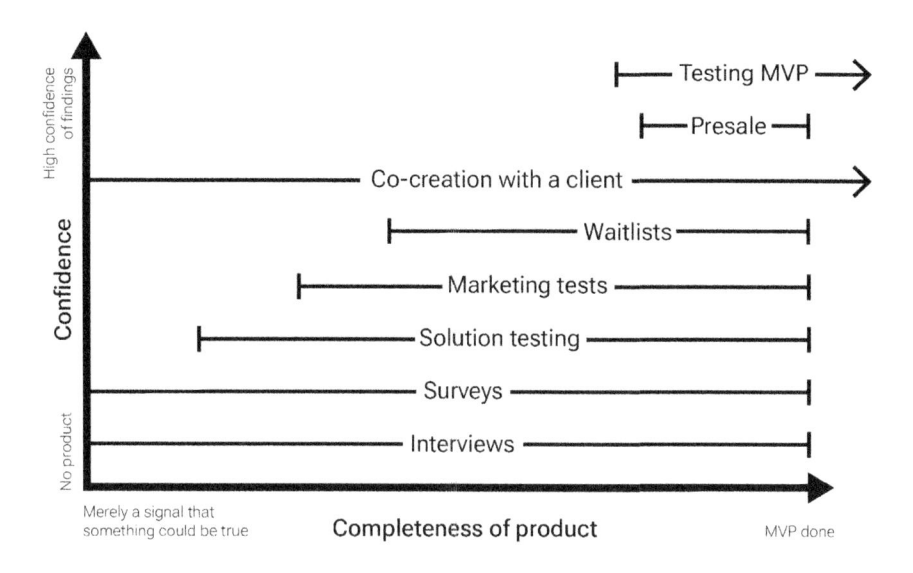

```
Confidence
High confidence of findings
                                            |— Testing MVP →
                                         |— Presale —|
            |———— Co-creation with a client ————→
                  |————— Waitlists —————|
                |———— Marketing tests ————|
           |———————— Solution testing ————————|
                  |————— Surveys —————|
                  |————— Interviews —————|
No product
         Merely a signal that
         something could be true   Completeness of product    MVP done
```

Source: Adjusted from Dr. Else van der Berg [19]

Now imagine confidence (C) on a scale of 1 to 5. Low C (1 to 2) means that a small number of people said something (e.g., you did five customer interviews), Middle C means that multiple people said it but have not really bought it (2 to 3), and high C (4 to 5), you have collected evidence that multiple people will purchase a solution.

This is how Jasper's team used validation methods for the ECP of their onboarding tool. Remember that their unknown, high risk assumption from assumption mapping was that non-technical founders in the UK are aware of their onboarding problem and are ready to act upon it now. This is what happened.

---

[19] Suggested further reading: Dr. Else van der Berg prepared a comprehensive handbook on research and methods that you can access here free of charge https://app-eu1.hubspot.com/documents/26963141/view/530524341?accessId=5d0f07

	C (1-5)	Short description
Interviews	1	Interviews are great for in-depth insights but only serve as the first anchor. Some early-stage teams have their number of interviews and findings as one of their KRs in their GTM journey. When doing interviews, it is vital to prepare great scripts. In GTM, we usually use the Mom test interviews.[20] Analyzing interviews is hugely important. You are searching for patterns, so you should use insights mapping. To capture everything, do not ignore nonverbal communication and sentiment as well. You can conduct interviews with field experts to
Surveys	2	You get more responses, but respondents still say they don't want to buy. To conduct a somewhat representative survey, you need at least 100 responses, or better yet, 1,000. An Instagram poll that 20 followers engaged with is not a good survey. You can use tools like Google Forms, Typeform, and Survey Monkey to easily create and analyze the answers. For optimal completion rates, stick up to 10 questions. Ensure that you attract the right type of respondents so that results will be relevant for your GTM. When analyzing a survey, make sure to segment the data and observe how different subgroups behave differently. There can be value bombs in answers to open-ended questions. Do not leave them out just because
Solution testing	2.5	Respondents are on a mission to finish the tasks, which is still not the real purchasing intent, yet this time, they do something and no longer talk about it. The most widely used ways of solution testing in GTM are beta testing, usability testing, and feature testing. Beta testing allows users to independently interact with the solution, whereas with usability and feature testing, a researcher verbally or technologically guides them through the process. Even if you are not developing a technology product, consider usability testing. It is very applicable for testing websites and apps and can even be done on a document like a PDF or presentation. A "magic number" for usability tests is considered to be five.[21] After five testers completed the tasks,

	Example
learn new things, with customers, prospects, and even churned prospects/customers (surprisingly interesting findings of why they did not go or continue doing business with you throughout your GTM journey.	Jasper booked 20 interviews with non-technical founders in London. He found the respondents on LinkedIn through accelerators and local meetups. He focused the interview on their problems with onboarding, Existing solutions to the problem, and what existing solutions lack. He did not pitch the tool. That was tough for him. Out of the 20 founders he interviewed in person, 12 were extremely interested in the solution, and one agreed to create the pilot. Jasper did not expect that.
they are more difficult to analyze. You will get a sample of a PMF survey later. Still, you can use them throughout your GTM journey to test marketing ideas, pricing, customer preferences, and room for improvement/innovation.	Jasper would like to learn what specifically are onboarding-related problems and for whom are the most painful. After conducting interviews with the founders, he still did not fully understand who exactly is his ECP. Therefore, we thought that he needed a bigger sample. He put together a survey focusing on verified pain points, what tools/solutions they are using/considering at the moment, and where they are getting the information for that. He posted a link to a survey in a social media group where UK founders exchanged information and got 272 responses. He was surprised to learn that a subgroup of UK non-technical founders showed especially high interest in the solution – fitness and meal planning apps.
a researcher found 85% usability issues. Further tests might have diminishing returns. Recruiting respondents that match your target group is very important in solution testing. Marketers, UXers, developers, and other digital experts should be excluded from the recruiter if they are not a target group.	Wow, that was interesting and very unlikely. Since Jasper already has a demo of the tool, he circled back to these respondents from the survey and asked them if they could do a usability test with their UX designer. Jasper aims to learn if this group of UK non-technical founders from the fitness and meal planning space understands how to install the solution. Out of 35 founders in the space who were invited to participate, six said yes, and one did not show up on a call. Jasper and his UXer had five usability tests with respondents. The task was to install an onboarding tool to their web app and set it up. Four out of five did it successfully. One did not know how to navigate his CMS and was anxious to do it.

	C (1-5)	Short description
Marketing test	2 (likes), 3 (clicks), 4 (sign-ups)	First, signals from the market and cold audiences come in that are informative but a signal if not associated with sales just yet. We measure social media responses, opt-ins, signups, or clicks in marketing testing. They are usually done in a way that they emulate the intended purchasing flow, but at the end, notify the user to "sign up" to be the first to know when it will be launched. It can also be a simple teaser on social media to measure the sentiment and interest in the innovation. A marketing test is often done in combination with a waitlist or a smoke test, where you actually sell the solution. Doing marketing tests is fantastic for messaging because you can test the offer, the
Waitlist	3.5	If done in a way that customers hit the "order now" button and know the price, it can be a great indication of the market wanting a solution. Based on my experience, the conversions to waitlists are between 10 and 30% if the messaging is good (includes benefits and some offers for early adopters). However, conversion rates to paid customers plummet if the waitlist audience is not well nurtured. People barely remember what they signed up for yesterday, not in six months of delayed launch. It is best to consider doing a waitlist in a timely fashion and update and nurture recipi-
Co-creation with a client	4.5	This is mainly used in B2B for complex projects. Congrats! That is already an actual purchase and solid validation right there. After all the long and hard work, it feels so good to have someone using and paying for the product. But be a little careful here, please. Two big mistakes that many technical teams make in co-creation with the clients are that they allocate too many resources towards serving that client and selling these pilots too cheaply. The first one is dangerous because it can divert the product development roadmap from its vision towards serving the market of one (that client). If you make a product, not a service agency, guess what you should be working more on. The second is very problematic to solve because "any client is better than no client," right? Not necessarily. With

	Example
wording, and even different audiences before the "big bang" you make with your lunch. It can be done with advertising, content creation on social media, email marketing, and on websites. The sooner you start doing it, the more insights you can gather for D-Day.	Jasper and his team were hyped. Maybe they have found the ECP! But are four people who said they would use it and pass the usability test enough to put it in writing? Not yet. The team needed further evidence. This is why they returned to survey data and reviewed where UK non-technical fitness and meal planning app founders hang out online. Two social media groups and one influencer in the space stood up. Jasper is very persistent. He convinced the influencer to mention their product in his newsletter, which was sent to more than 5,000 entrepreneurs weekly. 327 of them clicked on the news.
ents with updates and useful content. By doing that, they are more forgiving of delays that might happen.	Out of 327 clicks, 78 people actually signed up for a waitlist for the product. With emails, names, phone numbers, and company pages - it is finally getting real! The team could not believe it! After a little celebration in the office, they investigated the data a bit further. Wait! These people were not only from the UK. More than 75% of website visitors and singers came from the US. Is this audience really that different between the UK and the US? Does it even make sense to target geographically?
heavy discounts, you lower the reference price for future deals. It is really hard to make them pay more later. Such offers may also attract not the right talk of clients who act deviously and churn when things get normal. Co-creation should be a partnership that benefits both sides and is managed so that the company does not end up serving "the market of one."	Remember the guy from the usability test who was interested in doing a pilot project with the team? Jasper understood that he would have a much more convincing case if a client reference was attached to a launch and he could share real data. He called him next, and they agreed that some extra development was needed to do the integration. If a client agrees to commit to a year and to do a case study together, the team will do a technical setup for them. That was an extremely interesting experience because clients gave interesting insights; they wanted more customization to their brand colors, and something was not working well on mobile. Useful to know before the launch.

	C (1-5)	Short description
Presale	4.8	Already paid for, bravo, let's go and scale! A presale or a smoke test is an excellent validation that customers are willing to pay the price for the product. If you manage to presell and customers actually swiped their credit cards, you are in business. Pay attention to the offer for a presale. Usually, your most loyal followers will buy at presell. If you offer large discounts, you might leave money on the table. Other important things are to ensure that you have some targets on presale, that you can measure what is going on on the website, which will be hugely helpful later on the road, and that you have solemnly tested the funnel before the transaction actually happens. Expect the unexpected.
Testing MVP	3 (single feature), 5 (mash-up of features)	Congrats, it is not what they say, it is what they buy, and you will only retain them if you deliver on the promise. This is where life gets really interesting. With your product and website analytics in place, you can still use other methods such as surveys, customer interviews, usability tests for new features, and many interesting new options at this stage. You might want to use big quarry and data science to analyze usage patterns, and you can set up session recordings and heatmaps with tools such as Hotjar, CrazyEgg, and Clicktale. There is an exciting science of eye tracking that you could be interested in, and of course, the GOAT of all technical teams – A/B and multivariate testing. The key to implementing A/B (2 options), AB/C (3 options), or multivariate testing is to have a sufficient sample size. You want to conduct experiments that give you results with enough confidence while not leaving you out in the open. For

	Example
	Jasper and his team had a long talk. After reflecting that it does not make much sense to launch the solution only to the UK first because those founders are connected in international communities, they decided to launch a presale campaign targeted to the global fitness and meal prep app community. They had a waitlist, and Jasper was pinging that influencer twice a week to give them another placement in his newsletter to promote the presale (7 days from the launch) at a 20% discount for the first three months. The presale was okay, not great, but not terrible. They managed to pre-sell 61 3-month subscriptions for $99, and they were happy to get some budgets for advertising for the launch.
that, you need a sufficient sample. There are plenty of free online calculators of the sample size that you can use to plan that.[22] Many vendors, such as Google Optimize, Unbounce, AB Testly, VWO, Adobe, Optimizely, etc., for conducting split tests also have in-build calculators of the statistical significance of the results. Do not worry if the sample for slit testing is too large for now. Eventually, you will get there, and you can use other methods in the meantime.	It is finally launch time for the team! Based on alpha and beta testing data, usability tests, and co-development of the pilot with the project, Jasper and his team are finally ready to go to market with their MVP. Since the team is very technical, they measure all key metrics, but the issue is that they do not have the traffic to split test (A/B) test and get representative data. Instead, they went for an in-product survey on a pricing page. It pops up when the visitor demonstrates an exit attempt and asks: What is preventing you from subscribing today? By collecting 137 responses, they realized that most need to check with their development team if they can use this product. Jasper is hyped to create more technical documentation and a page for developers, which apparently also influences the purchase.

Source: Dr. Else van der Berg

---

[20] Fitzpatrick, R. (2013). The Mom Test: How to Talk to Customers & Learn If Your Business Is a Good Idea When Everyone Is Lying to You.
[21] Turner, Carl & Lewis, James & Nielsen, Jakob. (2006). Determining Usability Test Sample Size.
[22] For example: https://abtestguide.com/abtestsize/

Diligent research always reveals more than you ask it. Jasper and his team learned much more about their ECP and nicely narrowed down the Beachhead Segment from "non-technical founders in the UK" to a selected subgroup of such founders by using validation methods. Most early-stage GTM strategists decide to use two to three validation methods at first.

Experienced professionals will use more. Jeremy Epperson is the founder and Chief Growth Officer of a consulting firm. He has spent 16 years consulting and advising for the fastest-growing startups in Silicon Valley and has launched ROI-positive conversion rate optimization programs for 210+ startups in under 90 days. He suggests: "We do 6 to 9 research methods in the first 90 days of our projects. I know it's easier for a consulting firm with a dedicated market/customer research team to do this, but that's a quantum leap forward, and the insights collected on shorter timelines help paint a more accurate picture earlier in the process. In most cases, it takes 85 to 115 days to show the value of a growth initiative before it gets deprioritized or defunded. Speed is of the essence."

That was a great teaser for the last and most reliable way of validating your ECP – full-blown experiments.

Experimentation: Learning by Doing

"Observation and experiment for gathering material, induction, and deduction for elaborating it: these are only good intellectual tools."
Sir Francis Bacon,
the father of the scientific method and an English philosopher

There is no fine line between research and experimentation in GTM. While most growth experts say having a product-market fit is a prerequisite for using growth experimentation methodologies, I think differently. I have seen the benefits of using them hundreds of times, even in pre-product market fit.

Experimentation is a process of making decisions based on a scientific method by setting a hypothesis, testing it, and learning from it. By establishing an experimentation mindset, GTM companies can benefit from adopting experimentation methodologies and processes much sooner than often thought.

Back in 2016, I was working with a team on a crowdfunding campaign. To invest our tiny budget the best we could, we did a pre-launch marketing test to learn which audiences and messages would work best for our launch. We tested five possible audiences and invested $2,000 in ads. We found a clear winner – one audience that outperformed all others. Armed with these insights, we changed our messaging and the "look and feel" of our communication to better cater to that specific group. We rocked the campaign.

I am convinced our campaign wouldn't have been as successful if we had gone with the "one-size-fits-all" approach. To learn who "the one" is, we experimented and reverse-engineered the ECP from the results of an actual campaign instead of guessing.

Similarly, I tested two landing page versions to build a waitlist of subscribers for this book. The first landing page was very basic, with a vanilla design, and it converted at 35%. This is not great, but also not terrible. The second landing page was out of this universe with a very funky look and feel. This version produced signups at a whopping 47%, which I've never seen in my career since. I also did several polls on social media and tested models on LinkedIn posts before placing them in a book.

Bottom line: whenever you don't know something, it's easier to make the decision confidently by doing research and running some tests than holding on to an assumption on launch day.

In the previous chapter, you have already read about marketing tests, waitlists, presale, and testing MVPs as research methods. But Jasper's scientific mind is intrigued by the idea that he could also run some experiments to find the best shots of validating their high risk, unknown ECP assumption that non-technical founders in the UK know their onboarding problem and are ready to act upon it now.

The team made a simple experimentation plan to best test this assumption. You will learn more about the experimentation process in the last chapter of this book, but for now, let's see how to validate your ECP with an experiment.

Based on Jasper's observation, the target audience is already actively asking for tech tools in local Facebook groups, and the team will ask the admins of these groups if they can post their beta invite there. The team will use custom UTM links to measure which of the five selected groups responded best to their beta invite to inform further GTM actions. The team set up a hypothesis that it would be a win if the groups produced at least 200 applicants for the beta that were a close match to their ECP assumption. Upon further analysis of how the beta applicants validate and retain within a product, they can refine the ECP further. Here is a simple experiment card the team created to run this experiment.

Assumption	Experiment
Non-technical founders in the UK know they have an onboarding problem.	Post an invite to beta in Facebook startup groups.

We believe that	Involving	Will result in	We'll know that we're right when	Results
Our audience is already actively searching for onboarding solutions in local Facebook startup groups. This is why we will publish our invite there.	We'll ask admins from the five Facebook groups we validated with our customer interviews to see if we can publish there. We will also add different UTM links to understand which group attracted the most signups.	We will gauge interest from our target audience in the solution. It will also help us with early traction and to understand the target audience better.	The experiment is a success if we gain at least 200 registrants to the beta.	We got 251 signups, we rock! ✌️
Describe the experiment.	Who will be the participants?	Describe the predicted outcome you'll use to validate the assumption.	Describe how you will observe the outcome through measurable results.	After the experiment, describe what was actually observed.

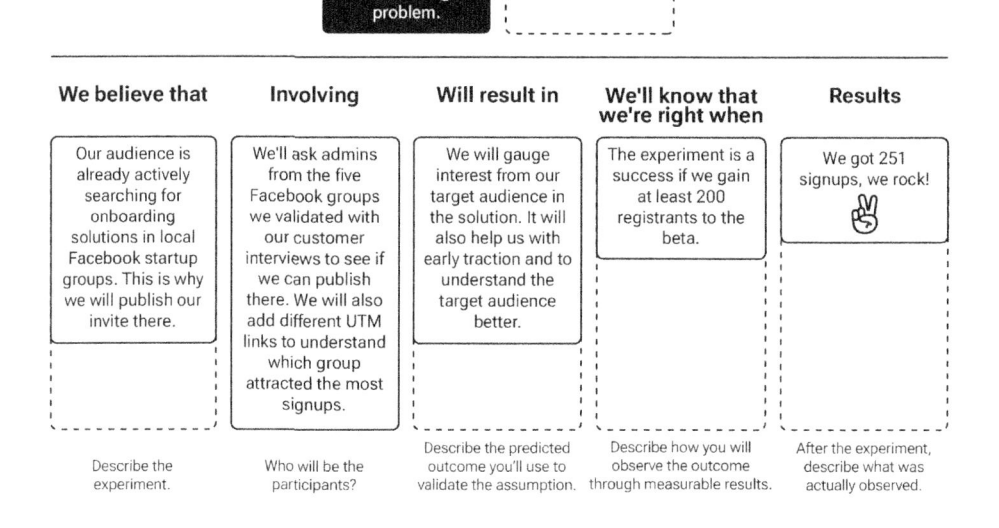

Adjusted from Peter Osmenda's Assumptions & Experiments

We actually ran this experiment with one of the teams I coached to get 500 subscribers before their Y Combinator pitch. It worked like a charm. We generated 643 relevant sign-ups and learned a ton from them. Prior to that, the team ran LinkedIn ads and got very poor results. We started to target a more relevant audience and created a more meaningful connection with them. $0 was spent; it all happened with some outreach and social media posts to relevant groups.

The last thought I would love to leave you with is my colleague Anuj Adhiya's view that the number of learnings is the most important metric when you're starting out:

"No single framework, no hack, nothing is ever going to guarantee success in GTM. But what it can guarantee is raising the odds of success. Ask yourself every Monday: 'Are we smarter this week than last week?' It doesn't have to be big, and it doesn't have to be small. If we cannot objectively say that we are not smarter this week, we are learning too slowly."[23]

Now that you have generated some evidence of what ECP is by doing assumption mapping, research, and experimentation, it's time to put a face on it and present it in a way that your team and other stakeholders can envision who is at the heart of your interest in your GTM.

---

[23] ProductLed Podcast, October 2022: https://productled.com/blog/howigothere-with-anuj-adhiya

Early Customer Profile (ECP)

"There can be only one."
Fictional character Kurgan in Highlander (1986)

One of the hardest elements of running a business is focus. Especially if you are a curious soul on a mission to help as many people as possible solve their problems. But remember the Beachhead rule – you start with a Beachhead Segment that you can win in the first 18 months. Later on, you are in a much better shape and position to conquer adjacent markets.

Having done the research or even launched some experiments as suggested in this chapter, you are ready to start crafting your GTM strategy around the selected Beachhead Segment because:

THERE CAN BE ONLY ONE

In a simplistic view, GTM should be laser-focused on one audience, one offer, and one channel. But the reality can be a bit more complex.

To find better-suited answers, this section:

- Establishes an understanding of why focusing on early instead of the ideal customer is the reality of GTM fields.

- Discusses two use cases (there are, of course, more) in which there definitely has to be more than one ECP profile in the minds and hearts of a GTM strategist.

- Proposes a framework for putting your ECP to words and colors based on insights from your research, experiments, and learnings, not based on stereotypes.

Sounds good? Let's go!

Early Customer Profile vs. Ideal Customer Profile

"The first adopters are true believers who see the potential and are willing to take a leap of faith. Their support and enthusiasm can ignite a revolution in the market."
Simon Sinek, renowned author, motivational speaker, and leadership expert

When creating "customer profiles," people can get carried away. Daydreaming of some ideal scenario in which Elon Musk falls in love with your product is aspirational, if not delusional, for most to believe. And not very likely to happen in the first 3 to 18 months of GTM. Forget the ideal user. Let's focus on the ideal customer you can successfully address, serve, and monetize in the next quarter or two. Here is a brief difference in early vs. ideal customer profiles.

ECP ≠ ICP

Early Customer Profile
- Early adopter who loves to try new tech.
- Easy to work with; they can totally self onboard.
- Generous and understanding in giving feedback; great beta testers. 🐴
- Will gladly endorse you if they are happy.

Ideal Customer Profile
- Would make a great logo on your website.
- Hard to close – Moby Dick Syndrome. 🐋
- Go big or go home.
- Requires proof of work.
- Takes time & compliance to onboard them.
- Once they are in – they are in it to win it. ✌

The GTM clock is ticking. Going all in to win a Beachhead Segment with an average purchasing cycle of 14 months might not be the best bet. Before getting a chance to convince the **ideal customer**, you will most likely have to win the hearts and minds of **early customers**.[1] Build an audience of people who will enthusiastically go on a journey with you and appreciate them.

Kevin Kelly argues that to build a healthy business, all you need at first is a list of 1,000 people who are all true fans.[2] After they experience the value you provide through content, community, educational materials, videos, or free versions of the product, they will likely buy from you once you present them with an offer. Some of them will stick with you for years and become the most valuable ambassadors of your product.

This is the other important criterion for the Beachhead Segment. It is very good if it offers potential for virality and word-of-mouth (WOM) to fuel the adoption of your solution. Early adopters usually enjoy making recommendations, writing online reviews, helping others understand and use solutions, or even participating in development. They feel proud if they have discovered something. It really makes them look good in their social circles.

Best-in-class GTM strategists not only know their ECP, but they become one with it. They understand their culture of communities, speak their language, and develop the ability to predict their needs and wants before they are even expressed.

Growth expert Ishita Jariwala ran GTM programs with thousands of early adopters, many of whom are engineers in the technology space for MongoDB and MathWorks. Ishita is an engineer by education, so she understands that technical users don't like traditional sales and marketing tactics. Instead, they are interested in two things:

1. How are you making them better at doing their job?
2. How are you making them smarter?

Early adopters need to see the product. They need to try it. They need it to solve their problem. They are eager to read, learn, and dive into the solution itself if they see the value. It can be a demanding crowd to win trust with, but when satisfied, they make a loyal user base and are passionate ambassadors.

---

21 Crossing the Chasm in GTM means winning Early Adopter and transitioning to Early Majority.
2 https://kk.org/thetechnium/1000-true-fans/

Other early adopters that might have vastly different preferences and needs later than adjacent mainstream markets are young moms, vegans, gamers, pet parents, brides, crossfitters, and/or peculiar compliance managers. They will see through hype and marketing BS, storytelling, and direct response copy (E.g., *"This offer runs out in 6 minutes! Hurry up!"*) because they genuinely want a solution to their problem. Not only do you have to know their problem, you have to fall in love with solving it and earn their trust before gaining permission to present the offer.

Let's say you are targeting engineers. You shouldn't invest in an ad campaign targeting people who like Star Wars, Game of Thrones, or Dungeons & Dragons. Learn the true sources they trust and find inspiration from. A simple email could be an amazing source of intelligence, like this email an engineer sent to learn more about where they spend their time.

From: **Engineer** (engineer@company.com)

I hope you are doing well!

I am writing to you because I need some help... 😊

We are in the process of increasing visibility of _____. We want to be present at important events, have articles in important magazines, follow certain channels, etc.

As there is a lot of things available and we want to systematically approach everything, I am asking you if you can answer/comment on my questions below:

- Which magazines from the industry are you (or the company) subscribed to?
- Which fares or conferences do you attend every year?
- Is there a special community where you get great information for your work, but is not well known to outsiders?
- Which channels do you follow on social media?

Now that you see the information I am looking for, please feel free to recommend something else as well. I hope you are able to help me here. 😊

Looking forward to your reply, and thank you in advance.

Br

Why bother doing hours of ECP desk research and hoping for the best when they are eager to tell you what is actually relevant for them?

Multiple-Player ECPs

"All of us start from zero. We take the right decision and become a hero."
Govinda, Indian actor, comedian, dancer, and former politician

In many cases, there will not be a single ECP, which is okay. There are certain product types, decision models, and business models that require interactions between multiple stakeholders. The value from such products can simply not be created and delivered to a single audience.

If you are GTM-ing for a product whose value delivery is conditioned from interactions of multiple players on the platform or selling to customers that make purchasing decisions in a larger group, pay very close attention to each of the stakeholders in the system. In such cases, you will have to win them. Let's explain both instances in more detail:

- If you are working on a GTM or growth strategy for a marketplace, social media platform, multiple-player game, collaboration tool, dating app, or any other product that requires "supply" and "demand" side or a large number of users interacting with each other, you might be dealing with the **Cold Start Problem**, as explained by author, growth experts and VC Andrew Chen.[3] Such platforms need network effects, and your job as a GTM strategist is to secure and grow all critical ECPs to deliver value through the platforms. Imagine that you would have to wait 45 minutes to get an Uber. That would be a very lame experience. Instead, the GTM strategy that the company developed was city-by-city expansion and securing a critical mass of drivers (even by subsidizing them) before launching a big acquisition campaign to acquire users. No drivers, no rides. There are no viewers without content creators, and there are no buyers without sellers.

- Decisions can be accepted by multiple people, especially when they affect a larger group of people (e.g., a company, a family, or a community).

---

3 Chen, A. (2021). The Cold Start Problem: How to Start and Scale Network Effects. Hardcover. Harper Business.

A **Decision Making Unit (DMU)** considers all decision-makers in a purchasing process.[4] DMUs exist both in the B2C and B2B buying processes.

DMU role	Buying a vacuum cleaner in my family (B2C).	A company with 500 employees is changing its accounting software (B2B).
Initiator first thinks of a purchase.	My husband wants to have a robotic vacuum cleaner because he is annoyed that he has to plug and unplug the vacuum when we are cleaning the house.	The Head of Accounting has recognized that the current solution no longer supports their processes with too much manual data entry. Some tasks need to be automated.
Influencer's views sway the purchase.	We visited some friends the other night, and they had a vivid discussion about robotic vacuum cleaners.	The Sales Director strongly supports the initiative. It would free some accounting resources to issue the invoice faster. Other accountants strongly dislike data entry.
Gatekeeper can say no to the decision.	Our dog doesn't like vacuum cleaners. She is attacking them. Robotics are not an option because she would chase it around all day long.	#1: A new budget will have to be negotiated with finance. #2: The IT department will have to evaluate compatibility with ERP and risk assessment.
Decider actually decides what to buy.	The husband agreed to a wireless vacuum cleaner as a compromise.	After the Head of Accounting presented a business case to the CFO and the CEO, they agreed to use it.
Buyer makes a purchase (can be different from the Decider).	He might mention this to his parents, who would like to buy a gift.	Purchasing department after procurement.
User uses or consumes the purchase.	Whoever is more annoyed by the mess that day.	Accountants at the company and their external partners.

---

4 McDonald, M., Rogers, B., & Woodburn, D. (2000). Key customers: How to Manage them Profitably. Butterworth-Heinemann.

If you suspect that your ECP is more likely a DMU than a single person, make sure you don't only focus your efforts on the Initiator. Instead, learn the dynamics of the DMU and make it easier for all members to embrace your solution. In the B2B case described above selling, the GTM strategy should serve not only the Initiator (the Head of Accounting) but also the internal team.

You can largely increase the speed and probability of winning if you pre-prepare comparison spreadsheets, along with easy-to-grasp, ROI-focused case studies for the Sales Director. Moreover, you can also target ads or send different emails that describe "what is in it for them" to each member of the DMU. Or you could pivot. If the Initiator struggles to move the deal using the ladder, you can address the Head of Sales or CEO directly with more ROI-driven messaging.

There are also multiple examples of businesses that serve multiple verticals and provide value to multiple segments. Most B2B SaaS companies have some breakdown of industry or SMB vs. Enterprise, etc., so that's common. The ecosystem is set so that the usage can grow with the product. Just like in the example of ECPs that we will describe next.

ECP Framework

> "There is only one boss. The customer. And he can fire everybody in the company from the chairman on down, simply by spending his money somewhere else."
> Sam Walton, American business magnate, and founder of Walmart

A visualization of an ECP can be a powerful tool to guide our decision-making in GTM and helps other stakeholders understand and embrace the selected Beachhead Segment and how it influences the business. Personas were intended to be a visual aid for helping you align with selected target audiences, but they don't do their job if they are completely vague and made up. Consider Prince Charles and Ozzy Osbourne (an epic LinkedIn meme). Technically, they are the same persona using the demographic segmentation, but would you really take them as the same audience in your GTM, or would you cater to them differently?

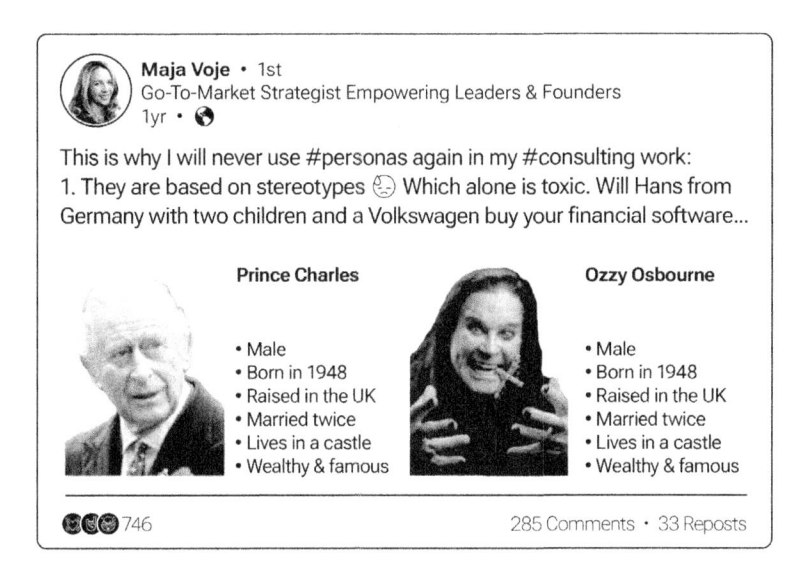

> **Maja Voje** • 1st
> Go-To-Market Strategist Empowering Leaders & Founders
> 1yr • 🌐
>
> This is why I will never use #personas again in my #consulting work:
> 1. They are based on stereotypes 😊 Which alone is toxic. Will Hans from Germany with two children and a Volkswagen buy your financial software...
>
> **Prince Charles**
> - Male
> - Born in 1948
> - Raised in the UK
> - Married twice
> - Lives in a castle
> - Wealthy & famous
>
> **Ozzy Osbourne**
> - Male
> - Born in 1948
> - Raised in the UK
> - Married twice
> - Lives in a castle
> - Wealthy & famous
>
> 👍❤️👏 746   285 Comments • 33 Reposts

These are the steps of how **not** to do personas:

- Your investor/consultant/trusted advisor tells you that you need to do them (hear me out, Jasper), but you see no point in doing it (hear this out, Jasper).

- You find some semi-applicable templates on the internet and DIY personas with whatever thoughts, opinions, and stereotypes you might have.

- You keep a very specific person in mind who is not really your target audience, but it would be so cool if that were the case.

- You outsource the task to "experts" who have never seen your ECP in person, are unfamiliar with your industry, and are not interested in conducting proper research.

- Or you gather the team in a room. Everyone pitches in their fragments of "reality" based on previous life experiences and opinions, and voilà – persona!

- Once you kind of think that you know what you are doing, you assign a designer to make them look pretty.

- Find an honorary place in an office where you display those "persona prints" so everybody can stare at them.

Personas are only a figment of imagination when they lack real data, research, and good GTM strategy judgment. Let's touch base on how to get to the "lovely poster on your office wall" that will actually make sense:

1. **Conduct research and experimentation.** Based on previous research work, you have recognized some patterns. Who are the customers who have the burning pain point and understand your solution to it in a heartbeat? You can either reverse-engineer them from actual data or find patterns by doing customer discovery interviews and surveys. Pay close attention to people who will respond first.

2. **GTM appropriate.** A good customer segment, according to the Beachhead Strategy, has a burning desire to solve a problem, is easy to access, has good growth, and WOM potential within the 18-month timeframe.

3. **Dive deeper.** Once you have a hypothesis of your Beachhead Segment, you want to understand and learn more about it. You might ask them how they first heard about a solution (channel), how they are currently solving a problem (alternative), what is insufficient in their current solution, and what is a promised land.

4. **Visualize**. Now it is show time, Picasso! Not until this point was there enough tangible evidence to start crafting a visual representation of your target audience. You are not doing it for the sake of doing it. Visualizing ECP is done to present your findings and effectively communicate them to others.

5. **Validate**. Okay, say you have your good-looking personas, now what? Start verifying if they are valid. Once again, you are up for some research and testing. You seek empirical proof to make decisions with confidence.

6. **Elaborate**. As you get new insights and information, your ECP will evolve. It is perfectly fine not to get it right at the beginning, but as you learn and grow, you will get closer to it. Make sure the ECP is not a poster on your wall but a living, breathing conceptualization of the person who matters the most in GTM – your target audience.

What to put in the visual representation? Here are some elements you can consider including. The elements vary from B2C and B2B.

	B2C Persona	**B2B Persona**
Demographic data	Useful for targeting them.	Assumptions will do.
Job and functions	Assumption will do.	Useful for targeting them.
Motivations and goals	Critical	Critical
Problems and frustrations	Critical	Critical
Dependencies in the purchasing process (DMU)	Optional – it is a more complex purchase.	Critical – you want to understand the DMU.
How they measure their success	Useful	Critical
Preferred technologies	Critical – there is no usage without habits.	Critical – it has to be compliant with their tech stack.
Brands they like and trust	Critical – are probably already using the alternative.	Useful – not everything is a direct substitute.
Influencers	Increasingly important.	Useful (if there are any).
Preferred channel	Critical	Critical

Based on this table, you can create the first prototype of your ECP. As you get more information and traction, you can update them with additional data. Patrick Campbell, founder of ProfitWell and strategy advisor at Paddle, shared a fantastic **MVP Persona Template for B2B SaaS Companies.**[5]

---

5 Campbell, P. (2023). Pricing in a Downturn https://paddle-7.wistia.com/medias/mk9ecwp-gy2

What's great about his framework is that it acknowledges the Early Adopters and nurtures a focus by defining **Anti Persona** and segments that are bad for your business.[6]

		Targets			Anti Persona
	Revenue	$1M to $10M	$10.01M to $50M	$50.01M to 100M	$100.01M +
Segmentation/ Qualification	Core Tools used	HubSpot CRM, HubSpot Marketing, Help Scout Support	HubSpot CRM or SGDC, HubSpot Marketing, Help Scout or Zendesk Support	SFDC, HubSpot Marketing, Zendesk Support	Eloqua, Marketo, Other CRMs
	Tech Attitudes	Early Adopters	Mix of Early Adopters and Early-t- Late Majority	Late Majority, Enterprise Style Clients	Late Majority, Enterprise Style Clients
	Internationalisation	U.S. Only	U.S., with expansion to EU and Canada	Multi Region	Multi-Region, but very specific needs in the Middle East and Sub Saharan Africa.
Acquisition	Value Props	"Seamlessly Scale"	"Seamlessly Scale"	"High Volume Ready"	"High Volume Ready"
	Pain Points/ Needs	Need an intuitive solution that plugs into their stack and automates.	Resolution time is the biggest deal here	No clear vendor to unify their stack, lack of dependability and stack scalability	Custom building solution around our products.
	Main Channels	Startup Program	Referrals, Events, Outbound	Partner Referrals, Outbound	Partner Referrals
	Purchasing Process	Touchless or minimum touchpoints (product-led)	Touchless or minimum touchpoints (product-led)	Procurement	Procurement
Pricing	High Preference	Core integrations, live chat support, contact management.	Core integrations, phone support, contact management, Analytics	Security, role management, dedicated CMS, API	Internationalization 24/7 support, very custom integrations.
	Low Preference	Security, Role Management	Security, Role Management	Live chat support, contact management	Live chat support, contact management
	Indifference	Analytics, API	API	API	API
Feature Preferences	Indifference Price Point	$257	$503	$1,878	$847
	Range	$189 to $304	$447 to $1,017	$1,024 to $4,783	$552 to $3158
	Likelyhood to Buy Score	3.9	4.8	4.2	6.3
	Discounting Needed	None	Token (5 to 10%)	Procurement (Raise list by 15%)	Heavy Discounts Needed
	Value Metric Preference	Contacts Bundle	Contacts Bundle	Contacts Bundle	Per User
Unit Economics	CAC	LTV	ARPU	$1,300	$5	$314	$2,025	$10,800	$625	$13,150	$36,450	$4,825	$38,422	$15,089	$1,033
	NPS	48	37	20	-25

Marketing Leaders (Director or Above) at Technology Companies

source: Pricing in Downturn by Patrick Campbell - https://paddle-7.wistia.com/medias/mk9ecwpgy2

Well-researched personas give GTM companies actionable and useful guidance for decision-making and are so much more than a bunch of stereotypes on an office wall. Yes, they do not look so pretty, but they are much more helpful for what we will do next.

Now we developed a deep understanding of our Early Adopters, we can start to develop products that will win their hearts and minds.

---

6 Bad for your business refers to segments that could be a good fit in theory but it takes too much resources to serve them, the sales process is long and difficult, they are just not compatible with the vision of the company or there is no joy and affection in serving this segment.

Key Takeaways:

- Winning GTM strategies are built around the selected **Early Customer Profile (ECP).** This involves crafting your product, offer, pricing, marketing, communication, channels, and messaging to suit their needs.

- **Research** will give you answers to the questions that you have in mind. Following the OODA framework - observe, orient, decide, and act – will help you infiltrate your customer's hearts and minds.

- **The Assumption Mapping** technique helps you find the most important assumptions, turn them into hypotheses, test them, and ultimately make better decisions. In this model, the focus is on identifying and examining your "leap of faith" assumptions. Those are highly important for your business, but you do not know (much) about them just yet.

- There are numerous research methods out there. Most GTM strategists select two to five that fit their needs and available resources. Most commonly used are interviews, surveys, solution testing, marketing tests, waitlists, co-creation with the client, pre-sale, and testing MVPs. The final selection depends on the level of confidence that you need to proceed with decision-making and the state-of-product you are given.

- **Experimentation** can be done before ever achieving Product-Market Fit (PMF). The use of the scientific method and experimentation process is highly recommended for GTM companies since it sets up a solid base for future growth teams at the company and helps you make decisions with (at least some) confidence. As long as you are learning, you are progressing. 50 to 90% of your experiments will fail if you experiment bold enough, but the good news is that you will still be learning a ton from conducting them.

- **ECP does not equal your ICP**. In GTM, you aim to win a Beachhead Segment that you can conquer in up to 18 months, and it will provide WOM, good references, and virality for further adoption. A client you can attract after five years in business is likely very different from your ECP. Best companies listen carefully to their ECP's feedback and sincerely appreciate their contribution to the development and adoption of the solution.

- You aim for one ECP. In most cases, that provides a very good focus and direction for the team. That is not the case if you need the network effects (supply and demand) side of the solution to deliver value, such as on social media, marketplaces, and social media platforms. There are also instances when ECP is not a single person, but it comes with DMU mode. It consists of all of the people who will play a role in the decision to purchase a product. They exist in B2B and B2C.

- **Personas** based on poor to no research and data are zombies on an office wall. Best ECP profiles are research-driven and closely aligned with what you need to support your decision-making in GTM.

To-Do List:

☐ Complete assumption mapping analysis for your GTM. You are welcome to conduct the entire analysis or stick to "desirable" assumptions that focus on the customer's problems.

☐ Select 2 to 3 research methods for your GTM planning. Have you done customer discovery interviews yet? Book the next one right now. You will learn a ton.

☐ Craft your first experiment to test your assumption for ECP – what needs to happen so you can take this decision with confidence? What is your hypothesis?

☐ Craft your ECP archetype based on the provided templates and your research findings.

Find all the worksheets, frameworks, and models mentioned in this chapter at *https://gtmstrategist.com/resources*. They are free and yours to benefit from.

CHAPTER 4

Product

"Customers are experts in pain, we are experts in solutions."

April Dunford,
best-selling author and positioning expert

You create and deliver value to customers through a **product**.

Ideally, products are developed to create value for a selected market segment based on research findings. In reality, many companies start thinking about GTM after they have already spent months or years developing a product. Once they "finish" the development or need an additional round of funding, they aim to seek a market segment that would reward them for their work. Here is how Jasper described their challenges:

To: **Maja Voje** (grow@majavoje.com)

Subject: **Launch time? Let's go!** 🚀

Hi Maja!

I'm sorry for not getting back to you sooner. Research of our ECP took longer than expected since we had to change the target segment and retest with them. As you know, our product is more or less ready to go, and since we are tight on budget, we need to validate it as soon as possible.

Our intended next steps and some questions are:

1. Tweak the product a little to fit additional requirements discovered in our research process – it should take a week at most. We got this

2. Set up product analytics to measure conversion rates – do you think Google 4.0 does the job, or do we need something fancier? Also – we do not have a budget for this, it should be free. And the costs of a solution should stay the same with traction. What tool do you recommend?

3. We still have not decided how we should charge for it. Should we go a little cheaper than our competitors?

4. What metrics and achievements will convince investors that we have product-market fit?

5. Also, do you know a good marketing agency or growth expert who could do the launch for us, and someone who can quickly make a landing page because our team is busy tweaking the product?

Do you have any tips or thoughts?
Thank you very much for your guidance.

Have a great week!

Jasper

Your work on improving the product is never finished, but many signals on this journey show if you are on the right track. GTM magic happens when the selected market segment loves your **Minimum Viable Product (MVP)**, finds value in it, and continues to use it and recommend it to others. You can measure many of these interactions by building an analytical system early on.

By multiple iterations of the product, you will eventually generate critical evidence that the selected market accepts your products. That is called **Product-Market Fit (PMF)**. It is the holy grail of GTM. Carlos Eduardo Espinal is an investor and managing partner in Seedcamp London who proposed a useful sequence to secure PMF called the **Product-Market Fit Cycle**.[7]

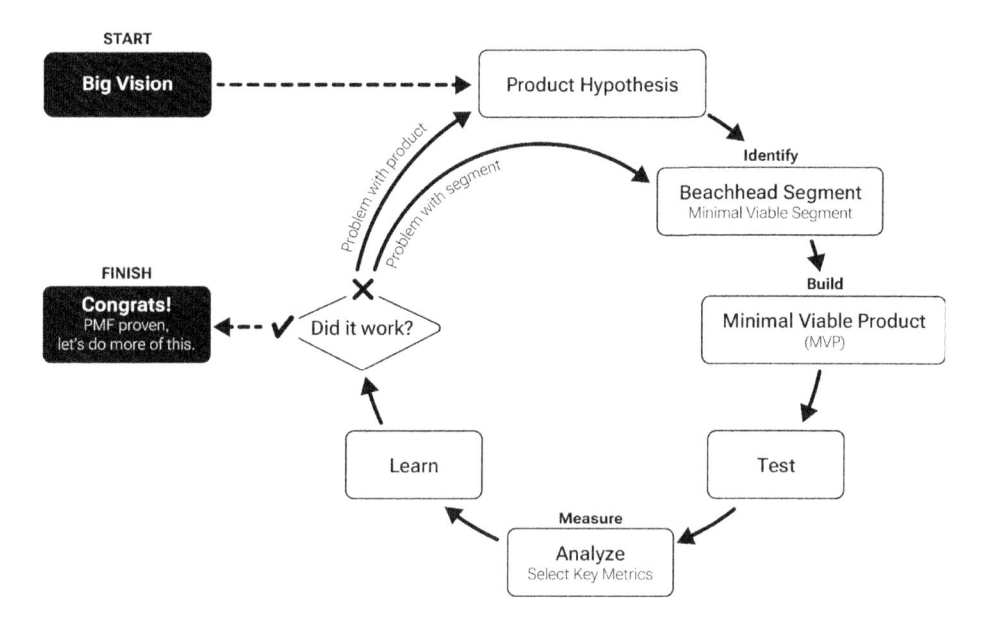

Adjusted from Startup Secrets: Go to Market Strategies by Michael J. Skok

You already have a big vision, your selected Beachhead Segment, and an understanding of your target customer's problems based on research. Now, it is time to incept a chasm-proof product. Here is your plan:

1. **Craft a Unique Value Proposition Hypothesis**: A value proposition is a clear statement that describes the unique benefit your solution offers to your target customers. It should be easy to understand, memorable, and compelling. To develop a winning value proposition, you must test your hypotheses against market realities. This will become your basis for positioning.

---

[7] Espinal, C. E. (2013). The Product Market Fit Cycle. Seedcamp Resources. https://seedcamp.com/resources/the-product-market-fit-cycle/

2. **Start building and ideating on your Minimum Valuable Product (MVP) and Minimum Valuable Business (MVB)**: Products that customers usually love the most are "SLEPPERY."[8]

   - **S**imple
   - **L**ow or no adoption costs
   - **E**asy to adopt
   - **P**roves value quickly
   - **P**lays well with others[9]
   - **E**asy to use
   - **R**OI is obvious
   - **Y** customers cannot live without it.

   We will tackle how to make your MVP "sleppery" enough to win the hearts and minds of target customers.

3. **Analytics**: GTM is all about testing assumptions and making decisions with confidence in uncharted territories. Best-in-class companies set up a system of metrics to measure performance from the get-go. It's time to learn analytics, key metrics, and GTM dashboarding. The analytical system should be aligned with your customer journey and provide an easy-to-grasp health check of your performance.

4. **Securing PMF in your GTM**: PMF is a mysterious place and time. It is easier to notice when you don't have it (low adoption, mixed or negative feedback from the market, low retention, slow traction) than to realize when you have it. You will learn established ways to measure PMF. It is not a "set it and forget it" mission. You have to defend it as the market is changing.

That is a lot of work to be done, but it will be a fascinating journey.

Ready? Let's dive into the wonderful world of product!

---

[8] Skok, M. (2012). Driving to Market - How to "Drive" Competitive Advantage in your Go To Market (GTM) strategies and tactics for Startups - Harvard Innovation Lab Series. Retrieved from https://www.slideshare.net/mjskok/goto-market#51
[9] Is compatible with other solutions that they use in their tech stack or services.

Why Should Customers Care?

"People don't buy products; they buy better versions of themselves."
Samuel Hulick, UserOnboard

The value your product creates is the pillar for everything you do moving forward.

That's why a strong value proposition creates an economic moat.

A value proposition is a clear, simple statement of the benefits (both tangible and intangible) that the product brings to customers.[10] It starts with **choosing the value** based on understanding the customer needs and continues by **delivering the value** through products, services, and distribution. Then, **communicating the value** is next via marketing and sales, and finally, **capturing the value** (which we will visit in the next chapter).

In the technology sector, most of us are very comfortable and enthusiastic to communicate about features and capabilities. It is easy to get hyped about AI-driven, next-generation self-hosted analytics, quantum computing, optimized cloud-based storage, etc. But quite often, communicating that alone on your website and sales materials does not land as well as expected.

Best products add value, solve customer's problems, and transform them for the better. Remember Super Mario, a popular video game from the 90's? First, there is a small version of Mario with regular characteristics and baseline capabilities. Once the player "consumes" a flower, the small Mario transforms into the bigger, more powerful version – he is super-charged, moves faster, performs the mission better, and boosts the players´ chances of winning. This effect is temporary, though. After some time, the player is back to small Mario, and the only way to return to previously known greatness is by consuming another flower.

---

10 Ballantyne, D., Frow, P., Varey, R., & Payne, A. (2011). Value propositions as communication practice: Taking a wider view. Industrial Marketing Management, 40, 202-210.

Person who's a potential customer + *Your product* (this isn't what your business sells) = *Awesome person who can do rad shit!* ← this is

Adjusted from The Elements of User Onboarding by Samuel Hulick

Positioning expert and best-selling author April Dunford suggests GTM companies consider two principles regarding communicating value:

1. **Do not overestimate the buyer's ability to translate features to value for the business**. A player does not want "a flower." Rather, they want a better version of themselves. The most effective way to spark their interest is to communicate what it can do for them instead of describing that the flower is red, yellow, and orange. It's our job to do that translation from features to value for them. What does that capability enable for the customer's business?

2. **Value alone doesn't win deals; differentiated value does**. Back to Mario, would the flower still be as desirable if "a mushroom" would do the same job? A player would not care much if they get supercharged by the flower or mushroom. The question to answer is not, "Why choose us?" The real question to ask and answer is, "Why choose us over the alternatives?" Your differentiated value is what you can do for a customer's business that no other alternative solution can. If every alternative on the market delivers on a particular point of value, that value becomes unimportant in a purchase decision. Your CRM makes it easy to track a deal. So do others. Your accounting system makes it easy to file taxes. Others do that, too. What makes yours the best for the customer?

Differentiated value is a pillar for building your **Unique Value Proposition (UVP)**, which is a statement that describes the unique benefit your solution provides to its ECP. It outlines the reason why customers should choose your product. The ideal UVP speaks to the point, emphasizes impact, and appeals to a customer's decision-making drivers. In GTM, we test multiple value propositions to find "the one."[11]

In B2B, the UVP is usually centered around getting the job done faster, better, and cheaper. But there are so many other options that you can explore – innovation, brand, quality of support, sustainability, customization, trust, etc. In B2C, the spectrum is wider and often includes intangible benefits such as an impulsive urge to buy, status, emotions, FOMO, and many others. In GTM, it is much more lucrative to solve real customer pain points than leaning on some "nice to have" features and solutions. The rule of thumb is that the more burning the pain is, the more likely the target market is going to embrace the innovation quicker and become a painkiller instead of a vitamin.

One of the best ways to find that is to ask your customers why they have selected you over other competitors. You can get wonderful insights from customer reviews or customer surveys. In addition, you can ask churned prospects why they did not end up buying from you and what prevented them from trusting you with their business.

Despite all of their research efforts, many companies struggle to define their value proposition. Their UVPs are packed with many "power words," such as purpose-driven, AI-enabled, frictionless CRM. Others try to address too many parameters at once and end up with undifferentiated vanilla statements such as a "user-friendly website builder" that is everything and nothing at the same time.

A tool that helps you find compelling UVPs throughout your product development journey is your Value Proposition Canvas, originally developed by Dr. Alexander Osterwalder.[12] Strategy expert Matic Moličnik and I revamped the original model to serve you better on your GTM journey, even if you are still figuring out what your product should be and we have tested it in practice. The model

---

11 Dunford, A. (2019). Obviously Awesome: How to Nail Product Positioning so Customers Get It, Buy It, Love It.
12 Osterwalder, A., Pigneur, Y., Bernarda, G., & Smith, A. (2014). Value Proposition Design: How to Create Products and Services Customers Want (The Strategyzer Series). Wiley.

helps you find the best candidates for your UVP that you can later test with your target audience.[13] It consists of two parts: **Customer Profile** and a **Value Map**. The most valuable outcomes of using this tool appear when you use real customer insights based on user interviews, not opinions. It's essential to know your ECP, so complete at least 10 interviews before you start this exercise.

We tested the modification of the model with multiple GTM companies, including Glimpse, a peer-to-peer app that provides live video of a location you might want to visit, such as a restaurant, wedding venue, sports event, concert, etc.[14] It's like a second pair of eyes that replaces the need to physically go to the venue to check it out. Brian, a frequent traveler who previously had a suboptimal experience in renting an Airbnb venue, will be our example here. He was willing to pay someone in San Francisco to stream the location of a venue he was interested in.

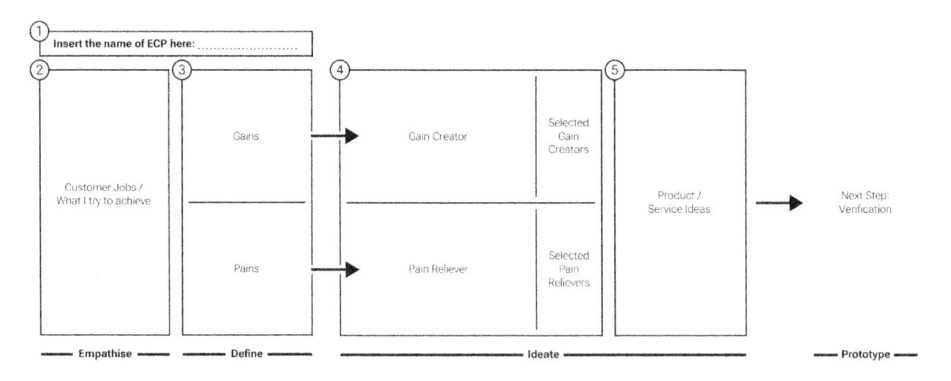

Start with a **customer profile**.

1. List out all of the **customer jobs.** What are the tasks the user is trying to complete?[15]

Brian has two jobs to be done: to get a realistic view of the neighborhood around the venue and to make sure it's safe and has good facilities.

---

13 You can download the original model here https://www.strategyzer.com/canvas/value-proposition-canvas
14 Glimpse is available on all app stores https://justglimpseit.com/
15 If you have done market segmentation based on jobs to be done framework, you are set up for a very good start. If not, you can learn that from doing customer discovery interviews.

2. Continue with listing the **pains**. These are the obstacles that are preventing them from getting a job done. It's also what annoys them about the current solutions they are using.

Brian is risk aversive. He not only wants to avoid a bad neighborhood, but he also wants to avoid bad service. Brian also has multiple other pains: he doesn't know anybody in the city to trust their opinion, and he doesn't like to engage in small payments because it takes time and effort to negotiate them. Moreover, he wants to be sure this is the location he is interested in and not some other street or even another city.

3. Finally, list **gains**. These are positive outcomes that customers aim to achieve by getting the job done, such as concrete results, benefits, and aspirations.

Brian wants to quickly get a realistic view of the neighborhood while remaining anonymous. He usually looks at recommendations from other users before buying products, but the lack of reviews is not a deal breaker for him.

Next is a **Value Map,** which shows how the business' products or services create value for the customer.

- **Pain Relievers**: How could you develop solutions to customers' pains? Each pain can have one or multiple solutions. There might also be pains that you cannot solve or decide that you cannot focus on solving them.

To address Brian's pain points, the app should connect Brian with people he doesn't know. They have to be at the desired location, marked live on the map, and willing to take a walk around the neighborhood for him. Last but not least, Brian needs to be able to quickly get a full refund if the service is bad.

- **Gain Creators**: How do the business's products or services create gains for the customers?

To make the solution more pleasurable for Brian, it has to include a two-way video and audio feed, plus an anonymous chat option. Provider ranking and customer feedback are also desired features.

- **Select pain relievers and gain creators:** Only focus on what is mission critical at first. This means selecting only the most impactful features out of all the ideas for pain relievers and gain creators. At this point, you should also consider which pain relievers and gain creators can be combined together to address multiple points with one feature.

Because Brian wouldn't use it if refunds are tricky, this must be implemented as soon as possible. A nice to have feature from the start is to rate providers after a call. However, with a risk-free and easy sign-up to the app, social proof for the app is not essential at this point.

- **Products and services:** Based on features and ideas, you can find out which ones will create more value and highlight them in your communication to a certain audience.[16]

To deliver even more value, Glimpse could add scoring mechanisms for scouts on the app based on the number of searches they have completed, along with star ratings to verify their reliability.

Last but not least, Glimpse needs to validate its value proposition for Brian by building a prototype of the intended solution and test it with more people who fit the profile.

Using the Value Proposition Canvas will bring additional clarity into what benefits and solutions you should be highlighting for your ECP. You can return to the tool when you get new market insights, create new solutions, or move to different market segments. It is useful on many different levels. But to be memorable and stand out, it is not only what you say but also how it makes a difference.

---

16 In the original Value Proposition model you start a value map by listing all the products, services and features and then explain how they create gain or remove pain. In our interpretation of it, you ideate on new products and solutions based on thinking what solutions could you develop or communicate better to close the value canvas loop.

Communicating and Testing your UVP

"What do I see and is it relevant for me?"
Your prospects when they first see your landing page

Clarity is the name of the game. A website visitor will leave your website after a few seconds if they cannot quickly grasp and understand what is presented, if it's relevant to them, and could add value to their life. Cold emails will never be answered if the recipient doesn't understand why they should care about the product to begin with:

"Dear {firstName}, does your {companyName} need expert SEO services? We are … " This is spam.

The simplest way to express your value proposition effectively is presented by Steve Blank, a professor, author, and the founder of the Lean Startup Circle.[17]

We help [X] achieve [Y] by [Z].

But there are other ways you can express it, and I've added some examples to the next page.

The key to a UVP's success is conciseness, powerful messaging based on benefits, and the clarity of added value for its target customers. You will learn more about how to put this into practice in the Positioning chapter. For now, let's remember that developing a UVP is an iterative process that consists of:

1. **Conducting customer and market research**: Gather feedback from your target audience through surveys, focus groups, etc., to understand the expected impact they will get by consuming the product and why they have chosen you over competitors. Do a sanity check with other alternatives on how to solve their problem.

---

[17] Team Asana. (2022). How to write an inspiring value proposition (with template and examples). Asana. Retrieved from https://asana.com/resources/value-proposition-template

1. The simple way
by Steve Blank.

> We help <u>target customer</u> achieve <u>customer need</u> by <u>product feature</u>.

Example: Automated CRO helps 6-figure ecommerce businesses to get to 7-figures by offering AI-based optimizations of copy for their website and ad campaigns.

2. Highlighting industry categories and benefits that customers value most
by Geoff Moore.

> For <u>target customer</u> who <u>needs or wants X</u>, our <u>product/service</u> is <u>category of industry</u> that <u>benefits</u>.

Example:
For 6-figure ecommerce businesses that are stuck on their journey to break into 7-figures (no matter what they have tried), Automated CRO is an AI-driven conversion rate optimization tool that optimizes your website and ads copy for higher conversions and running ad campaigns.

3. Comparison with competition
by Harvard Business School.

> - What are you offering?
> - What job does the customer hire you to do?
> - What companies and products compete with your brand to do this job for the customer?
> - What sets you apart from competitors?

Example:
Automated CRO offers a AI-based copy-writing service for optimizing websites and ad campaigns for higher conversion rates. It helps ecommerce businesses increase sales and squeeze more out of ever-more-expensive paid campaigns to break the ceiling of getting to 6-figures a month. Unlike agencies and freelancers, Automated CRO will do the job for a fraction of the cost, within seconds and reliably, based on learning from data samples of your best-performing campaigns. In time, as you feed it more data, it will only serve you better.

Adjusted from Value Proposition examples by Asana

2. **Identifying the key benefits of your product or service**: Based on the insights gained from market research, identify the key benefits that your product or service offers and how they solve your customers' pain points.

3. **Developing a unique value proposition hypothesis**: Based on your analysis of the competition and your key benefits, develop a unique value proposition that sets your company apart from others in the market. How you can take customers to the desired impact faster, better, more securely, conveniently, or pleasantly depends on what users appreciate most.

4. **Testing your value proposition hypothesis**: Same as ECPs, different value propositions could be and should be tested. Usually, there is one feature that makes a product stick, but it could also be a particular combination of UVPs. For example, one painkiller or one gain creator. One way to prioritize different value propositions is to use a Strategy Canvas.[18] When you are starting out, a combination of assumption mapping and experimentation will do the job.

5. **Integrating your value proposition in your messaging sales**: Ensure your verified UVP is integrated across all channels, including your website, social media, advertising, and sales presentations. Consistency is the key to effective messaging and an optimized buyer journey. Customers get confused and lose trust in buying if there are multiple UVPs scattered on their buyer journey.

6. **Continuously evaluate and refine your value proposition**: As the market changes, you enter new markets, and customer needs evolve. Be sure to continuously evaluate and refine your value proposition to ensure it remains relevant and compelling.

A polished UVP helps you attract the best-fit customers, develop better-converting offers, and stand out in a crowded marketplace. Nevertheless, GTM is not just about attracting ECPs to become interested in your solution. It is about building a product that delivers value and a sound business model to unlock the value exchange.

---

18 The Blue Ocean Team. (n.d.). 5 Compelling Strategy Canvas Examples You Can Learn From: Visualize your strategy and stand out in a crowded market. Blue Ocean Strategy. Retrieved from https://www.blueoceanstrategy.com/blog/strategy-canvas-examples/

Deliver Value

"Always deliver more than expected."
Larry Page, co-founder of Google

To achieve PMF, your mission is to build and deliver a product that users find valuable, are happy to return to, and will recommend to others. On this journey, you have a lot of assumptions to validate. Finding the best combination of product and market is a gradual process. It happens in iterations and is nearly impossible to strike right without repetitive field testing.

Testing assumptions and iterating on the best ways to deliver value is the name of the game in early product work. You do not need a full-blown product to start testing. You can start doing it long before a product exists.

Take the case of entrepreneur and B2B sales expert Tania Kefs as an example. Tania is the co-founder and CEO of the Paris-based startup Jurnee. The team develops and sells SaaS platforms for organizing and managing company team events. Tania previously led customer success and business development for a European unicorn company Aircall, a cloud-based call center software. One of her key learnings there was how incredibly effective cold outreach can be in attracting customers for new products.

She shares her GTM story: "Many companies spend a lot of time building a product, but they know very little about the market. When I started Jurnee, the first users came from reaching them with a PowerPoint presentation before the product was ever developed. I've always worked in tech, but I do not have a technological background. That didn't stop me from learning if the market was willing to pay for the solution. I crafted a list of potential customers that would benefit the most from the solution in my view. Then, they were sent an outreach message and an invite to consider a solution with my PowerPoint presentation attached. I directly asked the recipients if they would like to buy it.

At that stage, I envisioned how the product would look, but I kept the prototype as low a cost as possible. It was not a Figma prototype. It was a PowerPoint that I built myself in a couple of hours and sent it to my target customers. Then I received the first bookings for team events. So I was able to validate the need for the product by selling it before we even developed the tool. Once you understand that people are willing to pay fo it, you have verified your business model and can move forward with more confidence and funding for development."

Reflecting on Tania's case, the product and even its business model can be tested from the early stages on (we'll get into this in the next chapter). What is important in product development is to meet (preferably exceed) customers´ expectations. But product delivery mode plays an important role as well. It determines whether the solution will work for a client at a price point customers are willing to pay.

Some experts get it right from the get-go. Unfortunately, I had to learn that lesson the hard way by overinvesting in a product that the market rejected. I had a long-term successful stream with a-la-carte LinkedIn workshops and mentorship programs priced from $5,000 to $20,000. Clients loved developing a strategy based on examples, and more than 90% successfully implemented the newly acquired knowledge. I was excited about its potential to scale into an online course that could help more companies and no longer be constrained by my working hours.

I locked myself in my room for a month and created a $99 online course called the LinkedIn Lead Generation Masterclass. The idea was to position it as an entry product into my value added ecosystem. I thought it would be great to have the fundamentals pre-recorded and available to a wider audience. Then, later on, guide them on a more personalized journey. The critical assumptions I tested were:

- There is a market for a $99 online course.
- After completing the course, some businesses will be interested in workshops (which are already selling).
- I can make a funnel out of this with progression from online courses to high-ticket consulting, where we can avoid repeating the fundamentals.

The reality was different. The course was selling well. Within a year, 400 students took the course without any paid marketing. But completion rates were a suboptimal 8% at best.[19] That meant I would have had to sell at least 100 units

---

19 Based on industry benchmarks, this is not a terrible conversion, on mass learning plat-

of a course to get two consulting clients a month. Meh, there are easier ways to do it. I felt discouraged by this method of value delivery to create the desired impact. I knew the content was good, but the impact was not. Online learners, on average, don't execute at the same pace when compared to consulting clients, to my disappointment.

I decided to maintain the course as a mini-sell for those who would like to DIY it, but stick to a $10,000 to 20,000 consulting program for teams, where I could control the value delivery. DIY is still something that I would love to tackle one day at scale, but an online course wasn't effective enough as a value delivery tool. ROI-wise, the online course paid off, but I did invest quite a bit of time and resources into producing it. In retrospect, I wish I had tested the value delivery assumptions sooner using research methods such as a survey or presale before I went all into the fancy production and then the sales and marketing cycle.

But you can do it right from the get-go. Release your MVP out in the wild as soon as it's reasonable.[20] Gather and analyze feedback from your target audience before you go all in with marketing and sales. Identify areas for improvement and iterate on your MVP – adding, modifying, or removing features based on validated learnings. You are much more likely to hit the jackpot.

In some cases, you can still assume wrong. By testing the product early, you maintain a chance to pivot into a different target audience or solution. The sooner you start challenging your assumptions, the lesser the sunk cost of development in a non-optimal direction will be.

In GTM, we often decide to test the MVP and business model simultaneously. We are not only interested in attracting users, but we want to learn if we can create customers. If users actually pay for the solution, it's firmer evidence you are on the right route to PMF. Since the business model is the topic of the next chapter, let's learn how to develop an MVP first.

---

forms, the completion rates can be 2-5%, but my expectation was to have at least 10% completion rates because the course was selling at a higher price and I believe students would be more committed to finish.

20 Apart from some cases of complex value delivery to a user, very proprietary IP or innovations that are so profound that the user really has to experience them to understand them, the name of the game is to start testing and gathering feedback from the market as soon as possible.

Minimum Viable Product (MVP)

> "The minimum viable product is that version of a new product which allows a team to collect the maximum amount of validated learning about customers with the least effort."
>
> Eric Ries, best-selling author and entrepreneur

The key focus of an **MVP** is to validate your assumptions on whether or not you are providing the right solution or whether you should continue to iterate. The MVP has to get the job done. It has to provide value to the client. Everything in the product should be centered around the value you're inspired to create. If it does not get the job done, game over. No retention, no PMF, and no recommendations to drive future growth.

Creating an MVP is not as complex and lengthy as it first seems. Neither it is easy or breezy. A lot of thinking goes into products that we love. The job to be done in GTM is to incept a good enough version of a product to test if it delivers value to the target market and then iterate on it. Keep it simple and avoid unnecessary complexities whenever possible. Some teams can develop an MVP in a week or less (selling with a doc, building waitlists, or doing a presale) to speed up their learning process.

In practice, digital product development looks like this:

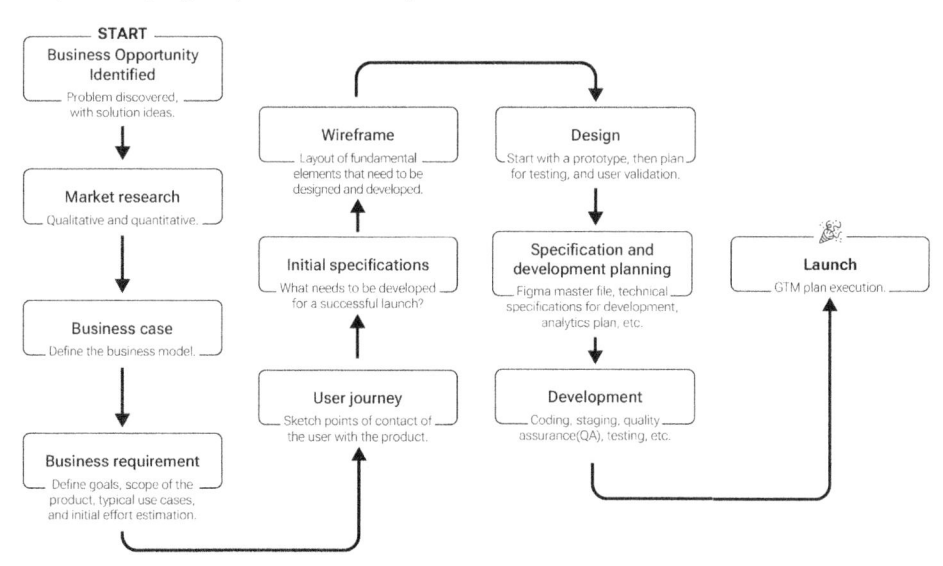

```
START
Business Opportunity Identified
  Problem discovered, with solution ideas.
        ↓
Market research
  Qualitative and quantitative.
        ↓
Business case
  Define the business model.
        ↓
Business requirement
  Define goals, scope of the product, typical use cases, and initial effort estimation.
        ↓
User journey
  Sketch points of contact of the user with the product.
        ↑
Initial specifications
  What needs to be developed for a successful launch?
        ↑
Wireframe
  Layout of fundamental elements that need to be designed and developed.
        →
Design
  Start with a prototype, then plan for testing, and user validation.
        ↓
Specification and development planning
  Figma master file, technical specifications for development, analytics plan, etc.
        ↓
Development
  Coding, staging, quality assurance (QA), testing, etc.
        →
Launch
  GTM plan execution.
```

GTM STRATEGIST

Let's take a look at the steps in detail: product development usually starts with the identification of a **business opportunity**. This is typically when someone discovers a possibility to solve an existing pain, maybe from his or her own experience or when talking with users. Maybe you have an idea of how to increase revenue or improve the value of your existing offering and thereby improve its competitive advantage. But numerous opportunities always pop up, and no company on Earth has the resources to jump on any of it. That's why it's important to evaluate the idea before you devote too many resources to it.

The next step is to do **market research** to get some rough estimations of how much potential there actually is. The first task is usually "desktop research." This is when you find resources online to try and calculate how many potential users there are for your product. Think of TAM, SAM, SOM, and other concepts we covered in the first chapter. This is followed by "competition research." Is there anyone already offering something similar? What are the alternative existing solutions? Finally, check on the "other end" of research, too: find some users and do interviews with them to gather their honest feedback on the proposed solution.

Next up is creating your business case. A **business case** is the first important document where you try and put everything on paper for a comprehensive team review – or for management approval. It is a structured document where you explain how the benefits and potential revenue of the project outweigh its costs. Think of it as a project outline: write down your vision or your "why" for the product and its UVP. This is also where you sketch the business model and GTM plan, even though they might adapt later in the product development process. Other parts of the business case include a project timeline and identification of possible risks. In the end, proposed success metrics (KPIs or OKRs) – how will you know if the project was a success?

Be careful when estimating potential earnings, and be realistic about all the costs involved, not just the direct cost of development. You need to consider the costs of bringing it to the market (e.g., marketing and distribution) and the marginal cost of each sold product/subscription. For example, if you plan to distribute an app in Apple's App Store, you need to know that Apple's commission is one-third of the end-user price. Pricing is a separate topic, and it is closely connected with positioning, which we will cover later in the book. But in the business case, you need to know some realistic scenarios to bring in revenue and to have started researching what value propositions your target audience resonates with.

It doesn't matter how confident you are in the idea; you need to bring your team members on board. A business case is all about a product pitch to the team that can help you realize it – be it team members, managers, or investors. A combination of sound numbers and compelling vision usually works best, in my experience.

Now that you agree on the vision and the outline, how will you put it into practice? After the business case is approved, the next step is to translate the business case to **business requirements.** What is the scope of the product? Do you have all of the people on board, or do you need additional hires before you proceed? Define the typical use cases and touchpoints of how users will interact with the product and provide a detailed estimate of your effort to get the MVP out in terms of resource planning.

User journey is the step where you sketch all of the points of contact between the user and your product. Where will they use your product? What will be their specific needs in this situation? Which channels will they use? Is it more likely to be through a mobile phone or desktop computer? In an office or somewhere else? Think about your ECP and have it in front of you while you and your team work on the user journey.

Next is to translate the user journey into **initial specifications** for what needs to be developed as an MVP. You need to be as descriptive as possible here so that everyone, from designers to software developers, are on the same page. A popular way to describe it, at least in agile software development, is with user stories – informal and general explanations of software features written from the perspective of the end users.[21] They usually follow this template:

"As a [user role], I want to [describe the user's intent], so that [describe the benefit that the user wants to achieve]."

---

21 Rehkopf, M. (n.d.). User stories with examples and a template. Atlassian. Retrieved from https://www.atlassian.com/agile/project-management/user-stories

An example of a sports tracking app with a social share feature would be: "As an app user, I want to share my results with my friends so they see my achievements." It will be up to designers and developers to find the best way to make it happen.

In the next stage, the UX designer will prepare **wireframes**. This is a layout of fundamental elements that need to be designed and developed. Wireframes can look like simple mockups of the app, but you should think of all the possible scenarios and paths within the product. When the wireframes are prepared, that's the best point to do a review of the effort estimation and see if the assumptions are still valid or if any additional resources are needed.

When the wireframes are confirmed, the **design** stage follows for detailed prototypes of how the final product will look like. When the first design is prepared, it's wise to plan for another round of user testing and to check with actual users on how they perceive and like it. Don't just take their words for an answer – observe how they interact with your product. Are the instructions and buttons easy for them to understand? Can they successfully finish their desired actions or do they get lost? Well-designed products should feel intuitive and should need less rather than more instructions.

Apps like Figma have become the standard for designing digital products. They enable easy collaboration between designers and developers but also enable you to present mockups to users so they can feel like they would be using the exact app or website.

When you make sure that early testers (who should be representatives of the actual target users) understand and like the design, the design then needs to be translated to **technical specifications and development planning** – this details what needs to be developed on the front end. Then you should also specify the analytics plan and other plans for the process, called backend development.

It is not the purpose of this book to describe the **development** stage in detail since it's usually an established process involving regular stages. What is important for you as the GTM strategist is to make sure the product is tested enough in the staging environment and that quality assurance is rigorous. However, in parallel, you should work on other parts of GTM for a successful launch. This means briefing all relevant teams on what is going to happen. If you have a customer support team, for example, they should be familiar with the product and have a list of expected frequently asked questions prepared with answers.

When the product is good to go as an MVP, it's **launch time** – your moment of glory!

Throughout the process, plan for regular stakeholder reviews and approvals. This includes user testing if the solutions (at the design stage, for example) are indeed aligned with their and your expectations. The process here might differ depending on your company. Still, usually, it is wise to do a joint check of specifications before the design starts. Then review the wireframes and final designs, and of course, be sure to complete rigorous testing to catch critical bugs before the launch.

Creating lovable products instead of tolerable products takes more work and heavy thinking, but you can get there. Remain laser-focused on your mission and committed to delivering value for your ECP. That's always the best lens to make decisions from. Diligently iterate on your MVP, the one that "does the job" to become loveable, worthy to return to, and recommended to others.

After being committed to creating added value, let's develop a system so you can identify early signals and meet some benchmarks that indicate you are doing an excellent job.

Metrics and Analytics

"In God, we trust. All others must bring data."
William Edwards Deming,
US statistician, engineer, professor, and management consultant

A **metric** is a quantifiable measurement to evaluate various aspects of a business. It provides specific and qualitative data that helps in monitoring performance, identifying trends, and making data-driven decisions. Metrics can range from numerical values to complex calculations. You can gain valuable insights into performance, identify areas for improvement, and measure their progress toward achieving goals if you know which metrics are vital for you to track.

A well-crafted **analytics system** is a compass on your way to achieving PMF and winning GTM. Many companies at the GTM stage need to develop their analytics system from scratch, which includes making some very profound choices such as:

- Determinate key metrics that will measure your GTM success.
- Set up and implement event tracking plans to capture vital touchpoints on the customer journey. How do you acquire customers? How many convert? How do they use and value products? Do they come back to it, and do they refer the solution to others?
- Choose the analytics tools and bring data from different sources together.
- Create dashboards that will help to make data-driven choices for the team.

That seems like a lot of work, but this work pays off because just putting a snippet of code to the website and following whatever numbers appear in that analytical tool can lead to false conclusions in your assumption testing.

One of the essential readings for all GTM companies that are setting up their analytics system is the book Lean Analytics.[22]

There is no universal way to set up an analytics system; each company has to build it around its customer journey, business model, and product development

---
22 Croll, A., & Yoskovitz, B. (2013). Lean Analytics: Use Data to Build a Better Startup Faster (Lean (O'Reilly)) 1st Edition. O'Reilly Media.

stage. Simply put, if you are not monetizing yet, you cannot measure revenue and profit-related metrics. Simpler metrics such as the number of insights from customer research per week (how it is changing in time), retention rates of your free users, and user satisfaction metrics will do the job for now.

The best analytical systems are designed in a way that they can be scaled once your business is evolving. Switching to a different system later on is a lengthy process and usually ends with a loss of some data. Let's learn from an example how to craft, implement, and use analytical systems that will support your decision-making on the entire GTM journey.

Choose the Right Metrics to Track

"What is the purpose of analytics? To protect you from lying to yourself."
Alistair Croll and Ben Yoskovitz, authors of Lean Analytics

There are multiple types of metrics. Overall, there are two differentiators – input vs. output metrics and leading vs. lagging metrics. **Input metrics** refer to the measurable and controllable factors or actions that can contribute to achieving a specific goal. They are under your influence and are considered the levers that drive success. For ChatGPT, the input metric is the number of research papers reviewed and incorporated into the language model's training data.

Output metrics, on the other end, represent the actual outcomes or results that are desired or expected. These metrics are the ultimate goals that a company aims to achieve but may not be directly controlled by you directly and solely. **Leading metrics** are forward-looking and predictive, providing early indications of future performance (e.g., number of qualified leads per week). **Lagging metrics** are backward-looking and measure past outcomes (e.g., monthly revenue).

To bring you the latest best practices, I interviewed Simon Belak, CTO at Zebra BI, who has helped dozens of companies set up or level up their analytics and built analytics tools used by the likes of Ikea, Mercedes, Volvo, Volkswagen, N26, Revolut, BP, Walmart, CocaCola, Pepsi, Microsoft, DHL, H&M, PWC, Deloitte, Nestle, Mars, and 3M. Simon shares the fundamentals of an analytics system setup for GTM companies:

"Many companies do not understand the nuances of how to set up an analytics system. The right question to ask is how you should be modeling your business, your product, and your market. Start from there. After you clearly understand that, you can confidently set up an analytics system that is needed to measure your progress. You set up a hierarchy of KPIs (causes and effects) for each of the vital areas and build dashboards that actually make sense to your business. It almost guarantees that you understand how the models work."

Here are some tips to get started:

- **Start at the end.** What are you trying to achieve (your KPIs)? Choose your One Metric That Matters (OMTM) and focus your GTM operational efforts around optimizing for it. OMTM is an actionable metric that addresses a bottleneck in your customer journey or strategic goal. According to Lean Analytics, a good OMTM is:

    - Understandable: everybody comprehends it in the same manner.
    - Comparative: it provides benchmarks to signal how good or bad is it going either based on past data, competitors, or industry benchmarks.
    - It is a ratio or a rate: which are easier to act on and compare.
    - Is behavior changing: we can actually act upon it; it guides our behavior.

    It is usually valid for two to six months, most often for a quarter. A team owns it. Different teams can have different OMTMs. Here you need to ask yourself: what does success look like in the next 2 to 6 months? Reverse engineer what is important to you. What needs to happen to get there?

    Simon led GTM for a product at Zebra BI, an advanced data visualization and reporting tool for Power BI, Excel, and PowerPoint. In the business intelligence market, the decision-making process is long and ambiguous. Under Simon's leadership, the team became radically focused on optimizing for the Bottom of the Funnel (BOFU) stage in product and marketing decisions.

    They prioritized doing the simplest tasks with immediate feedback to achieve their key GTM objective of getting 10,000 users in the following quarter. Having a clear objective brought everything else into perspective. It was easier to say yes or no to something once they could verify if it would help them achieve

10,000 users. The objective itself became a brilliant guiding mechanism on a journey in which they needed to validate the product offering the team was working on. Focus and interlinking the actions in a way to complement each other and take you closer to the end goal is a powerful lever of growth on the product-growth journey.

- **How do we measure that?** For most GTM companies, this will be some combination of profit, volume, and usage patterns, such as retention. **Retention rate** is a fundamental KPI for product stickiness. **Churn rates** and usage frequency are other important metrics to track. Long-term stickiness often comes from the value users create for themselves as they use the service.

- **You work your way backward**. SaaS, for example, is all about selling enough subscription plans. Some metrics in this way would be:

    - **The lifetime value (LTV)** of the client, and we should calculate this with margin, not revenue.
    - We divide the cost questions into two categories: how much does it cost us to acquire the user? This is known as **customer acquisition cost (CAC)**. And how much does it cost us to serve them? This is the operating cost, which consists of technology and office infrastructure, media buying, salaries, etc. This helps you determine your **gross margin**.
    - It is useful to also measure customer satisfaction, such as **Net Promoter Score (NPS)**, **virality coefficient (K)** and word-of-mouth **(WOM)**.
    - The opposite of retention is **churn**: how many users are we losing in a time period? If there is no preliminary data to assess churn, we can project it and correct it in the future.

After you select the scope of key metrics you want to measure across the customer journey, it is time to build, implement, and make the best use of an analytical system.

Connecting Your Business Model to Your Data

"Good analytics is the best friend of great decision-making."
John R. Talburt, an accomplished expert in data management and information quality

Most GTM companies are either undermeasuring or overmeasuring. Sometimes data-driven decision-makers think that having more data is a superpower. They gather data with multiple tools. This data is rarely centrally connected, and they scratch their heads about what is going on.

Say you have some data in Meta Business Manager and some in Google Analytics. The data on how many conversions happens to not match. That happens all the time in practice, the same with email marketing vendors, CRMs, and other advertising platforms. Each tool is overcontributing conversions to its advantage. Which data source will you trust?

Your job to be done is to create a single source of truth, a dashboard that displays critical data in a way that decision-makers can quickly grasp the information and make informed decisions. Better yet, data should be centrally gathered. Relying purely on vendor-fed metrics such as bounce rate, time spent on site, and other "in your face" metrics can lead to a very wrong basis for decision-making.

To build a reliable analytical system, you will most likely have to create custom events. Preparing and implementing tracking helps you plan, capture, and analyze non-standard event data that is specific to your business. Going into the nitty gritty of building an event-tracking plan beats the purpose of this book. But if you do not know where to start, use Amplitude's free event tracking plan template and adjust it to your business and tool stack.[23] I do that myself for most projects I work on, and it helps me tremendously to communicate with developers how to correctly and holistically implement the plan.

---

[23] Build an event tracking plan using this template https://amplitude.com/resources/event-tracking-plan-template and find recommended taxonomy for different industries here https://help.amplitude.com/hc/en-us/articles/115000465251-Data-planning-playbook#Next-Steps

Another great practice to find better insights is to "slice and dice the data." Data should be viewed and analyzed through different **segments** (geography, device, feature usage, company size, etc.) to get more actionable insights. It is better to see the data per segment or cohorts instead of observing them as a whole to avoid the noise of mixing together behaviors from vastly different segments. For example, if you are observing your analytics in Google Analytics, there might be important differences in conversion rates for different devices.

There are times in which it is better to work with less data if the data points are more similar to each other. I did a cart abandonment experiment with one of the teams that was selling computer cooling components. We implemented a simple exit survey, which was triggered when a customer showed the behavior of exiting a cart. It was a simple question, "Why did you decide not to finish the purchase?" Visitors were given multiple-choice answers:

a. I am still curating my basket.
b. I did not intend to buy it in the first place (just browsing).
c. Shipping is too expensive.
d. I could not find my preferred payment method.
e. Other.

After generating nearly 1,000 responses in a week, we analyzed the data. "Too expensive shipping" was the winner overall, with 43% of choices. We could say, "Great, let's implement free shipping across the website for the next promotion!" But the data had more to reveal. More than 78% of people who answered were from the US and Canada. Shipping is too expensive for a group of users, not the entire user base. We would be leaving money on the table if we just launched a site-wide free shipping promotion since Europeans did not care that much about it. This insight made a big difference. The same experiment could be done on pricing pages or cancellation pages. It is one of the most valuable experiments for optimizing BOFU.

For understanding retention, **cohorts** are essential. Here, you validate which groups of users get the most value from your product and, later on, try to attract more of them. The 80:20 approach to setting up a great analytics system is to have a good understanding of segments so that you can embrace these nuances in your GTM assumptions and hypothesis from the get-go.

I was helping with the launch of a Belgian running app, and the team decided to do a Meta advertising campaign for the launch to invite more runners to try out the app. We ran ads for two weeks and sadly realized that despite cost per install (CPI) looking promising, 92% of newly registered users never ran with an app. This could be interpreted on so many different levels. Luckily we did our "analytics system" homework and implemented event tracking in the app. After a deep dive into the data, we discovered that from newly registered users, a whopping 89% of them marked in the onboarding flow that their goal was to "run five kilometers without stopping."[24] They were not runners, and the app was best for active runners who were preparing for races such as a marathon or a half-marathon. That meant they messed up the targeting, not that the product was bad. The next campaign that we launched was a guide on how to get ready for your next half-marathon, and the results were much better in terms of activation and retention.

Most companies start tackling the analytics quest by asking which tools they should choose. When it comes to choosing analytical tools, Simon Belak believes that most work can be done with Google Analytics and Excel. It is not going to be pretty and fun, but it can fundamentally be sufficient in the GTM stage. The main pitfall when selecting the tools is that they will dictate what you can do. On the path of deriving an answer in an exploratory analytics phase, a person is lured to do an analysis that is easy to do with selected tools. To save time and effort, an analyst will avoid problematic pieces, leaning more towards the interfaces and data, which are easy to grasp from the tool. This is problematic because a company could be missing out on important dependencies and patterns that would be helpful for our decision-making.

While setting up analytics and metrics systems often falls in the "get something done and return to it when there is time" bucket, the investment into robust and reliable analytics systems pays big dividends down the road. Having a measuring plan for the main metrics and conversion events down your buyer journey will provide a valuable basis for decision-making. There are many tools available to ease the gathering, visualization, and interpretation of data: Google

---

24 Onboarding is a process of steps in the product that teach a user how to use the app and increase their chance to experience the wow moment - a moment of recognising the value added to the app. Activation is a point in which users experience the value of the product and for the running app, guess what - you have to run with it.

Analytics, Amplitude, Hotjar, Posthog, Metabase, Pendo, Smartlook, Mixpanel, and others. In essence, we separate analytic tools into two types of tools:

- **Session-based analytics**, where the user stays anonymous, and we can only track the behavior on the website or an app.

- **User-based analytics**, where you can track multiple sessions by a single user even though they might use different devices to understand the full customer journey.

By implementing different data sources (website data, advertising data, sales data from the CRM, social media data, data from your ERP, and other sources), you can build a holistic overview of your business. A free solution to do that is Looker Studio Overview by Google, in which you can integrate external data with Supermetrics, for example. But if you have the resources, it is better to build an internal centralized data storage and a team.

To get the analytics to the applicable layer for business decision-making, most data-driven teams use **dashboards** that are changed in real time. A dashboard in analytics is a visual representation of key performance indicators (KPIs) and data metrics, providing a centralized and easy-to-read display of real-time information for quick insights and data-driven decision-making. When set up right, you will have quicker, very actionable data to benefit your business. I've added an example of a dashboard below, so you can see how easy they are to use. Amplitude offers numerous dashboard templates for different business models – SaaS, B2C apps, ecommerce, B2B sales, channels, and departments.[25] It's really not as daunting as it sounds. I've found that templates serve as an excellent inspiration for you and your team.

---

25 Discover dashboard templates here https://amplitude.com/blog/analytics-dashboard

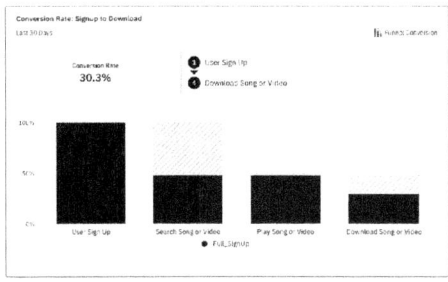

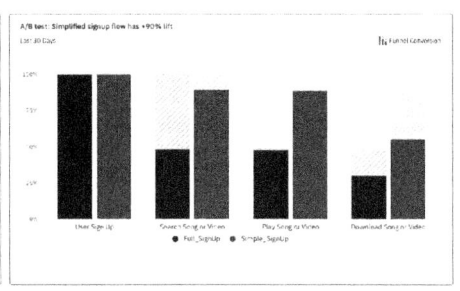

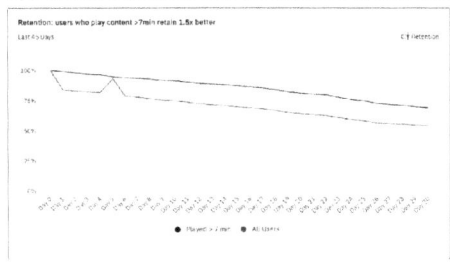

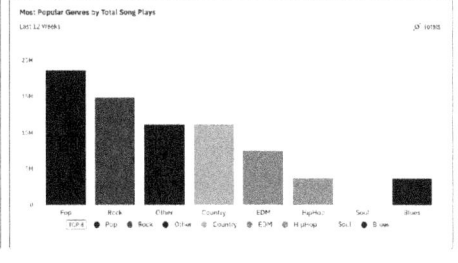

www.amplitude.com/blog/analytics-dashboard

This image is the courtesy of Amplitude

When planning a dashboard, make sure that your customer journey is well-represented and that you offer different interfaces to different decision-makers. A marketer will be interested in different metrics than a product manager. Curate the metrics that are relevant for their work, but make sure you understand their needs for decision-making and then craft a dashboard interface that suits them. There will be an overall view that the entire company is interested in, but for most departments, staying on the "need to know basis" and co-creating dashboards is the winning equation to success.

Once you plan and build crucial dashboards and data interfaces, make sure you incorporate a notification system to build a habit of reviewing them regularly, or start your team meetings by discussing the metrics on the dashboard. You can also color code some changes and metrics to give a data viewer a quick indication of which direction the business is moving. Eventually, you will learn and understand how metrics are correlated and what is consequential or coincidental.

The more data used, the more investment into more sophisticated tooling pays off. Simon says, "Most GTM companies observe the reds and greens when it comes to metrics, but it sadly provides very little-to-no insight into what they should be doing next."²⁶ He calls it "infotainment," a symptom of bad dashboarding and analytics. How this should be done in the right way is to inform a decision-maker what they should be looking for next and empower them to act instead of madly writing to Slack, "Hey, this metric is red! Let's have a red meeting." In time, you will understand how different metrics are interrelated and how they influence each other. For now, let's not panic too much if something is red. Take a step back, ask why, and create new assumptions to be tested.

The criteria for saying yes to something are radically different from other stages. It depends on you and where the market is at the moment. Is this even the right category of ideas to test? Is this approach correct? The changes in the product are relatively costly. Instead of spending your resources on random product tweaks to achieve 10 to 20% uplifts in certain markets, you should always question every assumption if it has the potential to bring a meaningful change.

Now that you are armed with insights and have your analytical system in place, let's find signs that your product is "perfect enough" to achieve the holy grail of GTM – PMF, where you bridge the gap of being celebrated by early majority customers and ready to scale further to the greatness it really deserves.

---

26 Red and greens refers to color coding of metrics in the dashboard. The benchmark is usually whether the metric is better or worse than in a previous period or given the min and max values that we set up to be "normal" for that metric.

Aiming for Product-Market Fit (PMF)

"The only thing that matters is getting to product-market fit."
Marc Andreessen, American entrepreneur, venture capital investor, and software engineer

Sean Ellis, growth expert and entrepreneur who coined the expression "growth hacking," states market fit is the prerequisite for sustainable growth and the most challenging area for driving growth.[27] It means that your product is a 'must-have' for people who try it and that it represents a large enough market to achieve your growth ambitions.

This notion became my prime driver on why I started to write this book in the first place:
"Everybody tells you that you need PMF, but no one clearly told you how to get there." I signed up for a mission to bring our methodologies to companies in the GTM phase who seek for PMF and welcome them to the growth stage once they are ready.

Searching for PMF and validating it is a unique courtship between each company and its market. Product expert and author Lenny Rachitsky conducted insightful research with renowned technology companies on how it feels like to achieve PMF. He identified three key learnings from the research:

1. **There is a strong market pull for the product.** Customers are actively asking and gravitating toward a solution. Some signals of a strong market pull include an inflection in organic growth, customers asking to pay for the product before you ask, customers complaining or even panicking when your site goes down, and people using the product even when it's broken. Ryan Graves, the former CEO of Uber, commented: "At Uber, we never really had a product-market fit problem — zero marketing budget, and we were growing like a weed. Word of mouth was uncontrollable, and especially as regulatory heat started, it's all anyone could talk about (it's how it felt). Marketing was free because the media loved the story."[28]

---

27 Ellis, S., & Brown, M. (2017). Hacking Growth: How Today's Fastest-Growing Companies Drive Breakout Success. Currency.
28 Rachitsky, L. (2020, September 29). What it feels like when you've found product-market fit:

2. **Finding PMF is a journey consisting of many milestones and small wins as well as learnings.** About half of researched companies found PMF immediately after launch, but half spent months or years iterating to get there. It took Netflix 18 months, Segment one-and-a-half years, Airbnb two years, Superhuman three years, and Amplitude four years to get there. Once they got there, though, PMF became obvious.

3. **The intensity of the pull depends on PMF** (how good your product is at solving the user's problem) and **initial market size** (is it niche or broad). Dropbox, Netflix, and Tinder were 10x better products within a huge market. They experienced sudden and broad pull. It took Chat GPT five days to reach its first million users and two months to reach 100 million. Instacart, Superhuman, and Substack were 10x better products, but a narrow set of initial customers created a steady and compounding pull.

By now, you understand the importance of PMF and that there is no single recipe for how to get to it apart from learning by doing. At this stage, you are interested in getting more hands-on information on how to know if you are on the right track to adjust your GTM moves.

Measuring PMF

> "Every time we launch a feature, people yell at us."
> Angelo Sotira, co-founder of deviantART

A VC group once asked me to supervise the collaboration between one of the startups they wanted to invest in and their selected performance marketing agency. The startup had a very prominent health-tech solution and a beautiful product. Yet, it was never seen by people outside of the founders' social circles. The VCs wanted to see if the team was capable of attracting 1,000 users to the product before considering investing in them. They chose influencer marketing and Meta advertising to achieve this objective.

Stories from the founders of Netflix, Uber, Airbnb, Substack, Stripe, Datadog, GitHub, Segment, Dropbox, Superhuman, Instacart, Nextdoor, and many more. Lenny Rachitsky. Retrieved from https://www.lennysnewsletter.com/p/what-it-feels-like-when-youve-found

After some strategizing and preparing marketing materials, the campaigns were ready to be launched. The company managed to get new users in at a tolerable cost regarding their expected LTV. Things looked good until they did not. Two weeks into the campaign, negative comments started to appear under ads that the product did not provide value and the tests were not accurate. Cold sweat. What to do? Shut down the campaign, delete negative comments, and reconcile with these buyers. Does it mean no PMF, a.k.a. game over?

We had to investigate what was going on. We did outreach to users who shared negative feedback and learned more about the issues they had. To the team's big surprise, most users were very helpful and understanding. Some of them did not even want a refund. Upon reflection, it was obviously too mature to do a full-blown campaign for that stage of product development, but I began to wonder if there might be an issue with the target group selected for the campaign. The agency went "mainstream" to capture seizable segments that are not necessarily early adopters. Are there data insights that show some user segments interacted with the product well? The next campaign could be directed to them.

Luckily, there was. We saw good retention for 35 to 45-year-old physically active males who are interested in taking supplements regularly. Even though the product was not in the best shape yet, they still used it. That leads us to assume that if we double down on that group and choose different channels and influencers, the product still has a fighting chance. We changed the strategy and relaunched for that audience. Conversions tripled. That group had more positive sentiments, and there was some WOM unlocked in their universe for the product. They barely pulled it off, but they did it.

Testing for PMF involves collecting data from customers or prospects and using that information to make informed decisions about how to refine a product or service to better align with market demand. Product-led growth and experienced product manager Leah Tharin suggests measuring PMF in three steps for each ECP separately:[29]

- **Proof of value experience**: Can you retain enough of such users? *(This is what should be done in the case above; the product was not yet monetization-ready.)*

---

29 Tharin, L. (2023). Leah's Product Market Fit Guide: How to find it, product-led. Leah Tharin. Retrieved from https://www.leahtharin.com/p/leahs-product-market-fit-guide

- **Proof of monetization:** How much are users willing to pay to get the value?
- **Proof of value proposition**: Do users experience the Aha moment?[30]

In GTM, not having a PMF is easier to spot than when you have it. Here are some of the signals to look out for if you have issues with PMF, and also how to recognize when you are on the right track.[31]

Customer journey stage	Poor PMF	Good PMF
Acquiring new users	Slow, expensive, difficult to spark interest.	Cost efficient, there is virality, WOM flourishes.
Activation	Even when you get people to give it a shot, they do not "get it" or are slow and unmotivated to move forward.	Users are so excited about the product they ask if/when they could get access to it or even prepay for it. They find it easy to understand and use the product.
Retention	Losing (nearly) everybody who comes back to the product.	Retention curves flatten at a certain point; you gain more active users than you lose them in a given period.
Monetization	The company is burning money. Prospects are hesitant to convert even when offered discounts and benefits.	There is or could be a profitable business model CAC < LTV.
Referral	Weak or non-existent. Low satisfaction scores such as NPS. Negative feedback.	Strong. Users are bringing new users to the product. Strong satisfaction scores.

---

30 The "wow" moment of a product refers to the specific point or experience in a user's journey where they are pleasantly surprised, impressed, or delighted by the product's features, functionality, or value. It is a pivotal moment that captures the user's attention and creates a positive emotional response, leaving a lasting impression and potentially leading to increased engagement, satisfaction, and loyalty.

31 Rachitsky, L. (2020). How to know if you've got product-market fit: Insights from Marc Andreessen, Elad Gil, Steve Blank, Andy Rachleff, Michael Seibel, and many more. Lenny Newsletter. Retrieved from https://www.lennysnewsletter.com/p/how-to-know-if-youve-got-productmarket

If you have an analytics system in place, you will observe retention and segment data to get insights. **Customer retention rate** is one of the most widely agreed signals of a PMF. Only users who appreciate the value-added provided by the solution will care enough to stick around and continue to use the product. Customer retention rate measures the percentage of customers who continue to use your product over time. The time period depends on the customer journey and usage patterns. While it makes sense to measure it in a shorter period (daily, weekly, monthly) for frequently used solutions such as social media apps or mobile games, there are more complex cases. A high retention rate could indicate that your product is meeting their needs and delivering value.

Here is an example from Brian Balfour that illustrates how Product A, which has PMF, flattens the retention curve while Product B plummets.[32] Some drop-off at the beginning is inevitable, especially with products that take effort and require habit development from a user, but if the retention curves normalize at some point, PMF could be just around the corner.

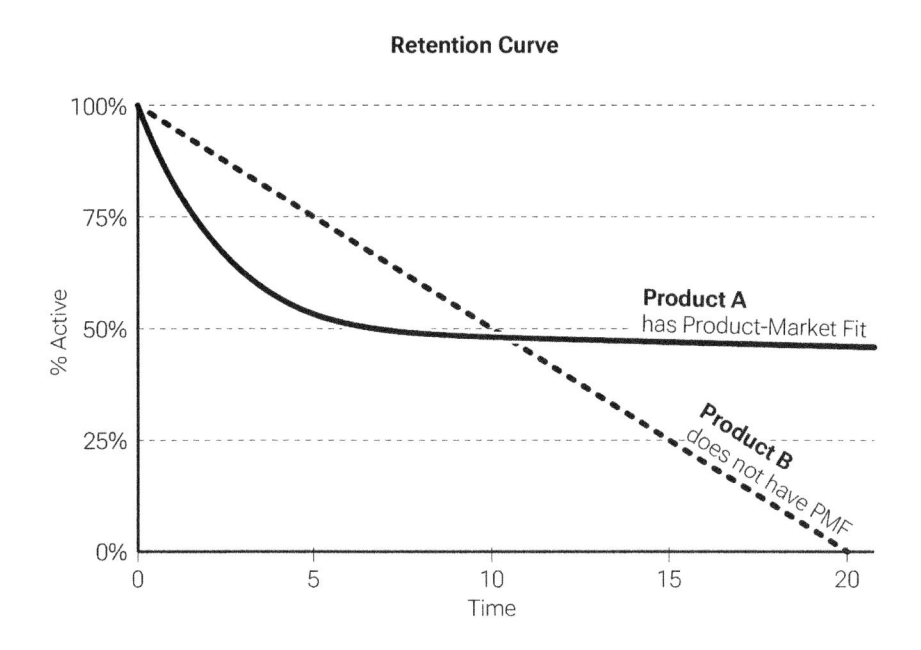

Retention Curve

---

[32] Balfour, B. (2013). The Never Ending Road To Product Market Fit. Brian Balfour. Retrieved from https://brianbalfour.com/essays/product-market-fit

Even if you cannot yet operate with reliable insights from product analytics or there aren't any, you can use a **PMF survey** developed by Sean Ellis to use on a customer/user base to measure if the product has the necessary PMF.[33] The survey contains eight questions:

1. How did you discover [ProductName]?
   - Blog
   - Friend or colleague
   - Google
   - LinkedIn
   - Twitter
   - Facebook
   - Other (please specify)

2. How would you feel if you could no longer use [ProductName]?
   - Very disappointed
   - Somewhat disappointed
   - Not disappointed (it really isn't that useful)
   - N/A - I no longer use [ProductName]

Please help us understand why you selected this answer.

3. What would you likely use as an alternative if [ProductName] were no longer available?
   - I probably wouldn't use an alternative.
   - I would use:

4. What is the primary benefit you have received from [ProductName]?

5. Have you recommended [ProductName] to anyone?
   No/Yes (please explain how you described it)

6. What type of person do you think would benefit most from [ProductName]?

7. How can we improve [ProductName] to better meet your needs?

---

33 You can create your own PNF survey here https://pmfsurvey.com/

8. Would it be okay if we followed up by email to request a clarification to one or more of your responses?

    No/Yes (please enter the best email for contacting you)

There are so many useful insights from this survey. From attribution (which channels did the users hear about you?) to insights on alternatives and value propositions. Now, let's focus on the second question, "How would you feel if you could no longer use [ProductName]?" Sean Ellis suggests that if more than 40% of your users would be very disappointed if they could no longer use the product, you have demonstrated a strong signal of PMF.

A great place to start is segmenting your data to users who would be very disappointed if they could no longer use the product and learn more about it. Gradually, you want to find more users like this. Worst-case scenario, you have to pivot the product, change your acquisition strategy to attract new users or tweak the messaging to set the right expectations. It's not easy, but doable. The sooner you get these signals, the more you can do to secure PMF.

In addition to these established methods, companies also use conversion data (conversion from free to paid, sign-up of purchases per segment), customer satisfaction measures such as NPS, and referral metrics (K, WOM, percentage of positive reviews) to signal PMF.

The route to ultimately confirming PMF can be long, but there are signals on the way to show you the best path. If PMF is the holy grail, what happens when you finally find it? Are you no longer in the GTM phase and can now move to the growth stage and forget about PMF? Not necessarily.

Life After PMF

"Product-market fit is a moving target."
Hiten Shah, Co-Founder of Kissmetrics, Crazy Egg, and Nira

Once you have built an MVP and proved the PMF, you should pay careful attention if you continue to provide value to the target audience and get value exchange for that. PMF can slip away. As you continue to develop the product, enter new markets, and grow your user base, PMF should be re-examined. Markets are changing rapidly. New technologies, competitors, and changed customer preferences can make the perceived product value by its target market obsolete. Therefore, continuous measuring of your PMF metrics makes sense to recognize the early signals that you double down your attempts to defend or rediscover PMF.

After winning PMF for your Beachhead Segment, you will aim to expand to adjacent markets to grow. Expanding PMF can take many shapes and forms, including:

- **Same use case, new segments**. Keeping the same value proposition while making it work for a new market, such as Slack launching Slack Enterprise or Instacart expanding to delivery from groceries to pharmacies.

- **New use case, same segments**. Expanding into a solution involves keeping the same market, launching adjacent products, and adding sales and customer support solutions, such as HubSpot.

- **New use case, new segment**. Diversification involves launching a completely new product to a completely new market, such as Uber launching Uber Freight and Transportation & Logistics Solutions for companies.

When evaluating PMF, always keep in mind that nothing happens in isolation in GTM. Remember the example of a health-tech team probably choosing the wrong channel to test, and that the model of a DIY at-home testing product did not fit the primarily selected target group? In the words of Brian Balfour, there are three other fits that you should consider:

- **Product/Channel fit**: are you delivering your offering through the right channels?
- **Channel/Model fit**: is the selected channel sustainable to unlock profitable business?
- **Model/Market fit:** is the end customer willing to pay what is sustainable for your business model?[34]

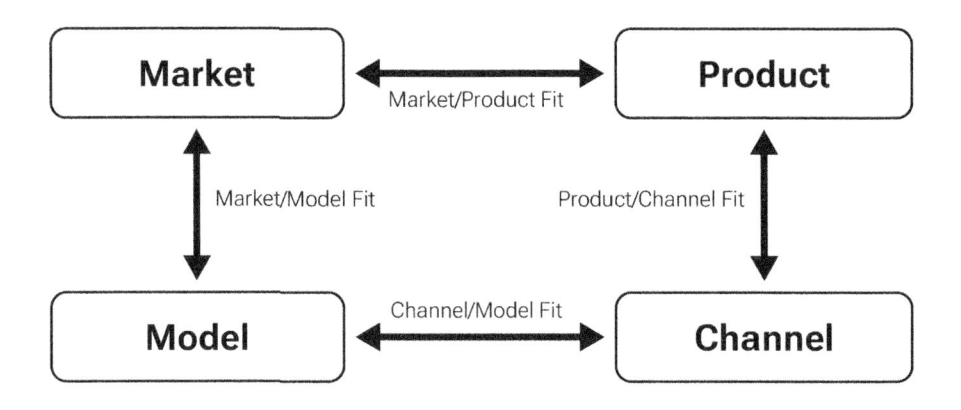

```
         Market/Product Fit
Market  ◄──────────────►  Product
  ▲                          ▲
  │                          │
Market/Model Fit      Product/Channel Fit
  │                          │
  ▼        Channel/Model Fit ▼
Model   ◄──────────────►  Channel
```

Source: Why Product Market Fit Isn's Enough by Brian Balfour

Robert Kaminski, the co-founder and partner at Fletch, whom you will meet better in the positioning chapter, beautifully explains this point using an example of communication platforms Slack, Discord, and Microsoft Teams. Technically, all these tools do the "same job," but they do it differently and serve different users.[35] Therefore, they are well differentiated and not often seen as direct substitutes.

---

34 Balfour, B. (2017). Why Product Market Fit Isn't Enough. Brian Balfour. Retrieved from https://brianbalfour.com/essays/product-market-fit-isnt-enough
35 Kaminski, R. (2023). How to use Positioning as a Differentiator. LinkedIn. https://www.linkedin.com/posts/heyrobk_positioning-product-marketing-activity-7033101814912737281-rtj8?utm_source=share&utm_medium=member_desktop

How to Use Positioning as a Differentiator

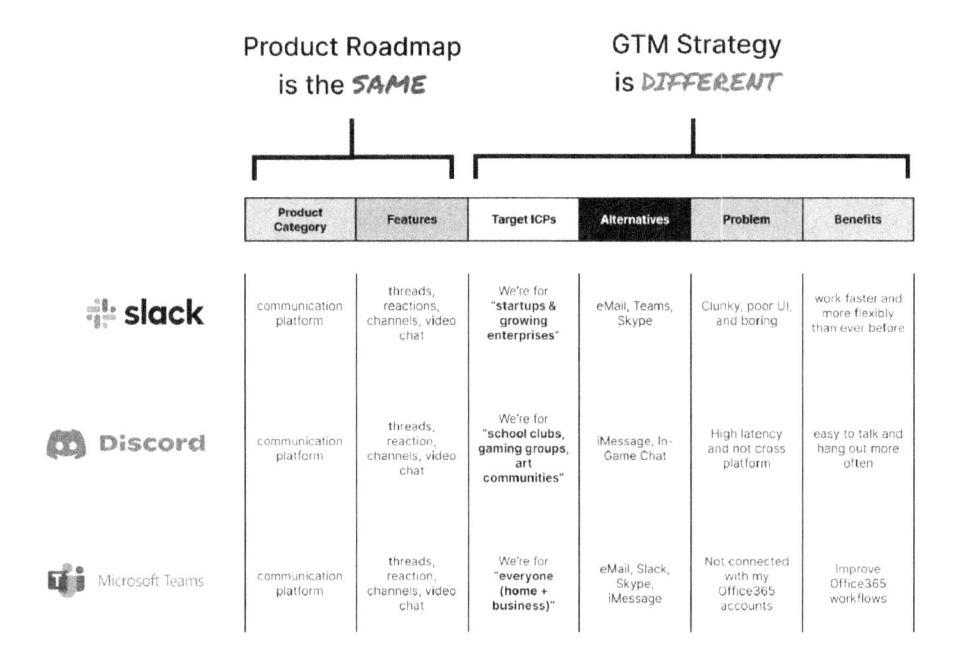

Product Roadmap is the **SAME**

GTM Strategy is *DIFFERENT*

	Product Category	Features	Target ICPs	Alternatives	Problem	Benefits
slack	communication platform	threads, reactions, channels, video chat	We're for "startups & growing enterprises"	eMail, Teams, Skype	Clunky, poor UI, and boring	work faster and more flexibly than ever before
Discord	communication platform	threads, reaction, channels, video chat	We're for "school clubs, gaming groups, art communities"	iMessage, In-Game Chat	High latency and not cross platform	easy to talk and hang out more often
Microsoft Teams	communication platform	threads, reaction, channels, video chat	We're for "everyone (home + business)"	eMail, Slack, Skype, iMessage	Not connected with my Office365 accounts	Improve Office365 workflows

This visual is the courtesy of Robert Kaminski and Anthony Pierri

To nail all four fits of your GTM strategy, you will next learn more about how to capture the value that the product creates and how much to charge for it. But first, congratulations on making it here.

Key Takeaways:

- GTM magic happens when the selected market segment loves your Minimum Viable Product (MVP), finds value in it, and continues to use it and recommend it to others.

- Value Proposition is a clear, simple statement of the benefits (both tangible and intangible) that the product brings to customers.

- A Unique Value Proposition (UVP) is a statement that describes the unique benefit your solution provides to its ECP and how that is better than anything else. It outlines the reason why customers should choose your product.

- Finding the best combination of product and market happens in iterations. You do not need a full-blown product to start testing. You can start doing it long before a product exists. MVP could also be defined as the minimum "tolerable" product to deliver value to get the job done. It is great for testing. Eventually, you will transition towards a minimum loveable product – the one that really excites the customers and starts testing the business model around it if customers are really willing to pay for it.

- A well-crafted analytics system is a compass for achieving PMF and a winning GTM. Many companies at the GTM stage need to develop their analytics system from scratch, which includes making some very profound choices, such as determining the key metrics that will measure your GTM success.

- Set up and implement event tracking plans to capture vital touchpoints on the customer journey. How do you acquire customers? How many convert? How do they use and value products? Do they come back to it? and do they refer the solution to others?

- Choose your analytics tools and bring data from different sources together.

- Create dashboards that will help to make data-driven choices for the team.

- In GTM, the most important metrics to observe are business-related metrics and build the analytics system around the business model. Will the product stick and provide value? How can you capture this value (monetization, business model) to cross the chasm and excel at your GTM efforts?

- Find your One Metric That Matters (OMTM) and focus your GTM operational efforts to optimize for it. OMTM is an actionable metric that addresses a bottleneck in your customer journey or strategic goal. A good OMTM, according to Lean Analytics, is:

    ◦ Understandable: everybody comprehends it in the same manner.
    ◦ Comparative: it provides benchmarks to signal how good or bad

it's going, either based on past data, competitors, or industry benchmarks.
    - Is a ratio or a rate: to make it easier to act on and compare.
    - Is behavior changing: we can actually act upon it, and it guides our behavior.

- A great practice to find better insights is to "slice and dice the data." Data should be viewed and analyzed through different segments (geography, device, feature usage, company size, etc.) for more actionable insights. It is better to see the data per segment or cohorts instead of observing them as a whole to avoid the noise of mixing together behaviors from vastly different segments.

- Aim for a single source of truth when planning your analytics system.

- By multiple iterations of the product, you will eventually generate critical evidence that the selected market accepts your products. That is called Product-Market Fit (PMF), and it is the holy grail of GTM.

- Finding PMF can be instant, or it can take months or even years. In GTM reality, it is easier to notice when you do not have it than signs that you are approaching it. But once you achieve it, you know you are there.

- Most companies measure PMF with retention curves, PMF surveys, or NPS. There are other measures to indicate signals of PMF, such as customer satisfaction and referral metrics.

- Once you confirm PMF, it is important to "defend it," and you are growing your business, and the market is changing. Create an ongoing system to measure it.

- Consider three other fits that you need to take into consideration: Product/Channel, Channel/Model, and Model/Market fit.

To-Do List:

- ☐ Fill in your Value Proposition Canvas.

- ☐ Craft your UVP hypothesis and create a plan for testing it.

- ☐ Develop your MVP.

- ☐ Choose metrics that are relevant to track across your customer journey.

- ☐ Develop your GTM dashboard.

- ☐ Decide how you will measure PMF.

Find all the worksheets, frameworks, and models mentioned in this chapter at *https://gtmstrategist.com/resources*. They are free and yours to benefit from.

CHAPTER 5

Pricing

"Price is what you pay. Value is what you get."

*Warren Buffett,
US investor and author*

Other GTM elements spend money. Pricing makes it. Pricing is a mechanism of value exchange between you and the client. Value is created through the product. You aim to get fair compensation for the added value your product has created.

Since you have tackled PMF so diligently, it's time to consider this question – will customers be willing to pay for the value your product creates? For most bootstrapping companies, it makes sense to start monetizing as soon as you have validated that the product can consistently deliver value to the target market.

Users can actually very much enjoy the free version of your product – but will they pay for it? Validating the **Willingness to Pay (WTP)** brings you one step closer to a successful launch and to the **Product-Market-Pricing Fit.**

When starting out on the pricing journey, many teams think like Jasper. They consider price as a number to stick on the product they have developed. But best-in-class products are developed with a WTP in mind. Pricing starts much earlier to build a sustainable business model and requires more profound thinking than sticking a close-to-competition number to it.

To: **Maja Voje** (grow@majavoje.com)

Subject: **It is time to set the pricing in stone** 💰

Hey Maja!

I have asked you this twice before, and I cannot shake off the feeling you dodged it.

Based on your previous inputs, we understand what the value proposition should be and how to set up the analytics system. But now we really have to set up the pricing to test our MVP and get some traction.

As I have explained, setting up the price 25 to 30% lower than our competitors will attract more users to our solution.

But I do not want to leave money on the table. What do you think about how much the subscription should cost and how to formulate packages?

Any input you can give will be appreciated, as always. But please remember that we are under time pressure here and needed pricing yesterday.

Say hello to your dogs, and have a fantastic week!

Jasper.

Jasper faces a lot of pressure. His investors require him to prove the product can attract users and be monetized. He is rushed into decision-making that would normally be done with some solid WTP research. Despite high-stake circumstances, he can still make smart pricing decisions.

Pricing is one of the most undervalued concepts in GTM and business in general. It is hard for most people to set it up in the first place, and they are hesitant to change it even if they discover it isn't the best choice. Many feel that changes in prices could jeopardize the relationships with existing customers or make their offer less attractive. That might be true in some cases. But this is what else is true: inflation, rising business costs, bigger payroll to cover when you are growing your business, and higher value delivered as you are perfecting your product. Pricing experiments are not merely to increase the prices at face value. They are done with the intent to optimize the bottom line of business in a given time period. And they are probably one of the most impactful changes that you can make in business.

These stats should motivate you to go all in on optimizing for pricing instead of shying away from it:

- Research has shown that **72% of innovation fails due to pricing, monetization, and business model** flaws. The key to crossing the business model validation chasm (when users are willing to pay what you offer) is early WTP research, according to Madhavan Ramanujam, who is a Board member and Partner at Simon-Kucher & Partners.[36]

- An OpenView Ventures SaaS Benchmarks Study indicates that one-half of the companies included saw a **25% increase in ARR** after they changed their pricing, which is a massive impact without any changes within the product.[37]

---

[36] Rachitsky, L. (2022). The art and science of pricing | Madhavan Ramanujam (Monetizing Innovation, Simon-Kucher) Appears in this episode. https://www.lennysnewsletter.com/p/the-art-and-science-of-pricing-madhavan#details

[37] Rachitsky, Lenny. 2023. "How to Price Your Product." Naomi Ionita (Menlo Ventures). Lenny's Newsletter. https://www.lennysnewsletter.com/p/how-to-price-your-product-naomi-ionita#details

- Paddle's study of more than 500 SaaS companies reveals that by successfully increasing monetization **by 1%**, research participants saw a **12 to 16% increase in revenue**, which is 4x the impact that you would expect to see if you focused on optimizing acquisition by 1%.[38]

This chapter was developed to provide you with actionable tools and examples to avoid these seven pricing mistakes and misconceptions that are often suffocating the growth of GTM companies:

1. **The solution simply does not deliver the promised value to users.** Most people will not happily pay for something they do not need or see value in. If you see a high churn of users, low LTV, high CAC, and low-to-nonexistent retention rates, it would be best to reconsider PMF before going all in on pricing. You can change the product (which is the most expensive), test a different Beachhead Segment (it may have a different WTP), actually lower the price point, or redo the offer at the same price and learn how to communicate it better.

2. **Setting up a price that is way too cheap.** If you think that charging a low price will automatically attract higher demand, you're wrong. There are price points where users find the product too cheap to trust its quality. In B2B, you want to avoid the situation that it costs the customer more to buy a product (internal costs such as procurement, compliance, time spent comparing the solution) than they actually pay for it. A team I mentored licensed their advanced analytic solution to a Fortune 500 for $30,000 a year. They believed that was a lot of money at that point. They soon realized that serving the client required so many resources that one of the co-founders had to spend nearly all of his time serving them. His ROI was worse than working full-time, and the company stagnated on its "market of one."

3. **Customers do not convert and say it is too expensive.** You actually have users, an audience, and leads, but it's very hard to close them, and they explicitly tell you the price appears too expensive. The anecdotal sweet spot in pricing is when customers complain about the price but still buy.

---

38 Campbell, Patrick. 2023. "Pricing in a Downturn." Paddle. https://paddle-7.wistia.com/medias/mk9ecwpgy2

It is okay to lose 20 to 30% of leads because you are pushing higher with the price to capture more value. If closing a deal is nearly impossible, the reasons might be:

- Double-check your messaging and offer any possible improvements in how you communicate value so it's clear to a prospect what they get for the price.
- Your offer needs adjustments. Consider creating a set-foot-in-the-door offer (smaller sell) or a free version of a product to demonstrate value before asking for larger commitments.
- You need a different segment. Is there a segment that reacts better than others to the presented offer? In that case, you could consider changing the target segment.
- The time to value it might be too long. The perceived upfront cost may appear too high before a client experiences any value. Consider different pricing models, such as recurring payments instead of upfront costs.

4. **One price fits all**: If the price is an exchange of value that most of us want to do at fair rates, consider this mental experiment. Let's say your product is used by independent developers as well as multiple product teams at a FAANG company. Netflix will get much more value from the product than "an indie developer who puts a personal credit card as a payment method." Should they be charged the same price? If you are serving different audiences, develop different packages for them. Primarily, you are building your business model for your selected Beachhead Segment, but with signals of adjacent markets with different WTPs, you can consider creating additional offers for them. Most companies offer a custom enterprise package when this happens.

5. **Giving away too many core functionalities for free:** Sometimes, the free version of the product is simply too good, and users have no real initiative to convert. If you see very high retention rates and user satisfaction metrics yet low conversions to paid, that might be the case. Usually, 20% of the features produce 80% of the WTP, and if you give it all away for free, what do you have left to monetize? It is vital for users to experience or trust value before buying, but what is beyond the paywall should elevate their experience to the next level.

6. **Waiting too long to monetize:** If you are delivering superior added value to users for (nearly) free or at a fraction of the value without charging users, that becomes a habit, and WTP decreases in time. Eventually, users learn to think, "Oh, this just works well for free." Many GTM companies monetize too late. They think that building a big audience and validating PMF is essential but then neglect early WTP testing and sustainable business model development. There is a big difference between wanting a product and being willing to pay X amount of money for it. Do you want an AI-based tool for optimizing your personal calendar? Excellent. Would you pay $100 a month for it from your personal budget? Probably not.

7. **"Set it and forget it" pricing**: You are constantly innovating on your product. Is it getting better and delivering more value? Has your team grown? Pricing should be revised every three to six months. Revising means not only increasing the price but also shaping new pricing packages, feature sets, offers, and other elements that create value based on your recent research findings or when you are launching something new.

To avoid all these traps and take a sensible approach to pricing, you will learn more about WTP research, price models, and pricing strategies in this chapter. Let's dive into how to craft winning GTM pricing strategies that will capture a fair share of the value you are creating and enable you to launch a sustainable business.

What Influences Pricing?

> "I made a mistake in pricing the product too low when we first launched. We thought that we had to be competitive and price it at the same level as everyone else."
>
> Elon Musk, CEO of Tesla and SpaceX.

They say pricing is an art and science, and we are going to focus more on the science aspect of it. Pricing is a core mechanism for capturing value; the price is a unit of the number we use for value exchange. In GTM pricing, we aim to find the best pricing that fits these criteria:

1. **Added value**: What are they paying for?
2. **Willingness to pay (WTP)**: How much will they pay?
3. **Competition and alternatives**: How much do they currently pay?
4. **Your positioning and unit economics:** What do you want and need them to pay?

Let's break each of these elements down and give you tools to make these decisions.

Added Value: What Are They Paying For?

> "Features perform actions. Products solve problems. Businesses deliver value."
>
> Eugenia Koo, Product Leader at Amazon

If conversion rate optimization (CRO) experts create $1,000,000 of added value in a month, would it not be a no-brainer to pay $10,000 for it? That would be a bargain. How about $100,000? Why not?

Sometimes, added value can be relatively easily quantified. Other times, it can be intangible. Can you put an accurate dollar amount on laughter, peace of mind, or personal growth? It is easier if the added value is agreed to be the "B2B holy trinity" of increased revenue, speed, or cost reduction. Sometimes, value added is delayed, appears because of a combination of factors, or it may not be in the client's interest to reveal this information.

The first step towards uniting this knot is to agree on what the value added is with a user and then measure it. A **value metric** is a quantifiable measurement used to determine and measure the value exchanged. It is a specific unit of measurement that aligns with the customer's perceived value and reflects the benefit or usage of the product. It makes it fair for a user. A good value metric is:

- Easy for the user to understand.
- Aligns with the value the customer receives in the product.
- Grows with the customer's usage of that value.

Value metrics provide fair grounds for pricing, and it's one of the most common ways to price products in SaaS. In a perfect world, you charge by a value metric, and this pricing strategy is called **value-based pricing**. Slack uses this strategy. Its value metric is messages sent – the more messages you send, the more you pay.

Customers buy because they expect the product to solve their problems or to get the job done. A unit of added value provided is one the fairest measures of value exchange to form price packaging around.

Here are a few examples of value metrics in action.

Product	Category	Value metric candidate
Loom	Video platform	Number of minutes recorded
Slack	Communication application	Number of messages sent
Stripe	Payment processor	Amount of revenue generated

Some value metrics are easy to set. Others are not.

When selecting a value metric, consider that it has to make sense to you and the customer. Look at benefits, not features. Pricing expert Madhavan Ramanujam, who has helped hundreds of businesses set up and revamp their pricing, describes a case when his client, the analytics enablement automation software Segment, placed pricing around the number of API calls. However, this metric only worked for developers and highly technical people, so it would have been better for the value metric to be the number of active users. It's the benefit over the feature.

Pricing expert Patrick Campbell suggests discussing value metric candidates with clients and asking them how they would like to be charged. What would be a fair exchange of value for them? You can also check how they are used to paying for such services today. Doing that establishes the notion of fairness; both parties acknowledge that value exchange happens and how to measure it.

Finding a value metric to anchor into your pricing can be a challenging task but a worthwhile journey. Therefore, many companies set up their pricing around value metrics but still charge a fixed fee plus a flexible cost to secure predictable revenue and remove the risk of usage decrease.

Even if value-based pricing is out of your reach, communicating value-added matters a lot in pricing. Based on Campbell's analysis of SaaS companies in the long run, value-based pricing and feature-differentiated service bundles still outperform other pricing models in SaaS with at least 30% more expansion revenue.

Once you have a value metric hypothesis, it's time to test it beyond agreeing on what to charge for.

WTP: How Much Will They Pay?

"You've reached the right price when customers complain, but 70% of them still buy."
Simon Belak, Data scientist and Lead at Zebra BI[39]

If you ask clients directly how much they would pay for your product, buckle up for some really strange responses. It is your job to set up the price points, not your users. This is why it's much smarter to ask this question using one of the recognized methods for price testing at a very early product idea stage. The most widely used methods for WTP include surveying or interviewing clients using pre-set questions. The two most widely used methods for testing pricing are Van Westendorp's Sensitivity Model and the Gabor–Granger method.

Van Westendorp's Sensitivity Model provides a multi-question model that indirectly measures WTP instead of directly posing the question to potential buyers.[40] Rather than asking potential buyers to identify a single price point, the Van Westendorp model helps assess a range of prices instead of just one. Here's how it works.

First, the following four questions must be posed at the end of the survey:

1. At what price would it be so low that you start to question this product's quality?
2. At what price do you think this product is starting to be a bargain?
3. At what price does this product begin to seem expensive?
4. At what price is this product so outrageously expensive that you would not even consider it?

This data is usually collected on a sample of a few hundred respondents. If you don't have the opportunity to collect it, you can also conduct interviews.

---

[39] In Simon's experience, the ideal closing rate is lower than 70% in a sales-led business model with qualified leads. If almost everybody accepts the proposal, that means that there should be a potential for price increase.
[40] Van Westendorp, P. (1976). "NSS-Price Sensitivity Meter (PSM)-A New Approach to Study Consumer Perception of Price." Proceedings of the 3rd ESOMAR Congress, Amsterdam, 139-167.

A good enough sample size in this case would be at least 20 interviews of ideal customers in your Beachhead Segment. Ideally more.

After results are collected, the values should be visualized on a line graph with price points on the x-axis and the percentage of respondents agreeing to said price point on the y-axis.

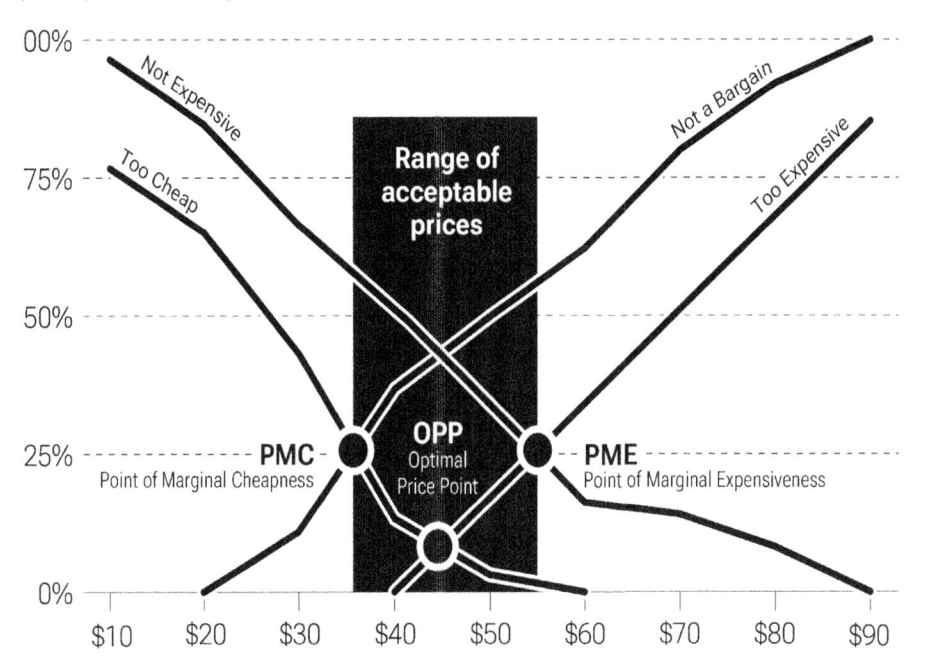

On this graph, you can directly see where users believe the product is too cheap and where they consider it to be too expensive. The method is most often used for established products that already have proven demand in the market, and consumers are at relative ease to express the price points.

How about if you are tackling something less known that is harder to value before you experience it? Meet the **Gabor-Granger method**, which can help you determine the price for a radically new product or service based on value perception.

When used on a big enough sample (at least 1,000 responses to a survey), it provides great insights into **price elasticity.** To conduct this survey, you need to find the highest price point that still seems somehow reasonable and determine five price points in between. Ask respondents to select purchase intent on a five-scale. For example, if you wanted to present a new gaming computer, you'd ask five questions:

- Would you pay $1,000 for this gaming computer?
- Would you pay $1,500 for this gaming computer?
- Would you pay $2,000 for this gaming computer?
- Would you pay $2,500 for this gaming computer?
- Would you pay $3,000 for this gaming computer?

If the respondent answers positively to all five questions, you'd know this person is willing to pay at least $3,000 for this new gaming computer. On the other hand, if the respondent answers negatively to the third question, then you'd know $2,000 is too much for this person, but $1,500 isn't. When you have at least 100 of your target audiences' respondents, you'll see the patterns. You'll determine the demand curve by calculating the cumulative percentage of respondents willing to pay at their respective price points.

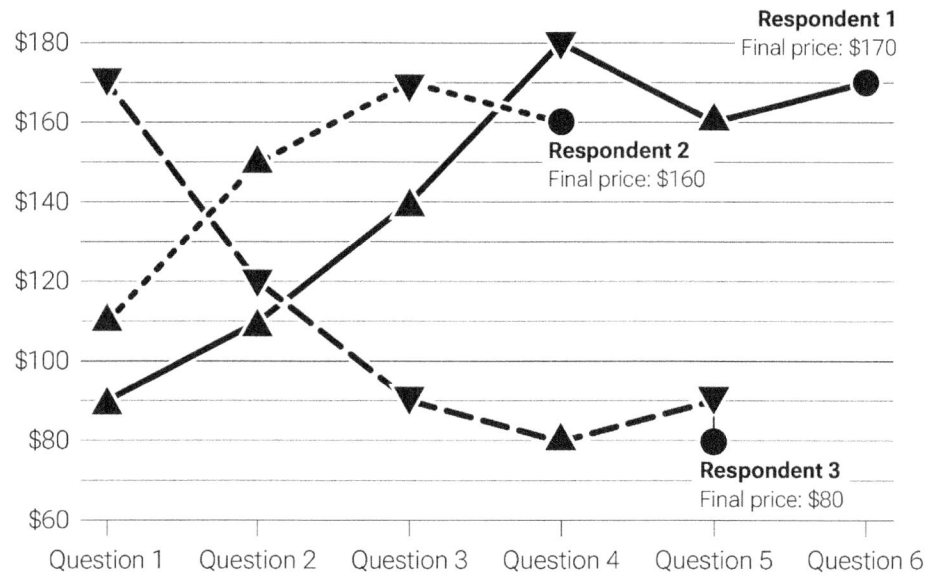

An even more reliable test of WTP is to presell the product and not ask the users if they would pay but instead invite them to pay and see what happens. However, there are natural ceilings to pricing based on customer expectations and the competition arena. In reality, most GTM companies are undercharging, not overcharging, but you can outprice yourself from the market if you are not solely offering a similar (perceived) value at a higher price point.

It is not only about the value per se but also about what other players in the space are offering when promising a similar value. In this scenario, always ask your users, "Why?" Why would they pay $500, but not $750?

If you are not "why-ing" at least 60% of the time, you are not curious enough, and you could be losing valuable learnings of where the psychological and market-determined price limits exist.

Competition and Alternatives: How Much Are They Currently Paying?

> "Often your toughest competitor will be the customers' status quo."
> Bill Aulet, author, professor, and managing director at MIT

The human brain is great at pattern recognition and solving puzzles. Every time we face something new, we tend to put it into an existing mental model. Well-informed users have reference points. They know what is a bargain, what is too expensive, and what is ridiculous to pay based on their available alternatives.

If you are entering the market with a rather undifferentiated offer in a crowded space, as a GTM company, the best you can hope for is roughly 10 to 30% cheaper or more expensive than the established competition. It depends on how you position yourself (more on that later) and what the actual value added from your product is.

For most users, the reference price is based on their experience and competitors' offerings. Old habits die hard. If customers have previously bought a solution similar to yours, they expect something within the range. You can research how much potential customers are currently paying for a solution they use and start to understand some limits of their WTP. The benchmark is set. There are budgets that decision-makers can use for buying products, and these budgets are hard to renegotiate when set.

Think of some hyper-competitive and consolidated markets, such as CRM solutions. There are some strong players, such as Salesforce, Hubspot, and Pipedrive, to name just a few.

Imagine going into that very saturated market and finding your place to compete. Here are the options:

- **Small businesses** would naturally search for free or very inexpensive solutions to start with. The value you have to portray to them would have to be 10x to conquer that market. Usually, their WTP is a couple of hundred dollars a month at best. More realistically, it's a double-digit number. If the annual deal is in the range of $600, you would have to attract many of them to build a sizable income stream to support your team. Are you comfortable that you can do that?

- **Medium-sized businesses** are more open to new players in the market, but their willingness and ability to pay is a bit lower. They might start with a free version and eventually upgrade to a $10,000-a-year solution. There is more competition in the space, but entry barriers are also lower. It might seem like an attractive space to investigate further.

- **Enterprise** would pay $200,000 or more for a yearly subscription to a CRM, but if you go there, you will be competing against Salesforce. Also, consider the sales cycle will be long and hard. It is doable but usually not the first bet for most GTM companies. You probably do not have the capacity to do that just yet.

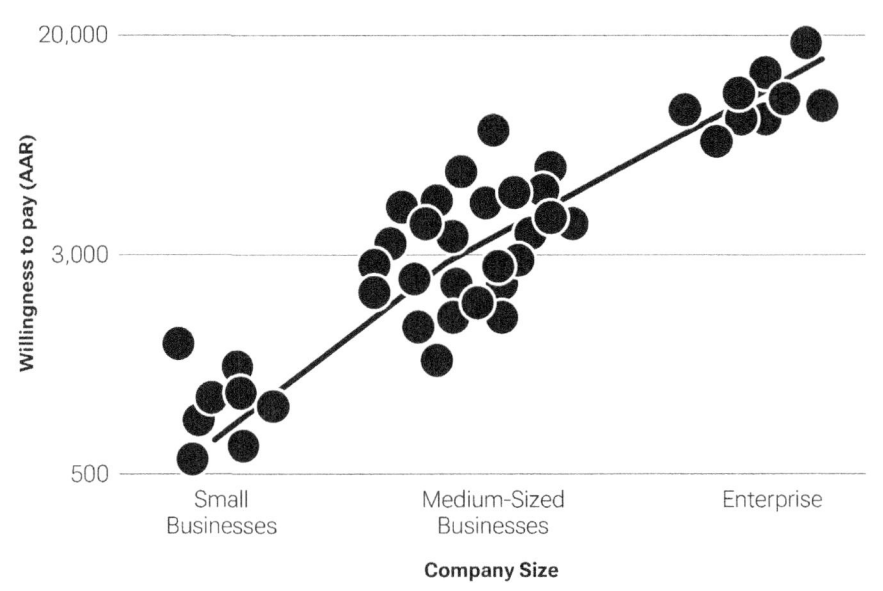

So, where would you place yourself in this arena? Definitely not at the lower end because it is a risky bet in most cases due to the 3 to 18-month lifeline in GTM. It takes economies of scale or very strong funding to pursue that. For most businesses, it is not sustainable to compete on price alone.

Can you go premium? Maybe. In some cases, you have either a really superior product or access to premium buyers. In this case, a prospect probably uses Salesforce. You would make a pricing decision like this: if Salesforce is priced at 100 points, how many points would you assign to your product based on the value it provides relative to Salesforce?

Given your resources, level of access, and capabilities, you will end somewhere in the middle (most likely). Unless you do something so valuable that competitors do not. In that case, you become a class of your own.

What Do You Want and Need Them to Pay?

"You are not optimizing for higher prices, you are optimizing for higher profits."
Simon Belak, Data scientist and Lead at Zebra BI

First, let's dive into the promised land: positioning of your product, as it will have a direct impact on its pricing.

Let's take a look at Apple's Vision Pro goggles. They start selling at $3,499. The competition – basic VR gear from Oculus – starts at $299. Apple's product is 10x more expensive. While Apple is a premium brand, and Vision Pro certainly is a technology innovation, it is fascinating how they positioned Vision Pro as an entirely new category of "spatial computing." When the product was first announced, Apple's CEO Tim Cook compared its cost with a setup of multiple high-quality computers, cameras, screens, and audio systems.[41] Suddenly, $3,499 becomes much more reasonable. With compelling messaging and the ability to deliver new value, you can ascend from the existing arena to a beautiful blue ocean where the hard limits no longer apply.

---

41 Apple. (2023.). Introducing Apple Vision Pro. YouTube. https://www.youtube.com/watch?v=TX9qSaGXFyg

Anchoring matters, but where to position yourself? Should you go with a high premium price, within the range of competitors, or a lower price and hopefully create faster adoption? Good news – we have an entire chapter on positioning later on.

For now, you need one more sanity check before calling the final shot on your pricing – do the business economics stand?

If you are bootstrapping, you have a couple of important jobs to do:

- Pay your team (payroll).
- Pay the bill (subscriptions, taxes, rent, etc.).
- Invest in marketing, business development, and sales, etc.
- Add value to the user (costs of value delivery).
- And a couple of others.

You could "pull it off" in the short term by promising shares to the team, not taking a salary yourself, working remotely, and investing your savings in the business. However, your job is to secure the business model and show some sign of a positive ROI to secure the existence of your company.

When deciding on pricing for your product, make sure to put together a sheet of expenses and a revenue projection as realistically as you possibly can. From there, try to reverse-engineer the quantity that you need to sell to get there in your GTM lifeline period (3 to 18 months) and prepare a couple of well-informed and research pricing hypotheses to test.

Let's assume that a team of five members who are working on an AI-empowered LinkedIn content creation tool has a lifeline of three months. Their objective is to validate that the product can be profitable because they have alternative projects to pursue if that's not the case.

Their simplified financial projections look like this:

	Expenses	Revenue Projections	ROI Projections
Month 1	$22,843	$0	-$22,843
Month 2	$20,643	$35,000	$14,357
Month 3	$29,843	$50,000	$20,157
Total	$73,328	$85,000	$11,672
ROI	115.92%		

A mission-critical pricing question is how can they secure $85,000 in merely months? Because in the first month, the product will not be ready. They have multiple options:

- They can do five custom projects for approximately $17,000 for larger companies to automate their LinkedIn content creation.
- They can sell 85 yearly subscriptions to SMEs for $1,000 each.
- Alternatively, they can sell 850 subscriptions at $100 each.

Ouch. These are hard tradeoffs, and these decisions will influence product development, service level, positioning, and much more. The sooner the team starts making these decisions, the better their chance of winning their chosen business model and pricing strategy.

But how do you make such choices, and what do you optimize for in our line of thinking?

Now, we get to a couple of pricing hypotheses. Let's pack them into some offers and start testing them. That's what is next: how do you charge for a product you have so diligently crafted to build a sustainable business?

Pricing Strategies

"Pricing is easy. But it is never easy."
Patrick Campbell, CSO at Paddle

Based on the research of 760 B2B SaaS companies, Paddle's researchers found the three most frequently used pricing strategies in GTM: competitor pricing (38%), value-based pricing (32%), and cost-plus pricing (30%). That makes competitor pricing a commonly cited pricing strategy. The problem with competitive pricing is that you are putting a higher value on your competitors than your customers.[42]

Sure, you can go ahead and copy some competitors or do pricing based on your gut feeling. It may work well, but are you willing to take that risk, or could you dive a little further to increase your chances of success?

Selecting the right number is never easy. "Cheap and expensive" depends on what you are offering to whom. Supply and demand curves do not always meet at the intercept of a minimum acceptable price to make a deal. Sometimes, the more expensive a product is, the more customers desire it.

There are only two fundamental strategies to build a sustainable business and get from the GTM to the growth phase:

1. **Optimizing for adoption**: Your GTM bet is to win a large number of clients with affordable pricing. You aim to create unit economics, upsells, network effects, and recommendations. Traction in volumes is essential for your business to establish a sustainable business model and its rightful place in the market.

2. **Optimizing for profit**: You selected a narrow subset of the target market's audience and differentiated your product so much that it provides outrageous value to the segment. The market is not price sensitive for the value they are getting, and instead of being in a constant cycle of sales, business development, and marketing, you focus on becoming the most valuable solution for your target market.

---

[42] Paddle. (2023). The state of B2B SaaS pricing in 2023. https://www.paddle.com/price-intelligently/state-of-b2b-saas-pricing-in-2023

Let's discuss them both and list pricing strategies that are commonly used.

Optimize for Adoption First

"Don't punish adoption – price should go up with value given, not adoption."
Simon Belak, CTO at Zebra BI

Growth Expert, Data Scientist, and CTO Simon Belak is a big believer in pricing for adoption. How different is it to optimize for adoption, revenue, or profit? He says the first question to ask yourself is, "What am I trying to achieve here?" That might be an odd question to ask because, obviously, the answer is to monetize and build a business model. But that isn't the entirety of the picture here. Pricing has two jobs to be done:

1. It's going to indicate what you are offering for the value you provide. It will have a significant effect on how the overall adoption will look and how it changes the customer journey of adoption.
2. Maximizing profits in the longer run.

You'll need to take a look at your business stage. If you have funding available and are post-PMF moving to the growth stage, you might want to consider optimizing pricing toward the biggest adoption possible. At that point, you want to attract many users to your ecosystem and push the adoption as broad as possible.

To ride the momentum and create a defensible market share, GTM companies can consider using a **penetration pricing strategy**. Penetration pricing suggests entering the market at a lower price than competitors in the hope of achieving the critical mass for innovation to work well and change customer preferences. An excellent example of this is Uber, which subsidizes drivers to drive in new cities to keep the prices reasonable for the consumer. This strategy is most obtainable to companies with funding to compensate for a loss at the beginning, as well as companies with high LTV and low churn. Sometimes, a critical mass of users is needed to unlock the next growth threshold. Before optimizing for profit, you have to optimize for adoption. Penetration pricing is also being used outside SaaS – in ecommerce, consulting, services, and digital courses.

Another strategy you can do is to give away a (part of the) product for free. This means you are investing in larger adoption and delaying monetization for later. The **freemium model** gets your foot in the door. Once they have adopted the product, users will consider paying for it. With this approach, you agree to be a **loss leader** who sells some of their entry offers at a loss or very low profit, which is later compensated for by higher-priced items. An example of this is Miro. They chose the freemium route and gave away some product features free of charge. The beauty of this approach is that potential customers could experience the value and expand their awareness of the tool, which unlocked virality for them. Once they saw adoption from enterprise clients, they sold them more premium services. There was some time when they were "leaving money on the table," but once they saw seven active users from the same company using Miro, the sales team was much more successful in closing the deals.[43]

In an adoption game, existing competition sets up the expectations about what buying the product should look like. Don't copy them, but work within the scope to (hopefully) outgrow their market share.

But what if you are bootstrapping and have to recover too much from development expenses and can't go all-in on adoption? What if your competitors are charging $10 a month per user, and you aim to charge $120? How will you justify this difference? That's what's up next.

---

43 Rachitsky, L. (2023). The ultimate guide to product-led sales | Elena Verna. Lenny's Podcast. Retrieved from https://www.lennyspodcast.com/the-ultimate-guide-to-product-led-sales-elena-verna/

Optimize for Profit First

"Lowering prices is easy. Being able to afford to lower prices is hard."
Jeff Bezos, founder of Amazon

In the long run, there can always be one cheapest solution on the market. It takes a lot of resources and scope to achieve economies of scale that make low-price positioning sustainable.

Big market share does not necessarily lead to high profits. Starting "low in price" in GTM can be a slippery slope. When you first give away something for (nearly) free, it is hard to raise prices in the future. You set up certain expectations and habits that are hard to change later.

It also takes money to make money. You have invested in developing a product, along with a marketing and sales plan. Especially if you are bootstrapping, you might be under pressure to recover this investment early on in your GTM.

Other reasons to consider starting with a higher price point are:

- Customers are willing to pay a premium for added value, especially if you are one of the first in the market.
- They are also willing to pay a premium for a good that is limitedly available.
- If the goods are temporarily in high demand and hard to access.

There are three pricing strategies to consider if this is your case:

1. **Skimming pricing**: When you are new to the market and create high value-added in a market with high demand, you can charge higher prices than existing alternatives. That might serve you well if you need to recover research and development costs to hit those green numbers. The premium comes from being the best, or the first, company to solve a specific problem. Skimming can not be defended in the long run because high margins and demand attract new players to the space, and competition increases. In time, prices will go down due to increased supply. But you can still use the skimming strategy when launching new products. Apple

launches a new generation of iPhones priced highly and eventually drops the price once new models are introduced.

2. **Premium pricing:** For some categories and target markets, the price can be whatever you and your customer agree on. When buying a luxury good, say custom-made giant yachts or super expensive Swiss watches, price sensitivity is low. How much would you pay for Warren Buffett to do 1:1 mentorship with you? What matters more is status as social signaling, exclusive access to a good that's in very limited supply, and the feeling of proximity to similar people who have access to it. Price, in this case, is whatever you decide and the market accepts. Sometimes, being more expensive even lures in more demand because of scarcity. But it takes commitment to superior quality, market access, and a lot of reputation building to get there.

3. **Dynamic model:** This means you are selling at different prices at different times to different customers with an aim to optimize profits. Amazon, Uber, and Booking.com make thousands of daily price adjustments to optimize business outcomes. Uber does this, too. The price rises if there is a sporting event and the rides are in high demand. Whereas in quiet times, you can get an Uber for a lower price.[44]

In business, multiple pricing strategies can coexist. You will learn later how to find the optimal combination with testing, but for now, how you set your price impacts your positioning and the type of customers you will be attracting. You can also change it later without hurting the brand by issuing cheaper product lines and subbrands once you have won your Beachhead Segment and want to conquer new segments. Nothing is fixed in pricing.

Now that you understand the strategy, let's look at *how* you can charge for your product.

---

44 Chen, A. (2021). The Cold Start Problem: How to Start and Scale Network Effects. Harper Business.

Pricing Models: How to Charge for Your Product?

"Your job isn't to build a product; it's to de-risk a business model."
Alistair Croll, Lean Analytics

Pricing has to be aligned with your customer's user journey. Is the value you are bringing to a customer's life a one-off transaction, or does it happen and increase with time?

There are multiple mechanisms of value exchange. They are called **pricing models,** and you need to take them into account when crafting your pricing strategy.

1. **Value-based**: This refers back to the value metrics we touched on earlier. You capture an agreed percentage of the value that was created by the product. A great example of this is Loom. Its value metric is the minutes of videos recorded. The price grows as the value grows in the product. I.e., the more videos a user records, the more they are charged.

2. **Usage-based**: This pricing model is based on how much usage the customer has in the product. A lot of cloud storage service providers, such as iCloud, use this pricing model with a value metric of gigabytes of storage. The more storage that's used, the more customers pay.

3. **Fixed**: Customers agree to a certain amount of money for a period of time. For example, Spotify Premium has a monthly fee of $6.99. With this model, you can still create different pricing packages so customers can choose one based on their needs.

4. **Hybrid Model (Usage-based or Value-based + Fixed)**: Most businesses end up with a mixture of the above and include a set amount of their value metric in a monthly or yearly fee. For example, someone pays a monthly or annual fixed fee for accessing Hubspot Marketing Hub for up to 2,000 marketing contacts (which is their value metric). In case there are more contacts, they'll pay more.

🧲 Marketing Hub™

Everything you need to capture leads and turn them into customers. Calculate your price ↓

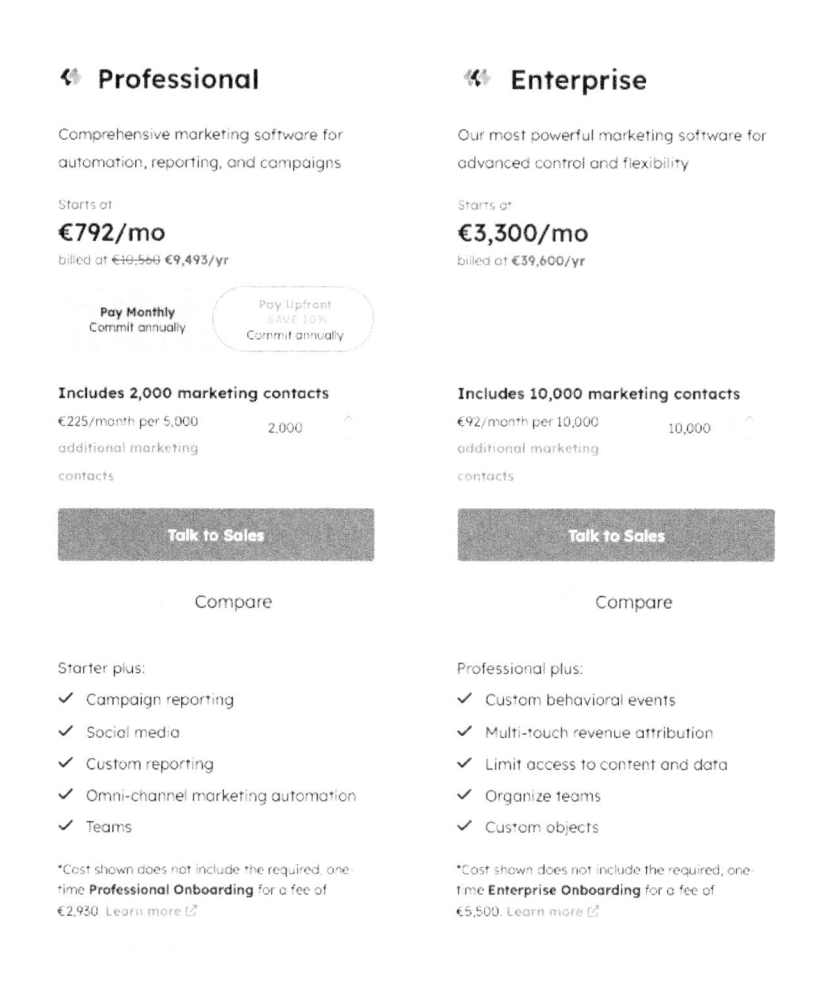

🧲 Professional

Comprehensive marketing software for automation, reporting, and campaigns

Starts at
€792/mo
billed at €10,560 €9,493/yr

Pay Monthly
Commit annually

Pay Upfront
SAVE 10%
Commit annually

Includes 2,000 marketing contacts

€225/month per 5,000 additional marketing contacts — 2,000

Talk to Sales

Compare

Starter plus:
- ✓ Campaign reporting
- ✓ Social media
- ✓ Custom reporting
- ✓ Omni-channel marketing automation
- ✓ Teams

*Cost shown does not include the required, one-time **Professional Onboarding** for a fee of €2,930. Learn more.

🧲 Enterprise

Our most powerful marketing software for advanced control and flexibility

Starts at
€3,300/mo
billed at €39,600/yr

Includes 10,000 marketing contacts

€92/month per 10,000 additional marketing contacts — 10,000

Talk to Sales

Compare

Professional plus:
- ✓ Custom behavioral events
- ✓ Multi-touch revenue attribution
- ✓ Limit access to content and data
- ✓ Organize teams
- ✓ Custom objects

*Cost shown does not include the required, one-time **Enterprise Onboarding** for a fee of €5,500. Learn more.

5. **Seat-based**: This value metric is tied to the number of users who need to access the product. If there are multiple users from the company, they would pay more than a single user. If there are multiple people in the account, the company could even grant them different access levels and price them differently. Miro prices their packages per user, but there is also a size limit to each package.[45]

---

[45] https://www.hubspot.com/pricing/marketing/enterprise?products=marketing-hub-professional

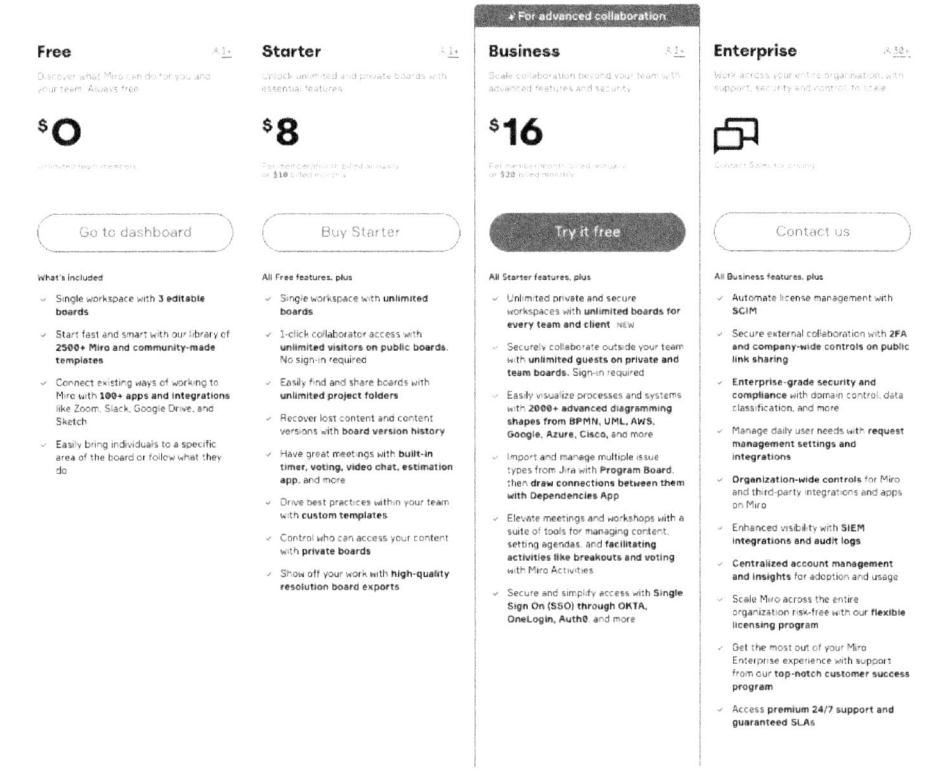

6. **Free trial or freemium model**: In addition to the paid version, there is also a free version of the product available that users can experience value. A free version is usually limited in features or available for a limited amount of time. Many companies aim to have some version of a free experience so a user can experience its value before committing to a purchase. Some prospects would simply like to try it before they buy it. Non-SaaS businesses can take advantage of offering free online courses, webinars, demos, and online courses. After delivering value to the customer, start to pitch more complex solutions.

Packaging: How to Package Your Product?

"Packaging can be theater, it can create a story."
Steve Jobs, Co-founder and CEO of Apple

Most B2B pricing packages are based on **Starter/Pro/Business/Enterprise** logic and center around time to access, typically monthly or annually. Each package has a value metric attached to it, along with additional features that serve and extra features that differentiate the packages to serve customers with different needs.

If we look at Zoom, their packages start with a free version to try, but it's limited to 40 minutes per meeting. As many of you probably know from personal experience, it doesn't look very professional if someone is in a rush to finish a meeting because they piggyback on a free tool in the business world. People who don't have an interest or the capacity to pay will gravitate toward another software that provides unlimited free usage.

Then there are those users who value advanced features possibilities such as recordings, team collaboration tools, and having the ability to host large workshops. They'll easily recognize the value of the advanced features on a Zoom call and choose the Pro or Business package.

Having 2 to 5 packages based on different usage needs and features is a great way to capture value. It's not always possible, but usually less is more. Remember the paradox of choice? The more choices given, the less likely people are to choose one. The fundamental job to be done here is to make the user understand which offer is right for them and how much it will cost.

For a customer, pricing creates inevitable friction in the purchasing process because they have to pay money and say no to other alternatives. Not only should you try your best for the pricing to be transparent and clear, but you should also make the communication rewarding or even celebratory.

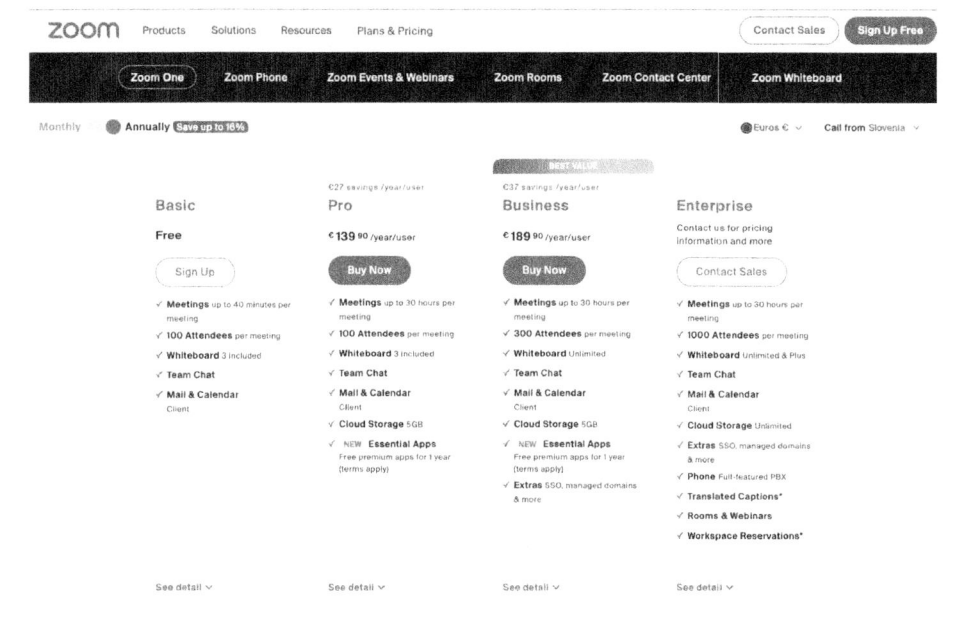

Your pricing page is one of the most important fields of optimization in your business. If you manage to make improvements there, the effect on the business can be tremendous. Even in B2B, customers don't solely use rationale when buying new products and services. Let's learn how framing your price can help you succeed.

---

46 https://zoom.us/pricing accessed in March 2023

Behavior and Psychological Aspects of Pricing

> "The reason it seems that price is all your customers care about is that you haven't given them anything else to care about."
> *Seth Godin, US best-selling author and former business executive*

Pricing gets really interesting when you observe the differences in customer behavior and learn about the psychology of decision-making. Let's start with a mind experiment to warm up for this topic.

Would you buy a yearly subscription for a low-carb home-delivered lunch service prepared by a chef for $1,850?

No.

C'mon, it is only $5 a lunch a day, and it's restaurant level!

Still no. I don't eat in restaurants every day, and I actually enjoy cooking or treating myself with a cheat meal sometimes. Bye.

But how about we look at it from another perspective?

How about a challenge where they deliver a weekly supply of restaurant-grade meals for a fraction of the costs of eating out?

A typical restaurant meal costs $14.99. They can do it for $5.99. How about giving it a week at $41.93? This means you save $63, on average, in comparison with takeout food. This is cheaper than three restaurant meals, and you get seven meals out of it!

Sounds better, doesn't it?

The point is the second offer is more expensive, but it sounds like a better deal because:

- There is a shorter time and monetary commitment at face value.
- Pitches the benefits and the costs of alternatives.
- You did the mental math for people. They don't have to calculate the costs of alternatives or the savings; everything is served to them to decide.

Meet one of the oldest tricks in the pricing books – **price anchoring strategy**. When customers are making decisions, they are always comparing us against alternatives. Yet, every customer wants to maximize their benefits. When presented with a set of choices, we learn to find the best value for us. This is why many software companies state that boldly on the pricing page and add a more expensive package to make the best-value deal seem even more appealing.[47]

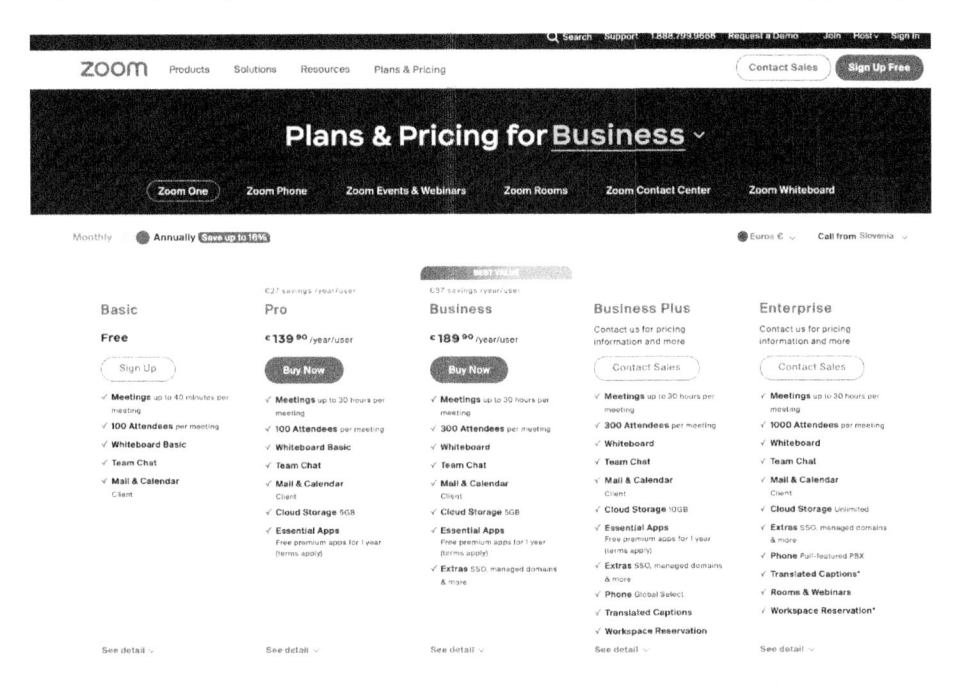

Consider the difference between Zoom's Pro and Business plans. The Pro is only $50 a year cheaper, but wow – you could host a webinar with 300 attendees! Even if I have one webinar a year, that is cheaper than paying for another tool to host it. How about buying the Business package instead of Pro?

In this instance, the Pro package could be a **decoy strategy**, a product priced in a way that lures the demand towards a more expensive option.

47 https://zoom.us/pricing accessed in July 2023

If Zoom was optimizing to boost Pro subscriptions, they could reduce the price of the Pro package or make Business a bit more expensive. Then, they would place the "best value" sticker next to the Pro package.

There is another interesting change in Zoom's pricing. Do you remember the Zoom pricing page from before? It had one less package than this one. In a span of three months, Zoom tested an additional package. There was probably more value to capture between the Business and Enterprise packages. It's a very smart idea to keep a swipe file of your competitors' pricing pages to find new ideas for pricing experiments.

Using anchoring and decoy strategies is possible if you have bundles and different packages for various market segments or usage needs. Instead of selling an individual offer and hoping that one size fits all, you bundle different variations of the products together, differentiate them, and price them differently.

You could sell a larger amount of goods, usually for a better deal to customers, and clearly communicate the value-added. Pricing expert Madhavan Ramanujam explains bundling and packaging per segment wonderfully with a McDonald's menu example.

In their menu, there are three categories of products:

1. Leaders: a burger such as a Big Mac, which is why you went to the restaurant in the first place.
2. Fillers: french fries and drinks.
3. Killers: if you bundle a killer product to the menu, it will kill the bundle. Think about coffee. If a customer wants it, they will order it anyway. But to put it on the main menu as a bundle with a Big Mac, it would not be a bestseller.

Last but not least, there is another mechanism that you are probably wondering about: the **discount strategy**. Though attractive for some customers, using large discounts to lure customers in GTM can backfire heavily. You could attract non-optimal market segments to your product that are extremely price-sensitive and always on the lookout to save some money.

That said, there are instances when using a discount strategy is sustainable for GTM companies:

- If you are (or will be) negotiating with a **decision-maker whose part of the job is to decrease the pricing.** You can account for a price bump in the initial offer and serve them the discount they require, which is usually in the range of 10 to 30% in B2B.

- If you have **multiple bundles,** you can present extra value by adding something to the bundle for the money instead of merely smashing the price. One of the best negotiation techniques is also to take away something from the package if the client pressures to lower the price.

- Discounts can also be given for **bulk purchases** and **longer subscription times** that will speed up the adoption and secure the revenue flow. This technique is great when you are selling a product that has marginal to non-cost duplication.

- If an early adopter commits to either co-create the product with you by providing you with feedback or agrees to a **case study or testimonial,** you can consider giving them a lower price because they are creating value for you.

If you are using discounting in the sales cycle, ensure your sales team has an agreed discounting policy and that it's not one of the core sales techniques. Otherwise, you might have a salesperson who offers so many discounts and free services that the company isn't making a profit but rather is operating at a loss. More about that in one of the next chapters.

Last but not least, there is also a strong psychological effect of how you communicate the price. Modern neuroscience has made great progress in how we react to prices.[48] You have probably heard about some of the specific tactics of psychological pricing, but still, let's throw in some ideas for you to consider if you want to test this territory of pricing:

---

[48] Coulter, K. S., & Coulter, R. A. (2005). Size Does Matter: The Effects of Magnitude Representation Congruency on Price Perceptions and Purchase Likelihood. Journal of Consumer Psychology, 15(1), 64-76.

- **$.99.** One of the ancient "pricing hacks" in the book. Should you end the prices with .99 because $9.99 appears less than $10.00? While the basic dynamics of this idea still work, consumers have become more sophisticated to "seeing through marketing lure." However, there is firm evidence done with a lot of experimentation that prices that are constructed of different digits perform very well, such as $297 instead of $300. It also has plenty to do with the overall number: $2.99 reads good, but $49.95 reads more expensive to most. The number of digits matters. You can test this in advance by using WTP research methods such as the Van Westendorp model.

- **Number of decimals and characters.** Most salespeople avoid listing $15,500.00 to communicate a price because it is a lengthy way to communicate the value. The more characters you can remove, the better it is expected to convert.

- **Make a unit of pricing displaying a small number.** For example, a monthly versus an annual subscription. While the price per annual subscription is obviously higher, if you reframe the annual price as a monthly fee and communicate the savings, it will look more attractive.

- **Reframe it to an even smaller unit.** This is called the Penny Effect. Instead of saying it costs $30 a month, you can reframe it to $1 dollar per day. If "for the price of a coffee a day" sounds too cheesy, consider communicating per-use cost.

- **Be careful how you portray small prices if your user is going to pay much more for their actual needs.** Simon Belak is not a great fan of sliders to calculate how much the usage of a product is going to cost a client. If you see the first offer at a price point of $200 per month and then move the slider to the volume of usage that you actually need, seeing your cost increase to $1,200 per month seems like a downer and can be a conversion breaker.

- **Do you communicate % or $ of savings?** The answer depends on how expensive an item is. If the solution costs $5 and you decrease your price by $1, a 20% price reduction should be more attractive than communicating a $1 discount. Oppositely, if the item costs $500, saving $50 seems more appealing than a 10% discount.

- **Do the math for them.** Our brains are made to calculate savings when considering offers. The easier you can make it for a customer, the more you make it attractive. Do not make them think about the purchase per se, and make them calculate the $ savings at the same time.

- **Test how to communicate discounts**. It also matters where you portray the promotional versus normal prices. According to research, discounted prices should be on the left, especially if the value of the purchase is high. Surprisingly, the font size, where you make the discount number bigger, plays a role. (I.e., only valid for Black Friday.)

- **Red or green prices?** Even the color in which you display the prices matters. There can be severe differences between cultures and genders. For example, studies have shown that women react better if the price is written in black or red, while the purchase intent of men rises if the price is written in blue, followed by red. Oppositely, the purchasing intent of women dropped below the average if they have seen the price written in blue.

There are multiple other experiments you can try. Since experimentation on pricing pages is one of the strongest levers to increase monetization.

Let's move to the most exciting part of pricing – experimentation.

Pricing Work is Never Really Finished

"Anyone can sell a Mercedes for the price of a Hyundai."
Larry Best, business executive and investor

Everything in business changes. In the GTM phase and beyond, there will always be new launches, new market segments to win, competitors' practices to conquer, and market changes.

As I am writing this book, an economic downturn is expected, budgets are tightening, and due to these expectations, many companies are removing and delaying purchases of everything that is not a necessity. Times will get better, as they usually do, but in the meanwhile, many companies will recession-proof their revenue streams by building less expensive products, offering deals for longer contracts, or adding additional offers to attract customers.

Pricing changes should not only be reactive but proactive. Smart GTM companies revisit their pricing at least once every six months and run pricing experiments to maximize their adoption and profit. However, many GTM companies struggle to start experimenting with pricing because they either do not know where to start. Others might be afraid they will lose some business, and others just want to "set it and forget it."

Rationally, you know that pricing is too important not to optimize. From Patrick Campbell's treasury of insights, we can grab another golden nugget that will be continually and increasingly important, "Experiment with price at least once a quarter. Set up a calendar reminder to do it. Growth is harder than ever. CAC went up 94% in the last five years, and WTP has dropped 70 to 80% in the last five years. AI advancement will make it even harder, and this trend will continue. Experimenting with acquisition is table stakes; real money nowadays comes from experimenting with activation, retention, and monetization."

When revisiting and experimenting with pricing, raising the prices is not the only option. The metric you should be optimizing for, in Campbell's belief, is revenue per consumer.[49] You might consider experimenting with a discount strategy and adding features to your offer. You could also try launching different offers for

---
49 Often measured as Average Revenue per User (ARPU)

different segments or even geographies. Oftentimes, WTP differs greatly between countries. New price ceilings can also be tested when you launch new products, add features, or once a customer reaches a new threshold of value.

But how do you get started with monetization experiments? What are the best testing methods to use? That's up next.

How to Run Monetization Experiments

"The moment you make a mistake in pricing, you're eating into your reputation or your profits."

Katharine Paine, founder and CEO of KDPaine & Partners LLC

The best method to test pricing is to actually encourage users to put their money where their choice is and run the actual tests (A/B test, multivariate test presale, etc.). In more controlled environments, prospects might try to appeal to the researcher or not take the research very seriously. A survey of how much people would pay for a product will provide less reliable results than actually using the dollars as an ultimate instrument of voting what value the market sees from your innovation.

Yet again, if the real testing is not obtainable to you, even doing a survey with the right target audience, in addition to competitor research, is probably better than "spraying and praying" that your conversion rate will play out as you imagined.

Whatever you will end up choosing to support your decision-making, it is likely to be much better than trusting your "gut feeling" or merely following the competition – especially when you might not have a long and valid trajectory in the industry. Here are some pricing experiments that best-in-class experts such as Patrick Cambell, Simon Belak, and Greg Leach recommend to kick off your pricing experimentation program:[50]

- For new offers, definitely start with WTP research. Test WTPs with interviews, surveys, or presale before making a final pricing call. If you are testing this onsite, aim for a sample of at least a couple of hundred respondents and a confidence level of at least 95%.

- Even small pricing increases from $49 to $50 can contribute to your bottom line if you have a large user base.

- If you increase prices, customers are usually not happy about it. To succeed in your price increase, make sure to communicate 30 to 60 days

---

50 ProductLed. (2023). AMA with Greg Leach Lead by Content Director at ProductLed Laura Kluz Replay. Vimeo. https://vimeo.com/838589845/c022cf8af5

before changes come into effect. The best way to structure the notifications that the price will increase is to:

- Remind them of all the value they got from the product, preferably share the numbers with them.

- Explain what will happen.

- Tell them why it's necessary and that you will continue to provide them with improved value.

- Set up clear expectations of when the changes will be effective and give them a way out if they can no longer afford or continue using the service. Thank them for their business and remain open for conversations.

- Each product and feature launch sets up a wonderful opportunity to test different packages and price points. Since you provide higher value-added due to improved products, services, or newly minted features, you have an opportunity to upsell existing clients and attract some new ones at a higher price point. When deciding if a launch is worth a price increase, WTP research again comes in handy.

- You might have features that are only used by a small segment of users. Based on your findings, you can shape custom packages that will serve them extremely well, and their WTP will be higher than if you push the offer to everyone from the get-go.

- Consider additional revenue streams. If you get a ton of leads that do not qualify for your product, those might be gold for someone else. For example, if people come to you for advice about a specific topic repeatedly, you might be able to sell that knowledge with a course. Do not get such opportunities to slip your funnel.

- Even when someone aims to cancel their plan, you can recover this account by offering a special deal or giving them a free upgrade if they continue doing business with you. Many will take you on the deal, and you saved the revenue. Even if they do not, make sure to learn what the reason behind their decision is to inform your pricing and revenue management experimentation in the future.

- Do not ignore churned users. If they have, at some point, stopped using your service, you can still send them updates and new offers if they agree to it. The game is not over until they explicitly say they do not want to be in business with you.

By using psychological pricing and these tips, you can shape a pricing experiment backlog that will keep you busy for at least a quarter or two. How about if the experiment goes wrong? In any healthy experimentation, seeing a success level that's more than 50% means your choices aren't bold enough. At GTM, you optimize for learning, and the faster and bolder you experiment, the more you learn.

Remember that pricing is a cross-functional sport. Most often in technology businesses, it primarily sits in product, not finance. But other departments, such as sales, data science, dev ops, customer support, marketing, and growth, can make a great contribution to shaping up and experimenting with your pricing. Before starting with any pricing changes or experiments, it is vital to get buy-in from all critical departments.

If you are selling to larger companies and enterprises, it is important that Sales is not only on board but also aligned with these changes. They will carry the consequences of these actions, and it may influence their performance. The primary buy-in, as always, comes from the founder or the CEO and has to be aligned with business objectives. If the metric you are pushing towards is to increase revenue per user, the alignment should not be an issue, but the metric should be reflected in OKRs and monitored in a period that makes sense.

It all comes down to how well you understand market dynamics, value metrics, price elasticity, and what you learn from experimentation. Instead of crunching another spreadsheet, you will get better insights by going out there, researching WTP, testing, doing it on a small scale, then looking at results and adopting your pricing accordingly.

As you well know, pricing is not done in isolation, and it is also used for signaling the quality and who the product is for. In the next chapter, you will get more insights on branding, positioning, and messaging so that you can communicate your intended price point with ease and confidence. But before you progress there, let's quickly recap this chapter to double down the learnings.

Key Takeaways:

- Pricing is a mechanism of value exchange between you and the client. Value is created through the product. You aim to get fair compensation for the added value your product has created for a client.

- Pricing is one of the strongest profit drivers in your business. Profitwell's study of more than 500 SaaS companies revealed that each change in monetization can have a 4x impact compared to optimizing for acquisition. From increasing monetization success by 1%, research participants have seen a 12 to 16% increase in revenue.

- Pricing is never done in a vacuum. Multiple factors influence it, including:
    - Added Value: For what value are customers willing to pay?
    - Willingness to Pay (WTP): How much will they pay?
    - Competition and Alternatives: How much do they currently pay?
    - Positioning: What do you want and need them to pay?

- A value metric is a quantifiable measurement used to determine and measure the value exchanged. It is a specific unit of measurement that aligns with the customer's perceived value and scales with their usage.

- WTP research is useful for informing your pricing and experimentation. The most common survey techniques to measure WTP are Van Westendorp's Sensitivity Model and Gabor–Granger method. But you can also use customer interviews, presales, and A/B testing.

- Most GTM companies have to operate within 20 to 30% +/- current price ranges for relatively undifferentiated and established competitors unless they can achieve the perception of being radically different.

- Most pricing models are either value-based, usage-based, fixed, hybrid, or seat-based.

- Your pricing and revenue-capturing strategy has to be sustainable and profitable, at least in the mid-term. You have to understand financials so that you can keep insights into how impactful and profitable pricing changes are.

- Transparency is very important. Customers are increasingly solution-aware, and they compare different options and search through online reviews before making product choices. Transparent pricing builds trust.

- Your pricing strategy is not limited to raising prices, and you can shape multiple offers that fit various segments and usage needs.

- Broadly, you have three options to determine the price range you will set:

  1. Penetration: you set the price lower or later down the customer journey to optimize for adoption.

  2. Skimming: you can outprice the competition to generate more profits and preferably also convince customers who are lured to exclusive values.

  3. Similar range as competitors: you create differentiated value perception using behavioral and psychological pricing.

- Pay attention to behavior and psychological pricing. It is not only a "how much" answer. Customers are comparing alternatives, and you should make their job as effortless as possible.

- Only use discounts if you need the project for a reference or if they buy in bulk or for a longer time period. Wherever you agree on a discount, the client should feel a slight pain of losing something from the original offer. For most, adding benefits to the bundle or tokens of appreciation for their business is a better call.
- Pricing experimentation is an increasingly important cross-functional effort. It's not solely the product team's responsibility.

To-Do List:

☐ Find your value metric.[51]

☐ Decide what methods you could be using to test WTP.

☐ Consider your positioning in the arena- what is your desired space to compete? Will you start with penetration or skimming pricing?

☐ Build your economic model for GTM.

☐ Prepare a swipe file and set up a reminder to review their offers and pricing pages at least every six months.

☐ Build an experiment backlog for pricing.

☐ If you had a pricing committee in your company, who would you join? Product manager, founder, CFO, growth director? Who should be on your team when you discuss pricing? Can you get these people in the same room and discuss the pricing learnings?

☐ Choose your first five pricing experiments to run and put them in your backlog.

☐ Set up a recurring calendar every three to six months to review your pricing.

Find all the worksheets, frameworks, and models mentioned in this chapter at https://gtmstrategist.com/resources. They are free and yours to benefit from.

---

51 Wes Bush, ProductLed. https://productled.com/blog/value-metrics-for-product-led-growth

CHAPTER 6

Positioning

"Positioning is the difference between customers that get what you do and customers that don't."

April Dunford,
best-selling author and experienced positioning expert

You now have a clear picture of your Beachhead Segment, the stellar product, and the selected price point. Now you're eager to introduce it to the market. On your sales and customer discovery calls, prospects "get it" after you put your heart and soul into explaining it.

The problem is – your outstanding performance on sales calls cannot be scaled. You must sleep, eat, and have at least a little fun while going to market. This is why it's essential to craft frameworks, elements, and rules that will help you scale your communication while keeping the DNA of your value proposition to a customer.

The goal of this chapter is to provide you with tools on how to scale your passionate explanation of your Unique Value Proposition (UVP) to enchant prospects on your website via marketing and sales materials – and we'll make it catchy.

There are three layers to this process. Most GTM companies, such as Jasper's, would begin with **branding** – how to create visual elements for their business. Most often, the burning question is if you should brand your website to your Beachhead Segment:

To: **Maja Voje** (grow@majavoje.com)

Subject: **Should we brand our website to our target market?**

Hey, Maja!

Thanks for your tips on pricing. I very much enjoyed the value metrics concept. After discussing it with the team, we will go with a free package, along with two additional packages based on the number of users going through our flow. That makes sense.

Now we are putting together a landing page, and I wanted to nudge you if you think we should build it around our persona (founders in the fitness and health space) or if we should go broader to not lose some other opportunities that might come to us.

Our technology can serve many more people, so why risk losing them?

Thanks again for your feedback and all the great insights so far.

Let's go to the market!

Jasper

Hold your horses once again, dear Jasper. Let's avoid the "putting lipstick on a pig" scenario by hiring someone on Fiverr to craft your visuals in a week. It's important to do this right.

But Jasper and his team don't have the time and resources for a fancy six-month branding project packed with workshops. For them, it's mission-critical to launch, and each day they don't, they burn their runway. It is also a cultural issue; their developers would laugh out loud if a branding consultant at a workshop asked them which animal they think best represents their company.

In this chapter, we focus on positioning, branding, and messaging. You have to start somewhere, and in time, it will evolve in parallel with your new findings on the GTM journey. Let's reach a consensus on what each of these terms mean and how they are different from each other.

1. **Positioning** is about identifying what makes a company's product or service unique for your target audience. Positioning answers the question, "What makes our solution different and better than others in the market?"

2. **Messaging** refers to how you communicate that identity and value proposition to your target audience. It "prescribes" the language and communication tactics you will use to consistently get your message across using marketing and channels such as website copy, social media, advertising, and public relations.

3. **Branding** is the process of creating a distinct and memorable identity for your company or product. It encompasses all the visual and non-visual elements that create the brand's identity, including the company name, logo, tagline, brand colors, and brand voice. Branding is how you get recognized and remembered by your customers.

Does a GTM company really have to do all this? Not necessarily from the get-go, but if you set up good fundamentals before sending your messages and images into the wild, you increase your chances of success. More importantly, you will be perceived as consistent and more trustworthy. The challenge of sending mixed messages and confusing prospects is high in GTM, where we fiercely test and learn. It also comes in super handy to have some guidelines written down when you are growing a team or working with external partners, agencies, and freelancers. It does not fall into the "urgent" bucket, but it definitely belongs to the "important" bucket of GTM activities.

Let's strike the agreement that it's best to do this before you go all in with GTM execution. You can use fragments of this chapter that make sense to you, or you can do the best you can now and return to the process later if you discover that your messaging is falling flat, conversions are not where you need them to be, costs of customer acquisition are unsustainable, and/or your target customers don't really understand or care about the value you are communicating to them.

The co-author of this chapter is positioning and growth expert Andrej Peršolja, who describes the experience of doing it with an app:

"When we co-founded KOBI, a mobile app that helps dyslexic children learn to read, we tried to penetrate the US market. According to research, half of the money spent on mobile apps worldwide is spent on that market, so the decision made business sense. However, we were struggling to attract attention. We couldn't get users to download the app or convert them into paying customers. So we knew we had marketing and conversion problems. We tried to grow our way out of these issues, but no matter what kind of tests we did, we couldn't get it to work. April Dunford's Obviously Awesome book changed my perception of things. In the book, April says something like, "If you have some loyal customers, but new customers don't understand what you do, you have a positioning problem." I was a junior marketer. I knew nothing about positioning. Because positioning wasn't taught in the startup programs that I went through. Most people sailed through it without giving it a second thought. So I dived into that. After doing a brainstorming session on our position as a mobile app, we managed to lower the cost of user acquisition by 52% by repositioning the product.

It's one of the hardest lessons I learned in marketing. It taught me to think about marketing and sales as amplifiers. At the core of the product, we have our position and our message. We want to spread that message into the world. Marketing and sales are helping us achieve that. But if your position is wrong, if your message is wrong, you are just spreading the wrong message. You are amplifying the wrong results.

So whenever you think you can skip this step, consider that you may be throwing away half your money through the window and into the wind."

Positioning: Be in Control of the Narrative

"Positioning is not what you do to a product. Positioning is what you do to the mind of the prospect. You position the product in the mind of the prospect."
Jack Trout, a marketing strategist and author of Positioning: The Battle for Your Mind[52]

According to April Dunford, a positioning guru and tech executive, positioning is making sure that your target customers understand what you do and why it's relevant to them in a way that differentiates you from your competitors.[53] In other words, positioning is not just about defining your product or service but also about understanding your customers' needs and desires and crafting messaging that speaks directly to them.

Imagine a cookie. Twelve cookies cost $2, which is $0.16 a cookie. But here is where the magic happens. Once you position a cookie for fitness, vegans, or snacks for babies, you can hit 10x more price points. Your choice will also influence the product development and selected marketing and sales channels. This is the power of positioning – it can be a cookie or a fitness/vegan/baby cookie.

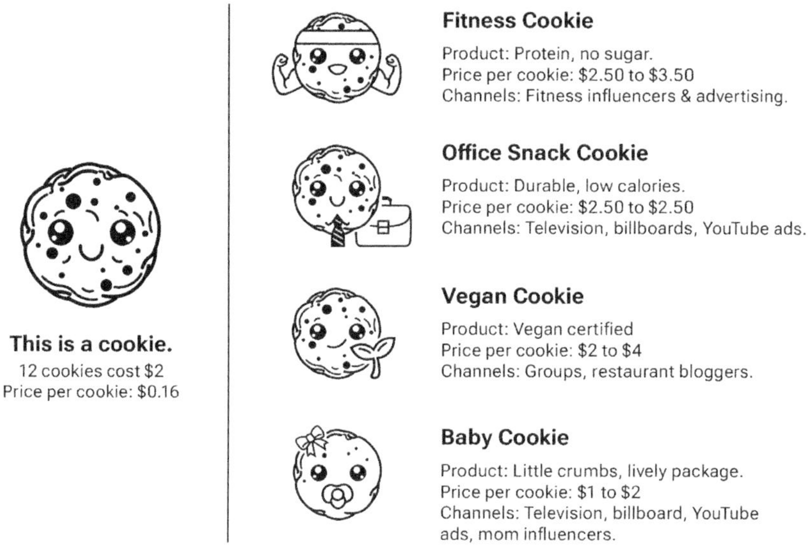

This is a cookie.
12 cookies cost $2
Price per cookie: $0.16

Fitness Cookie
Product: Protein, no sugar.
Price per cookie: $2.50 to $3.50
Channels: Fitness influencers & advertising.

Office Snack Cookie
Product: Durable, low calories.
Price per cookie: $2.50 to $2.50
Channels: Television, billboards, YouTube ads.

Vegan Cookie
Product: Vegan certified
Price per cookie: $2 to $4
Channels: Groups, restaurant bloggers.

Baby Cookie
Product: Little crumbs, lively package.
Price per cookie: $1 to $2
Channels: Television, billboard, YouTube ads, mom influencers.

---

52 Ries, A. & Trout, J. (2001). Positioning: The Battle for Your Mind. McGraw Hill.
53 Dunford, A. (2019). Obviously Awesome: How to Nail Product Positioning so Customers Get It, Buy It, Love It.

In simple terms, positioning is the answer to the question: what do you want your product to be known for in your target market's mind?

But the path to getting that answer is not always simple. You don't really have the power to control how your potential customers think. You can, however, provide the necessary context so they understand your product and what it can do for them. That context is your positioning.

Most companies and branding consultants just sail through positioning. They put down a positioning statement that is not really actionable or usable in any way. They follow a predefined template that worked for them once or even something they found on the internet.

Do you even know what the company does? How will that help your team stay focused and aligned on your business objectives?

Vanilla positioning often leads to messaging falling flat and simply not enchanting the target audience. The symptoms of bad positioning are:

- Not attracting enough leads.
- Attracting mixed audiences who don't want to pay your prices because they don't see you as a specialist in your field.
- Poor conversion rates.
- Poor engagement in the product.
- Long sales cycles.

Experiencing any of these?

You might still think: oh, positioning isn't important for us, so we'll just skip it.

The issue is that positioning happens. Always.

When was the last time you didn't have a "first impression" about something? When was the last time you had no opinion on a product? You might be indifferent about something. But that's still an opinion. And it is the worst kind of opinion because it's next to impossible to turn an indifferent lead into a customer.

The truth to the matter is that your potential customers and users will have opinions. They will position your product whether you want it or not. **So, it's better for you to be in control of the narrative**. Leave any room for interpretation, and your customers will make up their own minds about who you are and what you do. Who is on the riding seat, you or the customer?

An additional issue is that what works for one company will probably not work for yours. Even copying direct competitors with similar target audiences won't produce the desired results because the competition is already positioned as the go-to solution in the eyes of the customers, and you'll again just end up competing on price.

Deliberately positioning yourself provides real, tangible benefits. After working with more than 60 companies on their positioning, Andrej recognized three main benefits to really giving your positioning a serious thought and doing it together with the team:

1. **Improved marketing and sales KPIs**. Positioning is all about giving out the right context to the users so they understand the value of your product. The better you can do that, the better your marketing and sales KPIs are going to be. Testing this early is important so you don't end up overspending in marketing. Small changes in your positioning and messaging can lead to huge differences in conversion and acquisition rates.

2. **Team alignment**. What positioning strategy has to do is procure some team alignment. Creating your positioning strategy should align your marketing, sales, and development teams to all push in the same direction. When creating a position for your product, there should be consensus in the team on where the product should be positioned, creating a sense of unity in the team moving towards a common goal.

3. **Team accountability.** Positioning can easily be used to provide helpful, tangible documents for every department in the team. And most companies I take on as clients initially don't take it that far. So, by working through these templates, you can gain a tremendous advantage and avoid several problems along the way.

So, let's take control of the narrative to unlock these benefits.

Positioning Process

> "Positioning makes sure every effort you put in marketing and sales is substantially rewarded."
> Andrej Peršolja, positioning expert and practitioner

The best positioning embraces tons of different pieces and parameters that have to be tied together for it to make sense. And those pieces are moving.

This is why it's extremely important to develop your own unique position and let your copycats compete on price instead.

Your position on the market consists of the following elements, all of which we have already addressed in detail in the previous chapters of this book:

- Target audience
- Problem-solution fit
- Alternative solutions (your competition)
- Differentiated value
- Market category

Now, let's bring them all together and create a compelling, differentiated positioning.

Andrej Peršolja suggests doing positioning with a proprietary framework that is based on improving profitability by building your foundations and was perfected by working with 60+ companies.[54] It is proven to work and deliver results beyond "a sentence that you put on your website."

---

54 2023, Repositioning for Profit: How to Attract High-Value Customers and Increase Revenue, Andrej Persolja, ttps://apersolja.com/repositioning-for-profit/

Positioning Steps

In the positioning steps, you will take inputs (your target customer, your market, and your competitors) and position your product to deliver outputs that drive practical value for your company.

You'll also find an example of how to differentiate a product in a crowded market to make it clear how to build your product's positioning. You guessed it – the example we're going to use is a CRM software.

Step One: Your target audience

Your strategy, your product, and your positioning should start with the customer. Change your target audience, and everything else changes.

Therefore, we are focusing on that ECP.

Example: Say you're building a position for a CRM product. The CRM market is your typical saturated market with lots of competition scattered all across the board, with one major player holding a lot of market share – Salesforce.

Perhaps you find a niche in the small business industry. None of the competitors are really working for small businesses, and the founders of small teams are complaining about current solutions. So that's where you focus.

Step Two: Alternatives and the market gap

Next, go back to the chapter about your market and your competitors. You mapped out your competitors and figured out whether customers have unsatisfied needs they are complaining about. These are your market gaps. This makes sure your positioning works for the market. Next, let's test whether we can actually make that position happen.

Example: So you are building a CRM for small businesses. You do some market research and find that small businesses and consultants are complaining about how none of the CRMs are keeping them accountable. They don't even know when they have to follow up with their clients, and some that look good have too many features that customers don't want to pay for because they won't be using them. This is your market gap.

Step Three: Assets (how you will build your differentiation)

To become the best at solving a problem, you need to actually make that happen. You need assets to build your differentiation.

You can't say it's an innovative product if there is nothing innovative about it. You also can't position yourself as a tech expert if the founder is young and inexperienced.

Positioning is a story. That story needs to hold up. All of the elements of the story must be true, or your customers will get red flags when we tell them that story.

That's why in the third step, we map out every feature our product has and every ability you have in your team (a.k.a. an "asset") so you can pool together the strengths you have to work with.

Write down every asset your team has and every feature your product has.

Example: You are building your CRM with a small team, so agility and a lean process are assets. The lean process also means the product doesn't have a ton of features and is easy to use. Because AI is becoming more and more mainstream, we connected our CRM with AI as well. But really, the focus is on simplicity, ease of use, and on the features that matter most.

In this case, your assets listed would be:

- *Small team*
- *Lean process*
- *Easy-to-use product*
- *AI integration*

At this point, there is nothing special about your product.

Step Four: Turn your assets into benefits

Product marketers know features don't mean much to customers. They need a much more direct language, so it's important to explain the benefits they get.

We do that with a simple "so what" question. Take an asset and ask: "So what?" or "Why does the customer care?" Ask yourself the question five times, and you'll get a clear benefit a customer gets from your asset.

Example: What does the customer get from the CRM product?

- *Having a small team means we are quick to respond to user requests because there is not a lot of overhead or bureaucracy. A.k.a.,* **fast user support.**
- *A lean process means we are iterating the product in short stints with small but consistent upgrades. A.k.a.,* **quick product updates.**
- *There is not a lot of time learning or integrating the product. A.k.a.,* **an easy-to-use product.**
- *An AI integration means AI taking care of when to follow up with leads. A.k.a.,* **you don't have to know when to follow up with leads; the product takes care of that.**

So now we know what we can offer our customers, let's build our selling proposition statements.

Step Five: Build your Unique Selling Proposition (USP)

USP is a feature or characteristic of a product that distinguishes it from the competition and makes it more appealing to the target audience.

While your *value proposition* is your promise to customers, telling them what you will deliver or how you will make their lives better, your *unique selling proposition* tells your customers why they should buy from you.

Every asset you wrote down earlier has the potential to be developed into a differentiation statement, but it needs to fit two key requirements.

- **The asset needs to be viewed as valuable by the client**. If a customer receives fast service but doesn't care about speed, that's poor differentiation. The customer won't care, and you'll fall into the "nice-to-have" category. The first step is to filter out the assets and benefits your target audience doesn't value.

- **The asset needs to be unique to you**. The second requirement is that the asset needs to be almost exclusively unique to you or very few of the competitors. If too many competitors solve the same problems as you, you'll compete for market share, and you'll struggle to attract and convert users and compete on price. The second step is to filter out the assets and benefits that are unique to you.

What's left is your Unique Selling Proposition (USP). These are the product features and team assets you can use to build a market share of your own. Don't be nervous if you have two USPs here. One is good, two is better.

This helps you get your unfair advantage, giving you the unique ability to attract, convert, and retain customers much easier. It's why your customers will buy from you.

Example: In the CRM, you filter out the benefits your users don't see the value in:

- ~~Fast user support~~
- ~~Updated product~~
- No time spent on learning or integrating the product.
- Don't have to know when to follow up on leads; the product takes care of that and gives you reminders of when to do it.

Your users don't care about fast support or quick product updates when deciding on which CRM to choose. They just need a simple-to-use product that keeps them accountable. So, there is no use in building our differentiation on the first two benefits.

In the next step, you check the competitors. You find that tons of them claim to have a simple product. So we can't build our differentiation on that either. You can keep it as a benefit, though. That means we are left with an AI integration that sends them smart reminders. Your USP might be as follows:

- You don't have to know when to follow up with leads; the product takes care of that and gives you reminders of when to do it.

But what happens if you go through this exercise and realize there is nothing left?

If you are in a highly competitive market or have an undifferentiated product, you might struggle to find assets that are both unique to you and valued by customers. This means you'll end up competing on price, which inevitably leads to struggle. If you are having issues finding assets that are both unique and valued, answer this question: what is it that the current market is missing that is valued by the users? We also covered more on that in the previous Market chapter.

Once you have your answer, engineer the need backward. Ask yourself: what assets do we need to build a unique feature that satisfies that need in that market? And then build that asset until it becomes your unique asset that is valued by the clients.

Step Six: Merge your assets and benefits into a beautiful story for the customers

The final part of the positioning process is to merge everything together into a story that makes sense and then share that story through your channels. Here are the key components of your story:

- Your UVP: your main promise to the customers.
- Your USP: why your solution is better than other solutions.

You can now pack that unique story into any of the amplifiers: your marketing strategy, sales strategy, website, social media, PR articles, and your sales and investor pitches. The story is simple. This is why we do this. This is what we promise to do. And this is why customers will choose us over our competition.

Example: Let's unpack the CRM.

Your value proposition:
- *The only CRM that will keep your small team accountable.*

Your USPs:

- *No need to know when to follow up with your leads. Our AI assistant will suggest ideal follow-up times so you can close more clients.*
- *Stay on top of your follow ups with our smart reminders.*
- *Simply sign up and start using our product right away. No technical knowledge is necessary.*

You can easily see how this can now be turned into a landing page or a sales pitch.

Step Seven: Test your position

By now, you're well aware that all of our assumptions and well-educated guesses are rarely right. Before committing to one position or the other, it is wise to test it with your actual target audience before blasting it throughout all of the channels.

Andrej's best practice is to test different positioning with a simple landing page test. Create a landing page with one value proposition and USPs. A/B test that page against another landing page. Create ads to drive a meaningful sample to each variation of the landing pages. The meaningful sample depends on the use case, but try to aim for at least 50 conversions from the landing page. Often, you'll get a clear enough winner within a week; the winner has a higher click through rate on ads.

Alternatively, you can test this using other research methods such as surveys, social media, or email marketing. But that is a discussion we have already had – the closer you test for buying/using an attempt, the more confident you can be in the results of these tests.

Step Eight: Make positioning practical for your team

Positioning provides guidance for your marketing plan, your development plan, and your support team.

When you think about positioning, you should think about assets that you have on your team or environment, the features your product has, and what the benefits are for the user. It brings clarity and a sense of direction to business when done right.

When creating a marketing and content strategy, those assets, features, and benefits are what you should be talking about in your marketing. They should be used in sales calls, sales decks, and pitches. This keeps your position clear and consistent.

Let's look at the CRM example:

> *Your value proposition:*
> - The only CRM that will keep your small team accountable.
>
> *Your USPs:*
> - No need to know when to follow up with your clients. Our AI assistant will suggest ideal follow-up times so you can close more clients.
> - Stay on top of your follow-ups with our smart reminders.
> - Just sign up and start using our product right away. No technical knowledge is necessary.
>
> *From that, you could do a checklist for marketing:*
> - Does the post talk about the importance of accountability and following up?
> - Does the post show how simple our CRM is to use?
> - Does the post talk to small businesses?

Your marketing team can have this checklist pinned on the wall when creating a content strategy so your position remains clear at all times. The same checklist can be made for sales and even development teams.

To every great rule, there are some exceptions. If you are just starting out, if it really does not make sense to go very narrow, or even if your past positioning proved to be ineffective, the positioning steps can still come to the rescue, but a little differently.

Positioning Special Ops

"The essence of positioning is sacrifice. You must be willing to give up something in order to establish that unique position."
Al Ries, marketing professional and author of *Positioning: The Battle for Your Mind*[55]

There are three use cases to pay special attention to in positioning:

1. **Positioning for new companies and startups:** When you are creating a GTM strategy from scratch with no prior data, obviously, most of your decisions will be based on assumptions. Just like you shouldn't fall in love with your idea, you shouldn't fall in love with your positioning.

   When you actually launch the product, you will start attracting customers. Your goal in this first stage is to prove your idea can get traction. That means selling your product to whoever wants to pay some solid money for it.

   Embrace that initial chaos. But also, be prepared to pivot or change your positioning strategy if your angle of attack doesn't work. Perhaps your product will attract different types of customers than you anticipated, which means changing your positioning on the fly. That's completely fine, as long as you realize that at some point, you will have to make order out of the chaos.

   This usually happens when your product gets to about $500,000 to $1 million in annual recurring revenue. At that point, your growth might stall, meaning it's time to take a look at the data you gathered and reposition (or niche down) for your best-fit customers.

2. **Horizontal positioning:** There is no business sense of positioning vertically (per industry or demographic), but you want to keep your options more open and position horizontally, which means solving a specific need. In these cases, your target audience is too broad for efficient targeting, or the product is new, and the target audience isn't aware the

---
55 Ries, A. & Trout, J. (2001). Positioning: The Battle for Your Mind. McGraw Hill.

product exists. So, instead of starting with a specific target audience, we start with a use case that our audience has or has a habit that the product replaces.

Andrej helped a client called Elia nail their positioning. This startup helps non-English speakers improve their English with a Chrome extension. Elia's audience is broad – anyone who learns English and is not a native speaker is a target audience, from content creators, students, and business professionals. Because of the broad positioning, the startup faced user acquisition and conversion challenges. Some users converted instantly, while others left poor reviews. It was time to niche down and find users who loved the product.

Through a combination of product analytics, interviews, and surveys, the team concluded that people who used Elia as part of their workflow to speed up their writing and reading skills are the best target audience. That's still not one customer segment. But it is a specific use case.

The team came up with several different use cases where the users could suffer because of poor English skills. Consultants who need English to impress their clients, workers who struggle with productivity at work, and others who can't fit in. However, the test results were inconclusive. No use case really popped out as the clear winner.

The team stuck their heads together and rethought the problem. Most users were not aware of the product. They didn't even know you could install an extension that helps to find better words or explain the meaning of words directly in the text you are writing. This is why Andrej and the Elia team tried direct messaging. "Can't find the right words? Elia can help."

The test results were clear. The new messaging brought 12 times more people from the ads via the landing page to the web store compared to the first test.

The result of the positioning process was to position Elia based on a use case. Elia was repositioned from a language learning tool to a productivity tool for those who want to read and write in English faster.

3. **Repositioning**: If you happened to choose the wrong positioning from the get-go or did not really pay that much attention to it, you still have a fighting chance to get things right. If you are experiencing stagnant growth, it means your positioning isn't working for you (anymore). Stagnant growth usually hits you across the board. Your marketing KPIs are down (low CTRs, low conversion rates), and your sales suffer as a result. You are struggling to attract and convert users.

The reasons for a slowdown or stagnation differ. When Andrej worked with a Spanish SaaS company in the traffic acquisition space, tons of new competitors joined the market in a short period of time, leading to a loss of market share. The result of that was multiple pain points: ads getting more expensive while producing worse results and lower conversion rates (both organic and from ads), leading to lower revenue and decreased profitability. In plain words, it was more expensive to bring people into the website and more difficult to get them to convert.

Another reason for stagnant growth may be that user behavior changed, which was very apparent during and after the COVID-19 pandemic. During the pandemic, tons of users moved to online shopping, driving growth to ecommerce stores. After the pandemic, this behavior slowly returned to normal, leaving tons of competition to compete for fewer customers.

Another reason for stagnant growth might be that your product just attracted a mixed bag of clients in the beginning, which led to mixed feedback, affecting your product development and your marketing. Basically, the company ended up having a chameleon product that fits tons of customer segments but attracts no one because it's not specific enough.

In that case, it's time to reposition your product and niche down on a specific customer segment or their use case. The process is very similar to the positioning steps described in the previous section but with a different start. Because your product already has customers, you can use existing data to figure out your best-fit customers instead of relying on your hypothesis. So start with the analysis:

- Check your financial data. Which customer segments bring in the most revenue?
- Check your reviews and qualitative data. Which customer segments respond best to your product?
- Check your product analytics. Which customer segments have the highest lifetime value and use your product the most?
- What are best-fit customers solving by using your product?
- What's the problem-solution for your best-fit customers?
- How does your product help your best-fit customers?

By the end of the analysis, you should have a clear understanding of which customer segment is your best-fit client.

Next, follow steps two to eight from Andrej's positioning process.

As you develop your GTM strategy, please don't overlook the importance of positioning. By deeply understanding your target audience, identifying your unique value proposition, and considering the competition, you can create branding and messaging that speaks directly to your audience and sets you apart from the competition.

Keep in mind your positioning story needs to hold up. It needs to make sense to the customers, and you have to build the assets that will support your story. The better you present that story, the better your positioning, which means the higher price you can ask for your product, and the easier it will be to convert your leads into paying customers.

Okay, now you know what to say to stand out. But how should you say it visually and verbally?

Welcome to the wonderful world of messaging and branding built on top of your positioning.

Messaging: How Do You Tell It?

"The messaging has to come before the marketing and the discovery of the brand. This allows the foundation of what it will be built on to be understood as much as possible."
Loren Weisman, author and messaging and optics strategist

After you define your positioning, the next step is to put this information into practice in all your materials. You need to create compelling and relevant messages for each channel and situation that will engage your potential customers and drive the desired actions (for example, purchases or lead submissions).

Messaging refers to how you tell your story across **different channels to different audiences throughout their customer journey in a consistent manner.** It includes the tone, language, and key messages used in all communication materials, such as website copy, social media, and marketing and sales materials. Imagine messaging as a bridge between you and the consumer.

Based on research from the CXL Institute, messaging determines 80% of your conversion rate on websites.[56] Yet, messaging remains one of the most undervalued areas in business. Messages are often not being tested enough, leading to suboptimal conversion rates. Messaging should convey a message or idea to an audience in a clear, compelling, and memorable way. But how to do it, and perhaps most importantly, who should be responsible for it? Is it a part of the branding workshop, or is it the job of a CMO to do it? Or can you outsource it to a copy-genius freelancer?

Everyone knows they should use it consistently, but in reality, everyone is too busy writing their copy to follow the messaging guidelines (if they even exist), especially if you are working with a large team and external professionals. In this section, you will find the frameworks very helpful to align your communications and make them more effective and consistent. With the rise of AI-generated content and hyper-testing communication materials, it will inevitably gain importance in the near future, so it's better to learn the fundamentals as soon as possible.

---

[56] Schneider, E. (2023). Messaging Strategy: How To Win With Effective Messaging. CXL. https://cxl.com/blog/messaging-strategy/

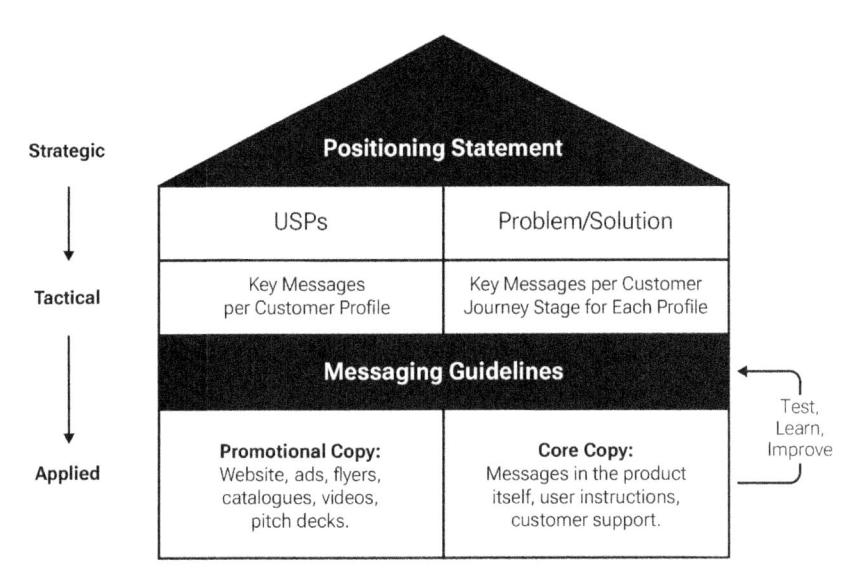

Strategic	**Positioning Statement**	
	USPs	Problem/Solution
Tactical	Key Messages per Customer Profile	Key Messages per Customer Journey Stage for Each Profile
	Messaging Guidelines	
Applied	**Promotional Copy:** Website, ads, flyers, catalogues, videos, pitch decks.	**Core Copy:** Messages in the product itself, user instructions, customer support.

Test, Learn, Improve

One statement you could put in writing, especially in the early stages, is a short pitch in the **"problem/solution"** form. What is the problem you observe many customers are facing, and how does your product solve it? That will help you nail the storyline of the presentations and pitch decks going forward. Some product managers even prefer to picture a "dreamland" of how the world will be improved with their product.

As a final preparation stage, define what some **key messages** are that should be communicated based on all the above, both to different customer profiles as well as across the customer journey. For example, a "money-back guarantee" is not something that should be part of the pitch when a customer first learns about you. But it can be a good statement to have closer to the purchase stage, to lower the resistance, and to improve the conversion rate.

Messaging guidelines are then a document where you put it all together. It is a short one or two-page document where you write down everything you defined: positioning statement, USPs, key messages, and also examples of "boilerplate" texts which you can use or adapt for specific purposes later - this refers to short product descriptions, a company description, founders' biographies, hashtags you are using, etc. You can find a template below. Having a document like this will help you keep your messaging consistent and also save you time when you need to produce new content. It is especially helpful when more people are working on the content, which is often the case.

Great messaging is distinctive and aligns with the tone of voice of your brand. This tone uniquely resonates with your target audience. In most cases, your messages should not read like a PR message; they should be genuine and in close proximity to your audience. Do not be afraid to stand out; be emotional, caring, bold, a bit quirky, or whatever your selected tone of voice is. It is best to provide examples of both good, "This is how we communicate," and bad, "This is how we absolutely do not communicate" tone of voice in your messaging document for everyone to learn.

Brand name	
Tagline/Slogan	
USPs	
Product Description (full)	
Product Description (in one paragraph)	
Product Description (a one-sentence pitch)	
About the company	
Founder's bio	
Descriptions for social media	
Hashtags used	
Emojis used	

Copy is then how you put it into practice. Messaging guidelines will help you produce better text on the website and in other promotional materials and presentations, But it will also keep the messages consistent in the product itself. It will help users have better product experiences, which should, in the end, reduce churn and improve customer retention.

It is important to note that the messaging work is never finished. Especially with digital tools and analytics, it's easy to measure conversions on specific parts of the website. But good old customer feedback in the form of interviews is always helpful, too. So, you have to always collect learnings and regularly update messaging guidelines and other assets. That's also the case if you pivot to re-positioning or start addressing other customer segments.

For the best practices when crafting your messaging, let's agree on some universally applicable good practices of messaging:

1. **Clear and concise messaging** is key to effectively communicating with your target audience. Avoid packing too many elements into the message by eliminating the fluff. Establish a core messaging brief and stick to it. Each message should have one key point. If you have more than three key points to the message, you likely are complicating it.

2. **Speak to your target audience** and address their specific needs, desires, and pain points. Aim to write in a way that mimics natural conversation and maintains a friendly tone that makes customers feel welcome. If your target audience uses buzzwords and industry jargon, you can too. If not, or if you are not sure, it's better to avoid it and double down on benefits.

3. **Be authentic**. Do not shy away from communicating your values, and use a distinctive tone of voice. Your message should showcase what sets you apart from your competitors, whether it's your brand personality, unique features, or a combination of both.

4. **Appeal to customer emotions and logic by using narratives and storytelling**: When it comes to an understanding of how people make purchasing decisions, some purchases have more rational and other irrational drivers. Our brains are wired that way so that it's often easier to understand and remember messages if they are narrated as stories. There is much you can learn from what is called a Hero Journey, according to Robert Kaminski, a messaging expert for Early Stage and GTM B2B companies.[57] Robert suggests communicating the following storyline in key materials, such as your homepage:

    - Persona: who is a "super specific" role or a team you intend to use the product?
    - Alternative: what are the current, insufficient ways of doing things?

---

57 Campbell, J. (2008). The Hero with a Thousand Faces. New World Library.

- Problem: what issues arise from the status quo that no one has managed to solve yet?
- Capability: how does your solution solve this problem?
- Feature: what are the superpower features that power the capability?
- Benefit: what are the outcomes of your solution?

Robert suggests five narratives that work well for attracting different audiences in B2B:

- **Tragedy**: A cautionary tale with a negative outcome. It is a fairly universal model that is powerful for convincing prospects they have a problem worth solving.

- **Overcoming the Monster**: A hero sets out to destroy evil. A strong structure, particularly for innovator prospects, highlights the flaws of the "current way."

- **The Quest:** An aspirational journey. This works best with early adopter prospects who care about unlocking new capabilities to create a "new way."

- **Rags to Riches**: An underdog overcomes adversity to win. This is a particularly useful structure when targeting under-resourced prospects (or small businesses) by showcasing superior features and benefits that give you a chance to compete with the dominant player.

- **Rebirth**: An event forces the hero to evolve. This is good for highlighting trends that are driving change in behavior.

Regardless of the narrative structure you decide to use in your messaging, be sure the story connects messaging elements in a believable way.

5. **Use Social proof and elements of persuasion**: It is one thing to say it, but it is so much more credible if you back it up with data, expert opinions, client testimonials, and case studies. To fuel your messaging, consider including Robert Cialdini's six Principles of Persuasion:[58]

---

[58] Cialdini, R. B. (2021). Influence, New and Expanded: The Psychology of Persuasion. Harper Business.

1. **Reciprocity**: People are more likely to comply with a request if they feel that someone has done something for them in return. If you have a very good offer or give high value for (almost) free, others will be compelled to repay you for your kindness. In biblical terms, give before you get.

2. **Scarcity**: People are more likely to want something if they perceive it as rare or in limited supply. If you limit the number of available units or put a time limit on the deal, the conversions will likely go up because you gave customers a reason to act now.

3. **Authority**: People are more likely to comply with a request if they perceive the person making the request as an authority figure. If you have an established expert or an influencer vouching and promoting your product, it will increase the perceived value added and boost conversions.

4. **Consistency**: People are more likely to comply with a request if it aligns with their prior beliefs or behaviors. If you incentivize a user to do something small for you first and later on proceed with a bigger task, it is more likely to succeed.

5. **Liking**: People are more likely to comply with a request if they like the person making the request. If you are on a good mission and have something that is emotionally appealing to people, like charisma or genuine community, to stand in your corner, the future looks brighter for your business.

6. **Consensus**: People are more likely to comply with a request if they see that others are also complying. The law of big numbers, a.k.a."Over 9,000 users have made $2 million last month by using this platform." It adds to credibility and trust.

After understanding the strategic part of messaging and best practices, you need to adjust it to different stages of the customer journey. If your target customers usually have different actors in their decision-making unit (DMU), you also need to adjust messages to each (technical benefits for CTO, financial benefits for CFO, etc.). We'll dive into that in the next section.

Messaging Tailored to Your Target Audience

"It is not our abilities that show what we truly are. It is our choices."
Albus Dumbledore, a wizard from Harry Potter

Best messaging is not you-based but customer-based. If you decide to use the Beachhead Segment, focusing on a single audience, you automatically avoid falling into the trap of "communicating too many things to too many different people." In case you have to do the messaging for multiple target groups, adjust the core messaging strategy to each.

But even if you are Beachhead-ing your GTM messaging, pay special attention to DMU once again. If there are multiple decision makers seeking different benefits or having distinctive requirements for value-added, your best shot is to adjust core messaging to become relevant to them. Robert Kaminski and his team analyzed the messaging for a video platform, Loom, that was being considered by an enterprise sales team with an aim to increase their success by using videos for personal selling.[59] Robert suggests using a value matrix to communicate effectively with different actors in the DMU by highlighting what they care about when buying a new productivity and collaboration tool.

- **Users** who care about the day-to-day experience.
- **Champions** who appreciate solving the problem and who are driven by the challenge.
- **Decision makers** are mainly driven by outcomes since their job is moving the needle.
- **Financial buyers** are primarily concerned with ROI.
- **Technical influencers** are concerned with the safety and effectiveness of integration in the existing tech stack.

This is how Loom can approach multi-persona messaging for a single use case in the DMU.

---

59 https://www.loom.com/

B2B Persona-Based Messaging

loom

Product Use Case: Using Loom to send personalized video messages to customers

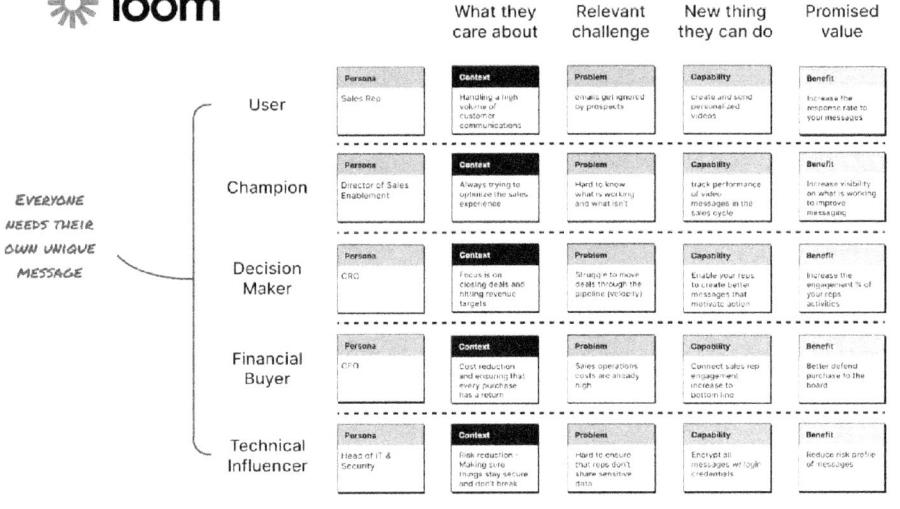

EVERYONE NEEDS THEIR OWN UNIQUE MESSAGE

	Persona	What they care about (Context)	Relevant challenge (Problem)	New thing they can do (Capability)	Promised value (Benefit)
User	Sales Rep	Handling a high volume of customer communications	emails get ignored by prospects	create and send personalized videos	Increase the response rate to your messages
Champion	Director of Sales Enablement	Always trying to optimize the sales experience	Hard to know what is working and what isn't	track performance of video messages in the sales cycle	Increase visibility on what is working to improve messages
Decision Maker	CRO	Focus is on closing deals and hitting revenue targets	Struggle to move deals through the pipeline (velocity)	Enable your reps to create better messages that motivate action	Increase the engagement % of your reps activities
Financial Buyer	CFO	Cost reduction and ensuring that every purchase has a return	Sales operations costs are already high	Connect sales rep engagement increase to bottom line	Better defend purchase to the board
Technical Influencer	Head of IT & Security	Risk reduction - Making sure things stay secure and don't break	Hard to ensure that reps don't share sensitive data	Encrypt all messages w/ login credentials	Reduce risk profile of messages

This visual is the courtesy of Robert Kaminski and Anthony Pierri

The next element to consider is that messaging varies across a customer journey. Robert emphasizes that good messaging is really about starting a conversation. If you resonate, you will earn a conversation. By leading with the right element, you can establish trust and earn the right to go deeper with a customer. Your best approach is to lead with your most differentiated features. Sequence the right message at the right time by considering the best practices for different customer journey stages:[60]

- **Awareness Messages**: Lead with the problem and use case. These prospects don't know about your product yet. The goal here is to qualify they have the problem for you to solve and to earn time for them to consider your product. You can't just jump right into explaining your product until you have landed this message.

- **Acquisition Messages**: Lead with capabilities. You've earned some time to deliver a product intro message. The goal here is to convince them to

---

[60] The steps example is primarily developed for SaaS companies, but you can apply it to other business models as well. For sales, you can assume that booking a sales call is an activation and you can move from activation to monetization directly. Feel free to adjust this model to your actual customer journey.

give your free product a try. Do not overwhelm your audience. Highlight your most compelling capability that aligns with the problem.

- **Activation Messages**: Lead with feature guidance. At this stage, you have earned a signup, but this is where the real work begins to get them to value. The idea here is to be a guide for your new user. Again, watch the amount of features you are pitching. You should focus on a single workflow that addresses the use case. There will be time later to introduce more stuff.

- **Habit Messages**: Lead with benefits. Your user has reached their first aha! moment. The goal here is to get them to continue to realize the value repeatedly. Show them how impactful their repeated use is for them. Metrics to back up these benefits can be powerful.

- **Expansion Messages**: Lead with adjacent capabilities. At this point, your user is a retained free user. The goal at this point is to start expanding their use towards premium features and capabilities. To do this, it is best to connect supporting situations and use cases to the habits they have already developed.

- **Monetization Messages**: Lead with scaled capabilities. The whole premise of PLG is to deliver value first, so when it comes time to ask for money in exchange for further scaling the value, it should be an easy task. But be careful of putting this message in front of users who haven't quite reached multiple aha! moments or formed habits.

The example below is for the meeting scheduling SaaS tool Calendly, with messaging variations approaching a salesperson.[61] Remember that the most effective messaging is about meeting the customer where they are with a focus on maximizing their value.

---

61 https://calendly.com/

Startup Website Messaging Guide
Each page has very specific purpose in your GTM

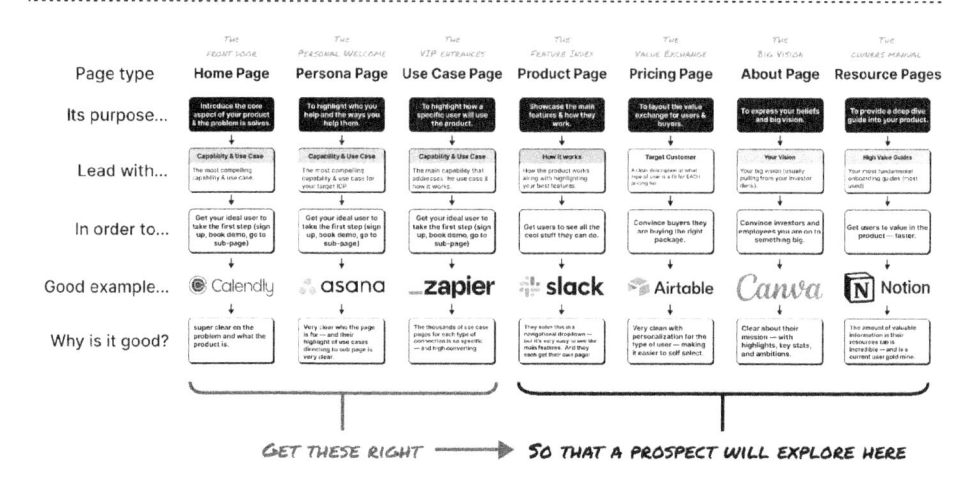

Page type	Home Page	Persona Page	Use Case Page	Product Page	Pricing Page	About Page	Resource Pages
	The Front Door	The Personal Welcome	The VIP Entrance	The Feature Index	The Value Exchange	The Big Vision	The Owner's Manual
Its purpose...	Introduce the core aspect of your product & the problem it solves.	To highlight who you help and the ways you help them.	To highlight how a specific user will use the product.	Showcase the main features & how they work.	To layout the value exchange for users & buyers.	To express your beliefs and big vision.	To provide a deep dive guide into your product.
Lead with...	Capability & Use Case — The most compelling capability & use case.	Capability & Use Case — The most compelling capability & use case for your target ICP	Capability & Use Case — The main capability that addresses for use case & how it works.	How it works — How the product works along with highlighting yo ur best features.	Target Customer — A clear description of what type of user is a fit for EACH pricing tier.	Your Vision — Your big vision (usually pulling from your investor decks).	High Value Guides — Your most fundamental onboarding guides (most used).
In order to...	Get your ideal user to take the first step (sign up, book demo, go to sub-page)	Get your ideal user to take the first step (sign up, book demo, go to sub-page)	Get your ideal user to take the first step (sign up, book demo, go to sub-page)	Get users to see all the cool stuff they can do.	Convince buyers they are buying the right package.	Convince investors and employees you are on to something big.	Get users to value in the product — faster.
Good example...	Calendly	asana	zapier	slack	Airtable	Canva	Notion
Why is it good?	super clear on the problem and what the product is.	Very clear who the page is for — and their highlight of use cases directing to sub page is very clear.	The thousands of use case pages for each type of connection is so specific — and high converting	They solve this in a long-toned dropdown — but it's very easy to see the main features. And they even get their own page	Very clean with personalization for the type of user — making it easier to self select.	Clear about their mission — with highlights, key stats, and ambitions.	The amount of valuable information in their resources tab is incredible — and is a current user gold mine.

GET THESE RIGHT ──▶ SO THAT A PROSPECT WILL EXPLORE HERE

This visual is the courtesy of Robert Kaminski and Anthony Pierri

Messaging in Action

"There are three types of people: those who make things happen, those who watch things happen, and those who wonder what happened."

Dan S. Kennedy, author, entrepreneur, and advisor

After deep diving into different personas that you need to address, it's time to get to the applied side of messaging – what do you actually tell to whom and where? In GTM, you interact with prospects and clients using different communication channels: on your website, in ads, social media, in PR articles, sales decks, and elsewhere. While your UVP should remain consistent throughout the channels, specific messages need to be persona, stage, and channel adjusted.

In the example below, you can learn how messaging evolves through different customer journey stages with Robert's example of some well-known SaaS websites.[62]

This structure allows consumers to scan the value proposition quickly and pick up on product features to decide if the solution is the right fit for them. Added visuals increase the ease of communication between the business

---
62 Source: Fletch.

and consumer. Peep Laja, a conversion optimization expert and the founder of CXL, suggests you start with the following formula on your web pages:[63]

- **Headline**. What is the end benefit you're offering in one short sentence? It can mention the product and/or customer. Make it an attention grabber.

- **Sub-headline or a 2 to 3-sentence paragraph**. A specific explanation of what you do/offer, for whom, and why it's useful.

- **Three bullet points**. List the key benefits and features. Consider a format such as "Accomplish X using our Y feature."

- **Visual**. Images communicate much faster than words. Show the product image, the hero shot, or an image reinforcing your main message.

- **Call-to-action (CTA)**. If the value proposition landed well with a website visitor, what's next? Help website visitors get further along their buying journey by clearly suggesting what the next recommended step is that they should take.

When developing your messaging plans, always adjust your messaging to the communication platform where a message will be broadcast. There might be a character limit, expectations, and best practices of how to communicate on a channel (for example, video, quotes, professional photos, etc.) or even an algorithmic push of new features that you can use to leverage your content. Hold a swipe file of other peoples' posts that inspire your work, but always adjust it to your tone of voice and the look and feel of the brand. One thing is universally true, though. Whenever you write for the web, keep your sentences short. It increases the accessibility of your content.

Merely posting consistently and "on-brand" on social media consistently will not guarantee the desired results. Take time and thought to develop a communication strategy and stick to it. Can your well-coordinated efforts still go to waste? Absolutely. You might scatter your messaging through too many channels, and not all of them are relevant to the target audience. Make sure to learn

---

63 Laja, P. (2023). Unique Value Proposition: How to Create a UVP. CXL. https://cxl.com/blog/value-proposition-examples-how-to-create/

before committing to a channel that the target audience is actually there and willing to interact with you on that platform.

Limit your testing periods for new channels. If you see mellow results for more than three to six months and barely any engagement or growth, don't waste more effort there. In GTM, it is critical to create an impact. Your efforts to move the needle might better manifest elsewhere. My best advice is to give promising channels a shot but evaluate them on a frequent basis to see if they are moving to serve their purpose. Optimizing messaging for different channels and developing clever content plans is a long-term game but only worth playing if a channel delivers on its potential.

Don't forget to test different messaging. Usually, this is done with two variations of a landing page and an ad campaign where you don't change a single word but the messaging and see what happens. You need to have enough visitors per variation to secure the statistical significance of these tests. We covered those details in the ECP chapter.

If this is not available to you right now, you can still consider testing messaging with a survey, focus group, interviews, or usability tests. You can even consider running a sequential test, where you measure before and after a change in messaging was implemented with your site or product analytics. Even high-touch methods can provide guidance or additional insights. One treasury of insights for testing is answers to "How would you describe X" questions from your existing clients.

Another great practice is to keep a repository of all messaging experiments with visuals and results of these tests (website, newsletter, blog post, social media, ads, sales decks, etc.), which is easy to navigate through and browse within.

I really believe that the key to organizational knowledge maintenance is being a good librarian. People come and go. Segments change. If the knowledge of messaging is kept within some clever people's minds, it is not scalable, and you expose yourself to the human factor danger. The more that can be documented and shared, the better chances are that the messaging will continue to evolve based on all the findings.

Branding: Express Yourself

"Your brand is what other people say about you when you're not in the room."
Jeff Bezos, founder and CEO of Amazon.

Branding, another mysterious animal in the GTM jungle. What is the brand, and how much does it really matter? How do you know you have a strong brand?

While I served as CMO at OriginTrail, many community members asked us to buy our swag and were proud to wear it. That was one of the biggest lessons I have learned from technology companies. Strong brands have raving fans, strong communities, and incredible word-of-mouth (WOM). How do we build a business that is strong enough for customers to crave its products and profoundly share their love for it with the world? Hello, branding!

Your brand is more than a shiny logo. Technically, a brand is a name and design that makes your product unique, recognizable, and distinguishable from other choices on the market. But a brand is also a set of associations, feelings, and expectations that customers and users start connecting with your product. All of these elements need to be managed and work together like a well-oiled machine to deliver a consistent experience for users.

Strong brands are built over time. In the longer term, branding leads to reputation. Established brands also have loyal customer bases, which can mean more revenue from repeated purchases or higher price premiums because customers are prepared to pay more for perceived quality.

Branding is also not just throwing money into awareness ads, which indeed have hard-to-measure ROI. A well-managed brand that knows its target users and is focused on communicating well can also mean lower advertising costs because you have loyal customers and have to invest less in attracting new customers or word-of-mouth spreads based on a good reputation.

Marketing expert and best-selling author Seth Godin stresses the importance of branding: "In a crowded marketplace, fitting in is failing. In a busy marketplace, not standing out is the same as being invisible. No one remembers a copycat brand. But everyone remembers a brand that stands for something, a brand that is different, a brand that is remarkable."[64]

That's why we started with positioning in this chapter. Knowing your target audience, position, and USPs will be the best foundation that will help you build a strong brand and not just a random logo. Now I have a confession to make. Similar to Jasper and his team, branding has always been one of the toughest business areas for me to tackle. I would choose accounting or legal work over engaging in branding workshops. The reason why I find it so difficult is because the process is difficult. I have problems expressing my design preferences, and feedback like "pretty or ugly" never helped anyone. For nearly 14 years, I have struggled to make branding decisions, but luckily, at this point in my career, I have a great team in my corner.

GTM Friendly Branding Process

"Products are made in a factory, but brands are created in the mind."
Walter Landor, brand designer and the founder of Landor & Fitch

Luckily, I am married to a person who is a Senior Brand Manager. Anže Voje has led and participated in more than 50 branding and rebranding projects, mainly with high-tech projects. When I no longer feel that I am able to express what I envision to a design team, Anže comes to the rescue.

64 Godin, S. (2009). Purple Cow: Transform Your Business by Being Remarkable. Portfolio.

Anže firmly believes that creating a brand for a GTM company or a new solution does not have to be complicated. By following a few questions, you can have a solid foundation for a brand that will resonate with your target audience so you can thrive in the market.

Meet Anže's GTM branding process:

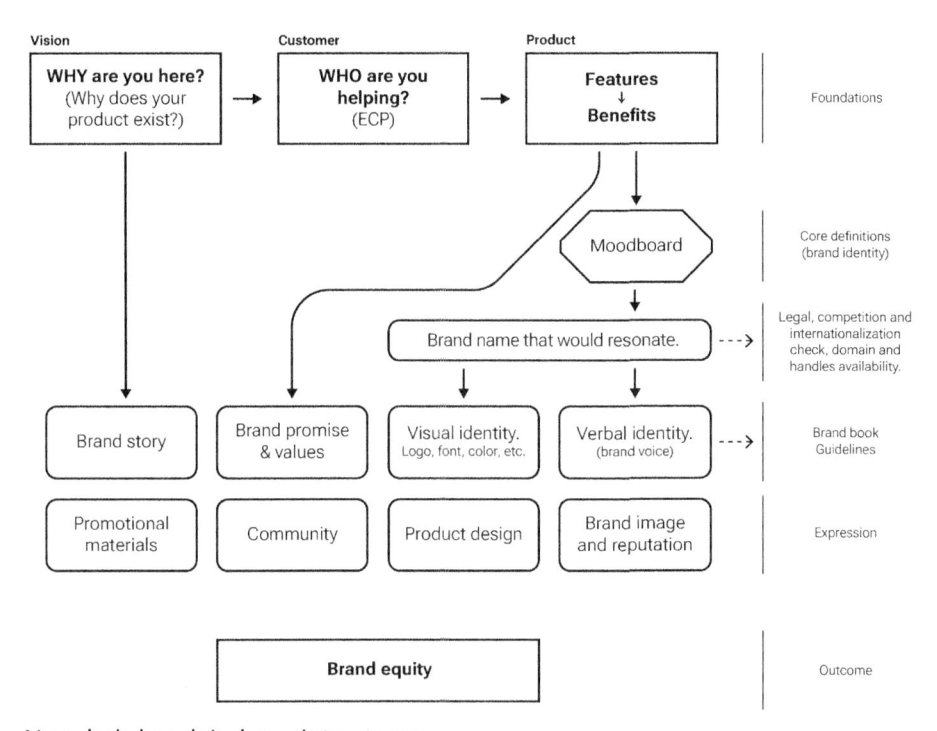

```
Vision                    Customer                Product
WHY are you here?    →    WHO are you       →    Features         │  Foundations
(Why does your            helping?               ↓
product exist?)           (ECP)                  Benefits
                                                    ↓
                                          Moodboard              │  Core definitions
                                                                    (brand identity)
                                                    ↓
                                    Brand name that would resonate. --→  Legal, competition and
                                                                          internationalization
                                                                          check, domain and
                                                                          handles availability.
    ↓                         ↓            ↓                ↓
Brand story          Brand promise    Visual identity.   Verbal identity.  --→  Brand book
                     & values         Logo, font,        (brand voice)          Guidelines
                                      color, etc.

Promotional          Community        Product design    Brand image          │  Expression
materials                                                and reputation


                            Brand equity                                     │  Outcome
```

Now, let's break it down into steps:

1) Foundations

There are three pillars you need to define at the beginning of the branding process, and we have already covered most of them in this book. It helps to have this information in front of you as your "North Star" of what your brand communicates to whom and why.

- **Vision:** Define why you are here as a company or why your product exists. How will it change the world for the better?

- **Customer:** Turn back to your ECP – who will your brand communicate with?

- **Product:** When talking about ourselves, we tend to be too technical or focused on the features. Features are important, but at this step, connect the features to the key benefits that your solution is bringing to the customers. These benefits can be either functional (e.g., time savings or cost savings) or, especially in the B2C segment, emotional (e.g., a sense of belonging).

2) **Core definitions**

Now that you have defined your three foundational pillars, you can define the core definitions of your (upcoming) brand. Here is where you can get more creative, so it's best to do it in a group with more people working on a project. You can start with a **mood board** – a collection of images or other brands that inspire you and feel relevant for your product, customer, and vision, no matter if they are in a different industry.

- **Brand name**: What will your product be called? It's the trickiest part, so maybe don't go with the first idea. Write them all down, give them a few days' thought, and maybe create some mockups when you work in parallel on other branding steps. But, most importantly, before setting the brand name in stone, check these to avoid problems and rebranding later down the line:

    - **Legal check.** See if your chosen brand name is not already registered or trademarked or if there are any legal limitations to using it.

    - **Competition check.** Is anyone else already using the same name?

    - **Internationalization check**. You might have checked the above for your home market or English-speaking environment. But if you're planning expansion to international markets in the future, it makes sense to do desktop research for other key markets. How does your name sound in other languages? For example, Chevrolet had a model named Chevrolet Nova, but in Spanish, "no va" translates to "it doesn't go," which is not ideal for a car brand.

- **Domain check.** In the end, probably lots of your communication channels will be digital, so it's necessary to check how website domains and handles of social media are available for your chosen brand.

- **Brand story:** Work further on your vision and explain your "why." As we have already learned, humans remember stories and narratives. Remember the hero's journey: tell your brand story in a compelling way. What got you started and why? Include the founder's story if it's applicable.

- **Brand promise and values:** What do you stand for as a brand? What is your core value? This can be aligned with the benefits you outlined earlier. Strong brands resonate with their customers when they overlap with both their customers' expectations or personal values but also with the product's functionalities. For example, Apple has a clear focus on privacy, which is also a feature of its products. FedEx's brand promise is that shipments will be delivered fast and reliably.

- **Visual identity:** This is the most visible representation of the brand: logo or other symbols that are used on your materials and products. It also continues with the choice of typography, the color scheme (on the website and other materials), the style of images, etc. At this point, you should probably discuss it with someone who has a design background, but the foundations should come from previous points.

- **Verbal identity:** This one is often overlooked, but just like people have different, distinguishable personalities that make them unique, so should your brand. When potential clients are reading your materials or engaging with your product, do you want to sound authoritative or funnier? It probably depends on the industry, too. For example, Google Chrome internet browser doesn't just write "Error" when something goes wrong, but instead writes "Aw, Snap!" This is much more casual, but it still relates to a frustrated user. A tagline or a slogan is another part of your verbal identity that encaptures your "why."

- **Establish brand guidelines:** The branding stage of the GTM strategy should conclude with brand guidelines or a brand book. It does not need to be complicated. To start, it helps to have a shared document where the foundations of the brand are defined - from values and taglines to design guidelines. This makes it easy to share with the team, external vendors, or business partners.

It also helps to translate the brand strategy into specific guidelines for frontline employees such as sales personnel or customer support staff. How should they greet the customer, and what voice should they use? That is where your brand will also shine and foster ties with your customers.

Brand guidelines ensure consistency across all marketing materials, from the tone of voice to the use of the logo and visual identity. Consistency is key to building brand recognition and trust with customers and partners. Having a great brand book makes onboarding for new employees and vendors much easier and ensures that everyone knows the dos and don'ts of your brand.

3) Brand expression

So, how does your brand come to life?

Some of the natural forms of brand expression are, of course, various **promotional materials,** but you should also think about **product design**. What form will the logo take, and what colors will be used inside of your app or on your physical products?

Brand image is the summary of impressions of how your brand is recognized on the market based on the experience of the customers with it. **Reputation** is a pinnacle of impressions, and a good reputation is something that is hard to build over years of hard work but can be quickly tarnished with some bad experiences that go viral. Trust is an important factor in branding, so a loss of good reputation essentially means lost trust. For example, Facebook (now Meta) suffered a huge loss of reputation in 2018 in a Cambridge Analytica scandal. It was revealed that Facebook had allowed the personal data of millions of users to be harvested without their consent by a third-party app, which then shared the data with the political consulting firm Cambridge Analytica.

The final outcome of the branding process in the long term is **brand equity**. Brand equity is a measure of how well a brand is recognized, trusted, and preferred by customers. Strong brands lead to higher perceived value, increased customer loyalty, and higher margins. With that comes higher revenue. In a nutshell, giving a thought about branding in the early stages of GTM means stronger foundations for long-term financial success.

According to Maja K. Ruzzier and Mitja Ruzzier, authors of The Startup Funnel, branding involves how you interact and build relationships with everyone involved with your company – from employees, customers, suppliers, and other stakeholders.[65] Branding encompasses everything your company does, whether it's planned or not. It's a comprehensive experience you deliver, where everything you do contributes to your story and visual elements. Customer experience is an important part of your company's success, and branding will help you define and sustain it. The more unique your branding is and the better it fits and engages with consumer desires, the stronger your brand will become. Here are some other best practices for go-to-market companies to consider when launching a brand:

1. **Align with the company's purpose and vision**: The purpose of the company should reflect its values and mission. The vision should describe what the company wants to achieve in the future.

2. **Create a memorable brand name**: A memorable brand name should be easy to pronounce, spell, and remember. It should also reflect the company's values and personality. You can use AI to help you find some candidates, but test them with your ECP to find the one that resonates the most.

3. **Design a distinctive brand logo and visual identity**: A distinctive logo and visual identity should reflect the company's personality and values. It should be visually appealing and consistent across all marketing materials. This can cost anywhere from $100 to $100,000. The price ranges vary heavily here. When choosing a partner to work with, make sure that previously determined brand elements are well documented and that the provider really gets the brand. Most will start with a workshop or a discovery call in which you should very actively participate. However, be

---

[65] Ruzzier, K. M. & Ruzzier, M. (2015). Startup Branding Funnel: Find your perfect brand-market fit to hack your growth. Meritum.

sure that you don't discuss for months only how your logo will look; that misses the point. The point is to get foundations for coherent communications no matter which platform you use for communications in the end.

4. **Communicate the brand**: Communication is essential in creating brand awareness and building customer trust. You will communicate the brand through various channels, including social media, advertising, and public relations. This is why it is important to develop brand assets that fit a specific channel. If a channel has a specific audience, such as developers implementing the solution, you can also tailor the channel brand experience more to their liking while keeping the brand identity intact.

You guessed it, branding is not a "set it and forget it" concept, either. After establishing the brand, it's crucial to maintain and evolve it over time. This includes monitoring and responding to customer feedback, adapting to changes in the market, and keeping the brand relevant as the market is changing and your company is growing. It's important to evolve the brand while staying true to its DNA.

Branding Special Ops

> "Your brand is a story unfolding across all customer touchpoints."
> Jonah Sachs, US storyteller, author, designer, and entrepreneur

It is not just about how the customer feels about you. It is also about how you make the customer feel about themselves.

In business, it is never (only) about you but primarily about the value you can deliver to your customer, the transformation to a desired outcome that you promise (and fulfill), and the vision of a better life for your customer. These aspects include an emotional component, not solely raving about the technical superiority of a feature and rational benefits. For example, if you are selling analytics SaaS solutions to a DMU in a small-to-medium business, you might face five members of DMU – here are their business vs. emotional benefits that they anticipate from your brand. Here's an example:

DMU member	Rational benefits	Emotional benefits
CEO	Faster, more profitable growth.	Proud to be an early adopter of a great solution.
CMO	Better reports and dashboards for an overall overview of the channel.	A real business enabler and problem solver.
E-commerce manager	Real-time reliable data on demand to make optimizations faster. Less dependence (waiting) on IT resources to get complex data.	I rock! I will get the best-in-class solution for analytics, and I can speak about our use case at conferences and look good in front of my peers.
IT	A safe and easy-to-integrate solution to the BI tool. Less overhead with "finding data" and more empowered business users.	It is a fun project to implement and has the potential to finally get rid of urgent requests from the ecommerce department that are messing up our development sprints.
Finance	Better economics for the long run, manageable expense that does not skyrocket with usage.	A business facilitator is included and respected in decision-making, not just "the bank."

You can clearly understand that emotional benefits would be much more appealing if you were buying such a solution, right? And they defer from one decision maker to another. While the brand promise has to be universally appealing and actionable for all ECPs and decision makers who participate in a purchasing decision, you can refine the messaging to each decision maker unit member to appeal to the specific benefits they are searching for.

Rebranding

Entrepreneur Sandra Šuc launched a mountain activewear brand called Alpine Princess a couple of years ago. Their primary market is females who love hiking and climbing. The niche brand is well-known for its high-quality materials and distinctive patterns. It took off well, but the company had a challenge entering the male activewear market. Would a guy wear an Alpine Princess? What about if a person does not identify with binary genders? They decided to rebrand to Alpine Nation.

It might happen that you already launched a brand, but it just doesn't resonate well. Maybe it's bland, and you're getting negative feedback from customers, or you see when you're trying to expand, there are legal or cultural limitations to use on some markets.

In that case, you can use the GTM branding process, as described above, to rebrand your solution and refresh your communications.

Sometimes, your early version of a logo and visual identity might feel outdated or not professional enough. In that case, you can go for a logo redesign and update of a visual identity, which is also a good milestone to catch the attention of the audience and make some buzz.

Complete rebranding would actually mean renaming your brand to a different name. In GTM, it is often due to a product pivot or service expansion. For example, marketing automation provider Sendinblue felt that it had outgrown its old name because they were not focused only on infrastructure for sending a newsletter. They recently rebranded as Brevo.

Brand Architecture

Finally, if you already have a company brand or are launching a complementary product, you might think about how to put them side by side. There are many ways to do that:

Corporate branding means that the company's products or services are all marketed under a single, unified brand name. The corporate brand is prominent, and individual product names may be secondary. For example, at IBM, the corporate brand is always in the front, and product names (like Watson) usually don't have their own identity.

At **endorsed branding**, the corporate brand endorses or lends its name to individual products or divisions. An example is Samsung Galaxy, where the Galaxy brand leverages the reputation of Samsung while distinguishing its mobile devices.

A branded house is a solution where a dominant or master brand is used across all products, services, and divisions, but the sub-brands also have more distinguishable identities. Amazon uses a branded house approach for its various services. Whether it's Amazon Prime, Amazon Web Services (AWS), Amazon Kindle, or Amazon Alexa, the core Amazon brand is present in all of its offerings.

Finally, **the house of brands** approach keeps product brands separate, with little or no reference to the corporate brand. In GTM, it can mean a fresh start, but a strong corporate brand with its reputation can help with the launch of a new product to the market.

However, there is no one-size-fits-all approach, so in the end, many hybrid solutions are possible, too.

High five, we made it! Jasper and I will still require some expert help to tackle our minds around all these concepts, but we have done positioning/messaging and branding in a single chapter, so at least you can avoid making some rookie mistakes in our GTM communication journey.

Now, let's finally go to the market. The next chapter will be about channels, growth models, and Growth Loops. I cannot wait to take you there. This field is my chosen profession and passion. But before we onboard that rocket, here are some reminders and a to-do list from this chapter.

Key Takeaways:

- **Positioning** is about identifying what makes a company's product or service unique for your target audience. Positioning answers the question, "What makes our solution different and better than others in the market?"

- Vanilla (bad, undifferentiated) positioning often leads to messaging falling flat and simply not enchanting the target audience. The symptoms of bad positioning are:
    - Not attracting enough leads.
    - Attracting mixed audiences who don't want to pay your prices because they don't see you as a specialist in your field.
    - Poor conversion rates.
    - Poor engagement in the product.

- Long sales cycles.

- Your potential customers will have opinions. They will position you whether you want it or not. It is wiser for you to be in control of the narrative. Leave any room for interpretation, and your customers will make up their own minds about who you are and what you do.

- One of the key steps in positioning is to turn your assets and features into benefits that are differentiated and relevant to your target market.

- USP is a feature or characteristic of a product that distinguishes it from competition and alternatives and makes it more appealing to the target audience.

- While your value proposition is your promise to the customers, telling them what you will deliver or how you will make their lives better, USPs tell your customers why they should buy from you.

- If you are an early-stage company, a startup, or a horizontal company serving multiple segments with the same product, positioning will be more challenging.

- If your initial positioning failed (or was never done in the first place), consider a repositioning project to change the tides.

- **Messaging** refers to how you tell your story across different channels to different audiences across their customer journey in a consistent manner. It includes the tone, language, and key messages used in all communication materials, such as website copy, social media, marketing, and sales materials.

    - Good messaging follows these principles:
        - It is clear and concise, with up to three key points per message, ideally one.
        - Speaks to your target audience and addresses their specific needs, desires, and pain points.
        - It is authentic. Do not shy away from communicating your values,

and use a distinctive tone of voice.
    - Appeals to customer emotions and logic by using narratives and storytelling. Our brains are wired that way so that it's often easier to understand and remember messages if they are narrated as stories.
    - Use social proof and elements of persuasion. It is one thing if you say it, but it is so much more credible if you back it up with data, experts' opinions, client testimonials, and case studies.

  - Messaging has to be aligned to the persona that it is for and the stage of the buyer journey that the customer is in.

  - There is a static part to messaging (what you always do, communicate UVPs, defend USPs, capture brand DNA with tone of voice and visual) and dynamic parts, which means different variations of messages, adjustments to platforms and target audiences, and different call-to-actions. The latter should be frequently and diligently tested.

  - Messaging does not set it and forget its mission. It is essential to ensure that your messaging resonates with your customers and achieves the desired results.

- **Branding** is the process of creating a distinct and memorable identity for your company or product. It encompasses all the visual and non-visual elements that create the brand's identity, including the company name, logo, tagline, brand colors, and brand voice. Branding is how you get recognized and remembered by your customers.

  - Your brand is more than a shiny logo. Technically, a brand is a name and design that makes your product unique, recognizable, and distinguishable from other choices on the market (competitors). But a brand is also a set of associations, feelings, and expectations that customers and users start connecting with your product. All of these elements need to work together like a well-oiled machine to deliver a consistent experience for your users.

- Strong brands are built over time. In the long term, branding leads to reputation. Established brands also have loyal customer bases, which in the end, can mean more revenue from repeated purchases or higher price premiums because customers are prepared to pay more for perceived quality.

- Here are some best practices for go-to-market companies to consider when launching a brand:
    - Align with the company's purpose and vision.
    - Create a memorable brand name.
    - Design a distinctive brand logo and visual identity.
    - Communicate the brand consistently across all channels you are using.

• By setting up strong guiding principles for positioning, branding, and messaging, you will be perceived as consistent and more trustworthy. It also comes in super handy to have some guidelines written down when you are growing a team or working with external partners, agencies, and freelancers.

To-Do List:

☐ Follow the positioning process by Andrej Peršolja to nail your positioning. Make sure to define your USPs in the process; they will come in handy everywhere. After you craft a positioning story, it is best to test it before incorporating it as a guiding principle.

☐ Follow the messaging process to define the fundamentals of your messaging strategy and put it into action by creating a messaging guidelines document.

☐ Consider different ways of storytelling – is there anything you can apply to your narrative?

☐ How about social proof – what evidence can you get from customers, partners, analytics, media, and other stakeholders that you can really deliver on your USPs? List these opportunities and make a plan for how to create social proof assets from them.

☐ Follow the branding framework to define the fundamentals of your GTM brand.

Find all the worksheets, frameworks, and models mentioned in this chapter at *https://gtmstrategist.com/resources*. They are free and yours to benefit from.

CHAPTER 7

Growth

"Poor distribution – not product – is the number one cause of failure."

*Gabriel Weinberg,
Traction: A Startup Guide to Getting Customers*

After making your best bets on all GTM elements, it is time to actually go-to-market. Your jobs to be done are:

- Identify **channels** where you can effectively reach your target market.
- Build a **multitouch strategy** to lead them through the customer journey.
- Hopefully, build some leverage, such as recommendations or virality to fuel your growth, often called **Growth Loops**.

I was pleasantly surprised by Jasper's email. He has come a long way in his GTM strategic thinking. When asking about channels, it seems that he has done some research about his customers, competitor monitoring, and even set up a budget. That is a decent start. His developers may not provide the best point of view to decide on channels since the team is aiming to attract non-technical founders from the fitness and health space, but let's celebrate Jasper's progress for a second.

To: **Maja Voje** (grow@majavoje.com)

Subject: **I was thinking IG Ads, Reddit, and Discord?**

Hey Maja!

After completing the positioning exercise, we know what to say to attract users.

That was helpful, thanks.

But which channels should we choose?

We can invest up to **$2,000** in marketing overall, and we should buy **IG ads** since fitness people are there. My developers also said there is a lot of discovery done in **Reddit** and **Discord** for that kind of product.

I also do not trust ads as a user and have blockers everywhere, so it is good to have a backup of some organic channels.

Oh, and a competitor also does **Google ads**, so should we throw this into the mix now or later?

I understand that we should not stretch ourselves too thin with channels, so I am pinging for your opinion if this is it before I hire a freelancer to kick off these channels.

Thank you very much for your help. The entire team is grateful for your guidance.

Best regards

Jasper

Jasper is laser-focused on selecting the best channel to attract prospects for their onboarding solution. Having read his email, he might have a bias towards low-touch channels, as many technical founders do when they are starting out. While it is great to start thinking about scaling, there are times when you have to use tactics that will not scale that do not scale (think fairs, conferences, personal sales, etc.).[66]

Let's review Jasper's case again. The team has a vision for building a Product-Led Growth (PLG) business, which means offering a free version of the product and providing them with value, with the goal that up to 15% of them convert. If a subscription costs $99 a month and the team is relying on ads to acquire users,[67] we are looking at these numbers after three months:

- A budget of $2,000 buys the team 1,400 website clicks.[68]
- Say that 9% of these users decide to try out the solution for free, which results in 126 free users.[69]
- Out of them, 30% successfully go through the onboarding, which leaves the team with 38 activated users.
- And 5% of activated users will convert to a 3-month subscription plan, which leads to two users.

Let's put these numbers together and see what that means for their business.

The team would make $297 in the next three months from each of those three customers. Yet, they would spend $1,000 on acquiring the customer through ads. Three months is a hard cut for them because it is their lifeline. While in some cases, that would make sense because the LTV could be very high, for Jasper and his team, these numbers don't look so promising.

They could bump up the price to earn more per client, upsell implementation services, or use free channels to reduce the overall cost per acquisition (CAC).

---

66 Graham, P. (2013, July). Do Things that Don't Scale. http://paulgraham.com/ds.html
67 Worse case scenarios are that there will be no virality, no recommendations and marginal success from social media.
68 Cost per click CPC is expected to be $1.4 in B2B based on Darragh, R. (2022). How much do Instagram ads cost? Startups.co.uk. https://startups.co.uk/marketing/instagram-ads-cost/
69 All PLG conversion benchmarks for calculation are sourced from McGrath, H., Townshend, C., & Poyar, K. (2023). Product benchmarks report. OpenView Advisors, LLC. https://openviewpartners.com/2023-product-benchmarks/.

But it's mission-critical here that CAC < LTV in the next three months. The rule of thumb for profitable SaaS is to keep CAC 3x lower than LTV.[70] Having tested the willingness to pay (WTP), they cannot really bump up the price. They will have to find cheaper ways to get users in the product to be in the green numbers. Their acceptable CAC at the moment is around $99 per client. Not $1,000.

By the end of this chapter, you will understand how to select the optimal channel mix for your product and build a growth engine that's fueled with growth loops to spin it faster. Your ability to attract prospects, activate, retain, and monetize them is the final frontier of GTM strategy elements before you go full into the implementation.

---

70 Skok, D. (2015). SaaS Metrics 2.0 – A Guide to Measuring and Improving What Matters. forEntrepreneurs. https://www.forentrepreneurs.com/saas-metrics-2-definitions-2/

Traction Channels

"Go where the audience is."
Common Sense

Most often, founders and experts start with a question: which channels should I choose at the very beginning of the GTM journey? There are so many choices. New channels emerge (and some die) faster than ever, and competition is flexing their biceps by rapidly experimenting and creating FOMO in the industry.

As always in GTM, your best friend when it comes to selecting a channel is focus. You can do anything, but you cannot do everything. To make smart choices about your initial channel selection, consider the following:

1. **Customer research is gold**. People are creatures of habit. Habits are difficult to change. Do you remember the PMF survey from the Product chapter? One of the questions was, "Where did you learn about the product?" If you already have customers, a waitlist, or prospects, you can simply ask them. Identify those channels where your customers will be willing to communicate and exchange value with you.

2. **Research competitors.** Research does not mean copying but gaining understanding. With tools such as Similarweb, Semrush, Ghostery, and others, you can learn which advertising pixels they have on the website, the tools they use in marketing, and where they are currently getting most of their traction.

3. **Consider your resources.** After understanding what customers prefer and what competition does, consider your strengths and weaknesses. Competition might have budgets to outspend you on paid advertising. But your product is highly praised and recommended in communities and independent influencers who do not accept fees for product reviews. Start by building on your strengths while understanding and defending your weaknesses.

4. **Do a sanity check of your unit economics.** Some channels are simply outside your budget or ROI constraints in GTM (Jasper's $1000 CAC, for

example). The ultimate goal of the company is to make money. If you sell at a loss, there is no company. It took Uber 14 years to generate its first operating profit[71]. You and I will probably have to do it much sooner.

5. **Find untapped opportunities.** In GTM marketing, the element of surprise can play a huge role. If there is a new channel or opportunity, larger competitors usually take much longer to react to it than your lean GTM machine, where you call the shots. You should think outside the box. If it is too expensive to have a booth at the conference, you can volunteer to work there or wear your company's t-shirt for the event.

6. **Aim for moonshots**. Spend 10 to 20% of your GTM marketing resources on "moonshots" or actions that can really move the needle in business. Most of them will fail, but if you win, you win big time. You cannot become a market leader by merely copying others and playing it safe.

Now, which channels should you choose? The Bullseye Framework from the bestselling book Traction by technology startup veterans Gabriel Weinberg and Justin Mares reminds us there are multiple channels and you cannot do them all.[72] Start by selecting best-fit candidates and run experiments on them to identify two to three channels that actually drive repeatable business.

For most GTM companies, early channel selection is not rocket science. The way you get your first 100 customers is different from how you onboard your 1,000th. This is what I like to say to my class of freelancers: "Your next $20,000 is hiding in your phonebook at any given moment." By simply making a list of 20 to 50 past clients, partners, employers, industry experts, and other stakeholders that can bring you business, it is almost inevitable to sell something. One of the mentees closed three clients a week by simply doing this. No posts on social media, no cold emails, just this. While great at the beginning to get the first sales in, GTM company cannot solely rely on selling through a personal network.

---

[71] Wilhelm, A. (2023, August 1). Uber is now a profitable, cash-generating machine. TechCrunch. https://techcrunch.com/2023/08/01/uber-profitable-earnings-analysis/
[72] Weinberg, G., & Mares, J. (2014). Traction: A Startup Guide to Getting Customers. S-curves Publishing.

Selling to friends is a poor signal of PMF but is great for building initial traction.

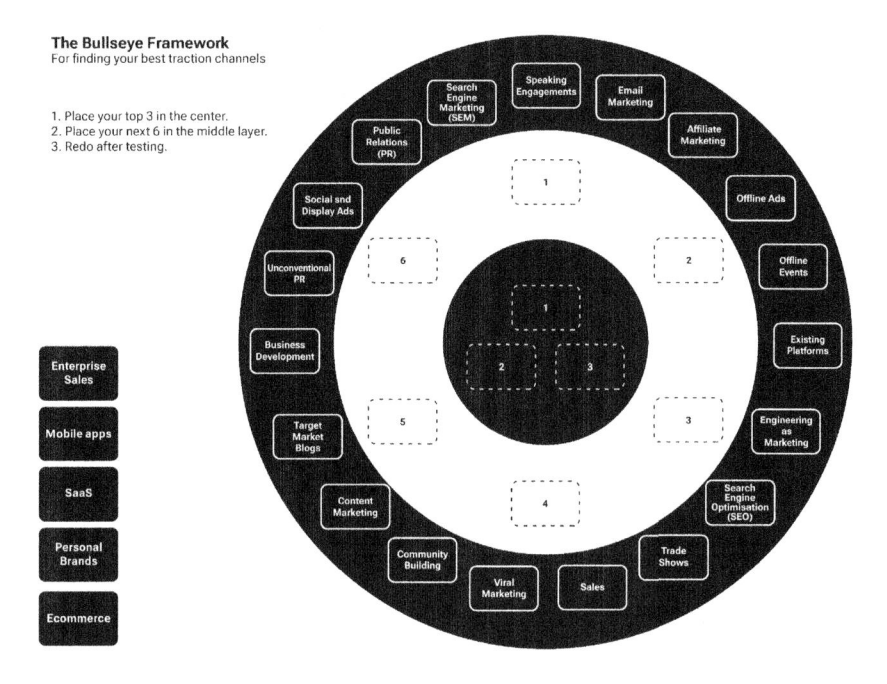

The Bullseye Framework
For finding your best traction channels

1. Place your top 3 in the center.
2. Place your next 6 in the middle layer.
3. Redo after testing.

Channels:
- Search Engine Marketing (SEM)
- Speaking Engagements
- Email Marketing
- Public Relations (PR)
- Affiliate Marketing
- Social and Display Ads
- Offline Ads
- Unconventional PR
- Offline Events
- Business Development
- Existing Platforms
- Target Market Blogs
- Engineering as Marketing
- Content Marketing
- Search Engine Optimisation (SEO)
- Community Building
- Trade Shows
- Viral Marketing
- Sales

- Enterprise Sales
- Mobile apps
- SaaS
- Personal Brands
- Ecommerce

Adjusted from Traction by Gabriel Weinberg

Sales are usually at the top of the "I do not want to do it, that's too cringe list." As a GTM strategist, it is invaluable to get hands-on experience with a channel before you can successfully outsource or scale it. Founder of Jurnee, Tania Kefs, believes founders are the best salespeople in early GTM: "You cannot bypass sales as a founder. Founders should know the customers' problems inside out. You can learn the core sales concepts quickly, but the magic happens when practicing them repeatedly. Eventually, you will learn how to best get in front of customers and what to tell or write to a prospect to sell successfully. It is hard work but worth doing because it is essential for your business. No sales, no business. However, the good news is that the more you do it, the faster you learn, and the better you become at it."

This applies to all channels. Whatever personal biases you have, do not overcomplicate the selection of initial channels to avoid using tactics you don't like if they are relevant to the customer and bring repeatable revenue to your business. You can always learn something new, get help in managing the channel, and get better at it by practicing the craft of using it. Countless founders and marketers have learned Google Ads, Meta ads, how to speak publicly, and talk to journalists because the cost of knowing this was simply too high, and they could not afford help from coaching from the get-go. You can do it too.

Before we move to the next subject – demand generation and demand creation – there are a couple of additional tips for channel selection and prospects and how they may evolve when you grow your business:

- **Channels are born and die faster than ever**: Remember Clubhouse and life-audio chat rooms? After viral growth at the beginning of this "invite-only" platform, it hit the growth ceiling in a couple of months. While it had PMF for some groups, the early majority that was hit did not find a good enough reason to stick around. Oppositely, TikTok grew from a niche lip-syncing channel to one of the most important mainstream social media channels in the marketing stack. If you are early on the channel, you may get a first-mover advantage and a big algorithm push of your content on an unsaturated channel. The reward might be worth the risk, but in the capacity that you can absorb even if all the effort goes to waste. Remember the recommendation of 10 to 20% of efforts for moonshots? It includes testing new channels.

- **The law of diminishing returns or bad CTRs:** Channels age, and you can outgrow them. Remain alert to the signals that a cornerstone channel is getting extensive and saturated. Growth expert and investor Andrew Chen says, "When you find a demand generation notion that works well for promoting your solution, the beginning of your investment there looks promising. In time, you can saturate the market, or a shiny new channel can lure your audience preference from it. You'll see diminishing returns or even negative returns."[73] Remember Facebook? The platform started out as a social network for selected colleges; very exclusive and super cool. Now, probably your grandparents, parents, and other respected boomer relatives are thriving at it, and lots of young people have moved elsewhere.

- **Some are here to stay**: Email is not dead just because it's an older, established digital channel. Some B2C companies get more than 30 to 50% of

---

[73] Chen, A. (n.d.). The Law of Shitty Click Throughs. Andrew Chen. https://andrewchen.com/the-law-of-shitty-clickthroughs/

their revenue from upselling existing customers via email and SMS. This nearly-free channel offers a brilliant bandage for ever-increasing CAC. In B2B, such channels are personal sales and events. There are successful companies that center all of their marketing activities on performing well at two industry fairs a year – the rest doesn't really matter much to them. Some channels stand the test of time and become a fundamental part of how we communicate, buy, and sell.

Oftentimes, GTM strategies only focus on building awareness and acquisition channels, where the battle for eyeballs, hearts, and minds of prospects is the fiercest. Can we make it a bit easier for you? Let's decide if we will be capturing or creating demand before you have a final say in the channel selection.

Generating or Capturing Demand?

"The way you position yourself at the beginning of a relationship has a profound impact on where you end up."
Ron Karr, marketing consultant, author, and speaker

In GTM, you have 3 to 18 months to win sufficient demand from your Beachhead Segment. Ideally, you would speak to solution-aware customers who are already actively searching for solutions, comparing them, and are able to make a purchasing decision relatively quickly. This is called **capturing demand (demand cap)**.

You guessed it – it's never that simple. If there is existing demand for your solution, the battle for attention down the customer journey is fiercer. Many companies are willing to invest heavily into winning those customers. Search ads in high LTV industries are a typical example of that. On average, companies are willing to pay more than $8 a click.[74] Some pay more than $30 a click. If there is high competition for a solution-related search term, a competitor with deeper pockets can outbid you just to win the business, often at a close-to-zero profit or even at a loss. The reason why they can afford to do this is because they can later recover their investment in a longer period of doing business with those customers.

Companies such as Jasper's cannot compete on budgets, but they have multiple other options to capture demand. They could go on marketplaces such as G2 or Capettera, where the companies are actively looking for solutions. They could do targeted outreach to decision-makers in companies that are preparing for launches, or they could ask for recommendations if "someone knows someone" who could benefit from this solution.

There is another way to tackle this challenge – **demand generation (demand gen)**. This is where you meet your prospects sooner in their buyer journey and help them navigate through it, or you create demand for a solution that is positioned differently on the market with little-to-no existing demand.

In demand gen, you invest in audience building and educating the market about a solution for their need or even about the problem. This might take longer, but

---
[74] https://www.statista.com/statistics/1115432/us-search-advertising-cpc/

it's great for positioning yourself as their long-term go-to because you have created enormous added value for them. The trouble with demand generation is if you can really afford to do it, it takes resources and time to do it well. In simple terms, it may take months or years to see a healthy ROI in your investment in podcast production, value posting on social platforms, or streams of high-quality video content to educate the market. It can happen much faster and be very impactful, but if you are pressured to deliver results in the next quarter, demand generation is a risky bet.

The decision-making process when selecting the demand-capturing channels can be described like this:

- **Is there an existing demand for your solution?** If yes, start with demand capture activities, then expand from there.

- **If there is no existing demand, is there a demand in an adjacent category you can piggyback on?** If yes, it's probably most cost-effective to start with demand capture activities there.

But if you don't find any existing demand that you could build on, start with demand generation activities.

Here is where it gets interesting. When choosing a demand generation channel, multiple factors influence your choice:

- **Audience type**: Part of their customer journey can you meet them? Are they unaware of the problem, problem aware, solution aware, in the comparative stage, or in the buying mode?

- **Market stage:** If you are one of the first movers in the market, it is almost inevitable that you will have to do some market education (or you can position yourself as 10x for an existing market and capture some of their demand). If the market is more mature, the battle for the final stages of the funnel is more aggressive.

- **Nature of the industry**: There are some industries and purchases that are done impulsively or out of need. Not everyone is super eager to do tons of research for purchasing their new broom, while in SaaS, customers expect extensive education and support resources.

- **Your business model and unit economics**: Some channels and opportunities to either capture or create demand are simply outside your reach, or they do not make sense unit economics-wise. You cannot and should not prioritize them in your GTM.

The key to choosing the optimal demand cap and demand gen channels for your business is to understand the customer journey, customer preferences, and the competitive nature of the industry. It is vital to do your own research. A simplified model for B2B SaaS could look like this. The placement of the channels is not fixed. You can experiment with placing them throughout the customer journey and test different journey-stage appropriate messaging.

Demand Generation | **Demand Capture**

- PR- Press, Podcasts
- Webinars
- SEO
- Cold Email
- Retargeting Ads
- Events
- WOM
- Direct mail
- Case Studies
- Display Ads
- Whitepapers
- Marketplaces
- Community Building
- External Communities
- Account Based Marketing - ABM
- Market Research
- Email Marketing Drip Campaigns
- Content Marketing

Awareness — Acquisition — Activation — Decision — Research — Action

A mental shortcut in GTM is to lean more towards demand-capturing channels first to pick up the low-hanging fruit before you are strong enough to climb trips. Yet, some channels work predictably well for GTM companies, and this is where we are heading next.

7 Growth Channels for GTM Companies

> "Finding the right growth model for your business can mean the difference between success and failure. It's not just about acquiring more customers or increasing revenue; it's about finding a sustainable way to grow your business over time."
>
> Claire Hughes Johnson, COO of Stripe.

Welcome to the endless rivalry of what the ultimate go-to growth model is. While marketing, growth, and sales professionals try to capitalize on the latest buzzword, others merely try to copy-paste what they have done in the past to their new project, creating "growth cults" that glorify one channel over everything else.

In most realities, marketing, sales, and product happily coexist and work well together. We all have certain biases and preferences, but you might be losing opportunities to do GTM the best you can if you automatically cut off some growth channels because you do not know or like them.

Almost no channel is too old-school or saturated to give it a shot if it's relevant to your target audience and you can budget it effectively in your GTM operations. Business development and sales don't only stand for taking your prospects to dinners and playing golf with prospects. Neither is it true that no one wants to talk to salespeople. If you would be buying a new car for your company, you may very much appreciate their guidance through all of the technical specifications. And we do not live in an exclusively digital world. Marketing with oldies such as billboards, flyers, fairs, and local outdoor advertising is alive and well. To my knowledge, people still visit stores.

After making peace with these unpleasant realities, let's make an educated guess about which channels will most likely help you build a sound growth model on your GTM journey.

Mark Roberge, founding Chief Revenue Officer at Hubspot, did us all a huge favor by creating a curated list of channels that are tested to work well for GTM companies.[75] I expanded his model based on my experience working with

---

[75] Roberge, M. (2023). 6 Demand Gen Channel Options for Startups: Which is Best for You?.

various companies from the technology sector – from enterprise to hardware, software, and open-source.

There are seven different proven GTM growth Strategies worth considering as a backbone to your GTM growth model.

1. **Inbound:** Content creation with the intent to generate leads.
2. **Paid digital**: Media buying to attract the attention of your target audience.
3. **Outbound**: Cold outreach to companies that match your target audience via email, social media, telephone, or even snail mail.
4. **Account-based marketing (ABM):** ABM is a strategic approach where sales and marketing teams work together to target and engage specific high-value accounts with personalized campaigns. The focus is on individual accounts (or a select group of accounts) rather than a broad audience.
5. **Community:** Creating valuable content and comments for members of a community.
6. **Partners**: Agreement with a comparable company to join marketing and sales efforts for mutual benefit.
7. **Product-led growth (PLG):** Development of a solution (usually a SaaS product) in a way that a prospect can self-onboard and get value before monetization efforts begin.

Always consider ROI within your GTM lifeline, which in most cases is 3 to 18 months. When I am working with GTM teams, we always develop these plans by reverse-engineering how to achieve a certain objective.

If a GTM team is developing a platform for peer-to-peer career mentorship, they have the following growth objectives:

- Objective 1: Attract 100 mentors to the platform.
- Objective 2: Secure 400 users for the launch date.
- Objective 3: Find three employers (partners) who will support a project.

Stage 2 Capital. https://www.stage2.capital/blog/6-demand-gen-channel-options-for-start-ups-which-is-best-for-you

We have to start with developing a program for attracting mentors. Remember the cold start problem? No great mentors, no users. This is how we develop acquisition experiment ideas to achieve these objectives:

- Objective 1: Attract 100 mentors to the platform.

    - Write an email to a team's pact mentors and experienced colleagues (60 contacts) if they would support us by joining the platform as mentors. We expect that half of them (30) will accept the invitation.

    - Post in three active local Facebook groups and invite their members to join as mentors. We select a group of developers, growth experts, and UXers. We expect to attract at least 40 mentors from this action.

    - Make a partnership with a local student organization that arranges 150 mentorship couples to pitch you to their mentors. We expect to attract at least 50 mentors from this collaboration if done well.

Based on the projections, we could attract 130 mentors to the platform by simply sending out a couple of emails and posting them to relevant communities. No advertising, PR, or daily posting on social media to an audience that doesn't really exist. What is mission-critical for them at the moment is to get mentors.

The team will deal with more sophisticated growth methods later on their journey, as they will be attracting mentees and doing partnerships with employers to gain their support fees for sharing job opportunities there. No users, no sponsors. And that is the exact order they should tackle it.

Marketers and growth experts in early-stage companies often believe that "doing the job" is to post regularly, arrange talks at conferences, and send out a newsletter. In GTM, the only work that really makes a difference is helping the companies move towards the objectives and measuring that on the go so you can make better choices. Marketing as an ongoing, predictable activity comes later (if the objectives are achieved).

OK, rant over. Let's dive into each and explore real-life examples so you can decide which ones will help you reach your GTM growth objectives.

Inbound: Give Before You Ask

Inbound gained popularity in the early 2010s when Hubspot showcased that it can work wonderfully well for winning leads, especially in instances of longer and more complex sales cycles. By providing value in the forms of ebooks, tools, video content, cheat sheets, and presentations, you can reach prospects sooner and start creating a meaningful relationship with them that will hopefully result in sales.

And Hubspot absolutely walked the talk here. These days, whenever you search for relevant terms in the field of marketing, there is a high probability that a Hubspot article is going to pop up on the first page. In addition to creating a fascinating volume of helpful articles, Hubspot elevated the game by developing downloadable ebooks, guides, checklists, and even online tools such as their free Website Grader, which continues to help millions of businesses grade their technical performance, SEO, usability, and security.[76] Such helpful feedback is a great touchpoint for the user that adds valuable information and, therefore, the ecosystem of the Hubspot brand.

But it takes a lot of work to create great content and free tools to deliver value, doesn't it? Generating ideas, copywriting, keyword research, design, posting regularly on social media, committing to doing a podcast, or publishing daily updates on stories in the hope of attracting new customers seems like a long(er) game.

And there are times when it doesn't work well or is done poorly. It is so important to measure the effectiveness of your lead generation program in GTM, not only in the number of emails that you generate but also to observe what's going on with these leads and if they are converting.

Andrej Peršolja, a Growth and Positioning expert whom you met in the previous chapter, was trying to penetrate the US market with an app called KOBI, and they started with an e-book focusing on how to help dyslexic children to read.[77] Their CPC was great: they got a click for 50 cents (and that is really good for the US

---

[76] https://website.grader.com/
[77] You can watch a full workshop recording to learn more about this case on Andrej's YouTube channel https://youtu.be/yLCgFzj_lyg?t=467

market!), but the users who downloaded the e-book were not downloading the app. That was a problem they later solved with better positioning and funnel tweaks, but it's a lesson learned for us – lead generation programs in GTM should be measured in their entirety. People who come to your webinar to learn something will not automatically be eager to buy from you after consuming one hour of your content.

Inbound usually works well in SMEs and mid-market (marketing software, technology providers, legal services, agencies, etc.). It is often used in B2C as well when selling a solution that needs an additional touchpoint before making a purchase. It works best if your Total Addressable Market (TAM) is big enough. If you are dealing with a lead list of 200 companies that you could potentially sell to, personalized direct outreach may be a better option.

Inbound also comes to the rescue if your target audience is bombarded with offers or nearly allergic to outreach efforts. Groups that come to mind are developers, marketers, product managers, CEOs, Head of Sales, etc. They will do their own research prior to the purchase, and it's in your best interest to provide them with helpful guidance and goodwill for the sale to happen. In this case, you should consider whether or not you want to gate content. While "submit the email to access the resource" was alive and well ten years ago, many people these days prefer to experience value before risking being called by a sales agent or bombarded with business development emails.

Make your inbound assets customer journey appropriate. Depending on the lead generation program you run, the cycle to actually convert the business can vary significantly. You can use inbound evangelism, spreading awareness for the solution, or do a neck-to-neck spreadsheet comparison in addition to your competition. Choose wisely. Some will be more valuable than others. If you develop a tool for changing an electricity provider by providing information on how much you could save with this decision, it is likely to work faster and better than if you conduct research on why people hesitate to change the provider and present it as an infographic on social media. Those tools target prospects at different stages of a customer journey.

Before going all in on inbound, you should have reliable analytics and a CRM in place. If your lead generation program works well, you can get a lot of "noise" in your funnel. Do your business developers a favor and check earlier if the lead is a good fit for the solution and has a willingness to buy. You can do that with qualification criteria, in the form of online surveys, email drip campaigns, or by inviting them to view new content that aims more at ready-to-buy customers.

It's unrealistic to expect that a founder or CTO will be able to spend 10 hours per week writing technical blog posts, as this is not a priority for most business leaders. While you can outsource some of the content creation workload, it's important to recognize that if you work in a complex field of business that few mainstream writers and designers are familiar with, you may not be satisfied with the deliverables. Therefore, it's important to develop structured ways to acquire the knowledge, resources, and inputs needed to deliver high-quality content.

Content marketing, SEO, and lead generation are often delayed gratification channels. Most companies invest 3 to 6 months of work before validating the results of these efforts. While inbound can be an effective way to attract new audiences and build long-term assets that can contribute to brand recall for years to come, most GTM companies recognize that achieving tangible results requires a significant amount of effort. Publishing one blog post per week will not yield significant returns in a timely manner. But in addition to SEO, there is another amplifier that you can consider using. What if you could "buy" the relevant audience to speed up your GTM traction?

Paid Digital: Pay to Play

Most GTM companies operate with very limited budgets and "spray and pray" that advertising dollars land well. This is why we approach every decision on where to invest with caution. Is your audience really addressable on this platform? Is this type of channel customer journey appropriate? How much should you invest in the channel to see relevant results?

There are six types of paid channels to consider:

- **Search Engine Marketing (SEM):** This is also called "Google Ads" since Google dominates more than 85% of the search market.[78] Moreover,

---

[78] Statista. (2023). Market share of leading desktop search engines worldwide from January 2015 to March 2023. https://www.statista.com/statistics/216573/worldwide-market-

YouTube provides advertising tools to content creators to monetize their audiences by displaying ads. Many GTM companies, where demand capture is the name of the game, swear by this channel. Instead of building demand and inspiring afflicted buyers to consider a purchase, SEM's superpower is to enable quick testing if there is some existing demand for the solution and address prospects within the later stages of their buyer journey when they are actively looking for solutions. Before running a campaign, you need to do your research. With tools such as Google Keywords, Semrush, Moz, Ahrefs, and others, you can get actionable estimates of search volume for specific terms with a **Cost per Click** (CPC) and intelligence on competitors to make educated decisions.

- *Example: A company is testing demand for their new device that helps system engineers monitor changes on the network and sends alerts if there are irregularities in the system. They should consider Google ads because their target audience is already searching for solutions.*

- **Social media ads:** People use social media to kill boredom, connect with others, get inspired by content, find random snippets of great advice, etc. Ads on Instagram, Twitter, Reddit, X (ex-Twitter), Facebook, LinkedIn, TikTok, and Snapchat (and whatever comes next) are great for creating awareness. They're typically a go-to solution for GTM companies that can sell their products almost "impulsively" to large audiences. Have you ever gotten the urge to buy the cutest pair of socks with your pet's photo while scrolling Instagram? That's an impulsive decision. But social media ads might also serve you well if the buying process is more complex. By carefully engineering a tour campaign, you can target prospects at different stages of their customer journey with different messages. Most social media platforms offer powerful ways to target audiences that are hard to find elsewhere. Every social media advertising tool has a specific interface and best practices that you have to learn, but the good news is there are many free and paid tutorials on how to do them effectively.

  - *Example: A consultant is promoting their free consultations with LinkedIn ads, Meta ads (Instagram and Facebook), and X ads to find new clients.*

---

share-of-search-engines/

- **Influencers:** In the 2020s, working with influencers skyrocketed. Their audience leans on them when they need inspiration, guidance, trusted reviews, or simply some entertainment. In numerous launches that I have participated in, influencers were often one of the key channels and strategies of not only how to get attention at scale but also how to build trust and affinity for the product really fast. Materials that were created by influencers can also be scaled beyond their audience and reach. From a simple "promo code shoutout" to advanced techniques such as dark-posting (advertising on Meta on behalf of the influencer), influencers are getting too important to ignore not only in B2C but increasingly in B2B. People trust and form relationships with people.

  - *Example: An analytics software provider launched a great research report that presents the state of the market. To get it in front of a more relevant audience, they partnered with influential professionals in the product-led space to share the report on LinkedIn. The compensations were negotiated individually, but on average, the company paid $500 to reach 10,000 people on LinkedIn.*

- **Affiliate programs:** This refers to a marketing strategy where companies incentivize content creators or agencies to promote their products or services and earn a commission for each sale or conversion they generate. Good news! You can apply for an affiliate link for this book, and whoever buys from it will pay you 20% of the created revenue. It sounds like a great deal because you would probably pay more if you went with classical ads and are only rewarded when you make a sale. Promoting a program is valuable, so why not compensate for it? Affiliates are often used in conjunction with influencer marketing, paid media, sales/business development, or inbound.

  - *Example: A marketing agency is setting up email marketing accounts for clients. They play a significant role in deciding which platform the client will use. The agency is motivated to push Klaviyo for ecommerce clients because they get a percentage of the revenue that a customer brings in. If you are consulting clients, you should consider finding such affiliate programs and using them with diligence and the best care for the customer's needs. You can find the deals at platforms such as Partnerstack.*

- **Public relations**: Trust in traditional media is still double that of information coming from social media platforms because it is edited and curated. Media power brands like TechCrunch, Forbes, The New Yorker, Economist, and Bloomberg add enormous credibility to your brand if you are featured there. Sometimes an interesting opportunity emerges, such as an ad in your local newspaper or a specialized magazine that is (you guessed it) relevant to your target audience. If you can be featured by a national or even international media outlet, it boosts your credibility and stays well-indexed when people are searching for your brand for years to come. But control expectations, please. Do not simply assume that after a media powerhouse features you, sales will magically explode. Rome was not built in a day, and it is unlikely that a single article will magically transform your business.

    - *Example: A steel producer is searching to expand to a Mexican market. In addition to business development efforts and sales representatives, they have also contacted local media to present their investment to the market and emphasize that new jobs will be locally created. The team did meetings with 50 relevant leads that week. Out of them, 37 prospects have mentioned they have heard of the Mexican market because of the media feature. Prospects were more likely to respond to sales messages by a business development team after the media feature.*

- **Other digital media buying:** If you learned that your target audience searches for information outside of mainstream social media and other forms of media (i.e., specialized blogs, forums, news sites, closed communities, etc.), it is smart to investigate media buying opportunities there. In the current media landscape, there are usually options to buy display ads, banners, or native placements as sponsored articles in media. Another more scalable option is to go through programmatic advertising – automated bidding and placement of ads on a given platform that usually has access to a wide range of online media, other websites, and apps. Examples of programmatic networks are Outbrain and Taboola. You could also consider paid listings on platforms such as G2 or Capterra or paid placement on popular marketplaces that see a lot of traffic in your industry.

- *Example B2B: A company that offers software for logistic companies will likely achieve the right decision-makers if they invest in media buying in professional websites such as Supply Chain Dive, Logistics Management, and Transport Topics. They might pay $2,000 for 100,000 monthly impressions of a banner on the website. It means a CPM of $20, which is probably more than the company would pay for 1,000 impressions with Google Display Ads, but the website guarantees a more specialized and targeted professional audience.*

With paid media, it is important to ensure your target audience really pays attention to these channels and is in the "mood" to have a conversation with you there. I don't want to see ads for bananas as a perfect office snack on LinkedIn.

When deciding on what paid channels to prioritize, there is no magic formula to perfectly allocate a budget, but let's assume that you could consider investing 80% of your budget to verified channels (i.e., your audience is there, and you have a fighting chance with your budget. You can also experiment with reaching new channels, offers, and USPs, but that would be your experimental budget (up to 20%). The lion's share of it should be fueling educated guesses to secure your GTM traction. Once you see a paid opportunity that could be leveraged because you saw traction, it would be smart to renegotiate or redistribute the budget. The best GTM budget management is to be flexible and to ensure a lean decision-making and approval process. You are still testing multiple assumptions, and therefore, you need flexibility to act and relocate fast.

How do you make these decisions?

In media buying, a lot of experts and practitioners praise their excellence with low CPCs and CAC in their monthly reports. It looks cool on paper, but would you rather have:

- $500 CAC on an "expensive channel" to win a customer who spends $30,000 with you, or
- $50 CAC on "cheaper channels" to attract a customer who only spends $200?

What are you optimizing for? Alone, low CAC can be a slippery slope. LTV should not be overlooked. Also, consider the scale of the channel: can it produce enough such opportunities to fuel your GTM journey, or is it an outlier that is difficult to scale? Decide how long to value the channel as well. It can be anywhere from less than a day to two years in a B2B enterprise. Most startups settle with the idea to decide on what their test budget is. Say it's $2,000, and they run ads for a week or two. They'll want to look at not only purchase, but also meetings with qualified leads, report downloads, or webinar attendees. These can all be used to signal that the channel works well for you.

Your payback period is a helpful metric (a.k.a. the time it takes to recover your CAC investment per channel). Many GTM companies have a "rule of thumb" CAC, which is basically a cap on investment.[79] Think hard about what you are optimizing for and how to value channels before making a final call.

How about if your audience is really difficult to reach or expensive to target with paid media? Could you contact them directly instead? In GTM, we are more wired to proactively push the traction ourselves. So that might be an interesting option to explore.

Outbound: Proactively Reaching Out

For most of you, this will be outside your comfort zone since outbound has a "bad rep." No one loves the "Dear sir, may I interest you in our SEO services for your website" direct messages on LinkedIn, but many people do outbound poorly or misuse it. Before shaking your head, consider that Oracle, SAP, Cisco, Dell, Microsoft, Google, Accenture, Deloitte, Amazon Web Services, and many others consider outbound one of the key channels to winning new business.

Outbound refers to contacting larger bases directly and sending out messages in volumes to see what sticks. The recipients of these messages have not yet expressed an interest in the product, but you believe they would be a good fit for your offer. Outbound can be done via email, cold calls, direct email, social media direct outreach, or SMS marketing.

---

[79] Especially in GTM, CAC should not be calculated based on media buying spend but should include other costs such as wages, tools for optimization etc. that were associated with client acquisition.

By using a relevant contact list that expresses at least some interest or affinity for the area and personalizing the message to their context, you can create outbound campaigns that add value to your prospects and spark interest in your product and services. Even if you have a strong personal bias against the channel and claim you would never reply to a cold email, you should give this inexpensive and potentially highly scalable channel at least a fighting chance to become part of your GTM.

But how do you execute outbound as a GTM company so that it does not mess up your domain reputation or, worse, personal reputation? I had a word with a colleague of mine who created a $6 million B2B pipeline in 30 days with a single outbound campaign for a client.

Growth expert Jaka Berdnik previously worked for Microsoft, and he co-founded a company called Automatic Content. He kindly shares some processes and tools around how to plan an outbound campaign so you can execute one successfully.

Tools are usually the sexiest to start with, so let's begin there. To set up an outbound email campaign, you will need these main types of tools:

1. **Lead generation tools**
    a. Existing databases
        i. https://www.uplead.com/ (good for IT)
        ii. https://d7leadfinder.com/ (good for small businesses)
        iii. https://www.leadfuze.com/ (Has extensive search abilities)
    b. Email finders
        i. Hunter.io
        ii. Rocketreach.co
        iii. apollo.io

2. **Email automation / Cold email drip campaign**
    a. Instantly.ai (great for beginners)
    b. Lemlist.com (good for ABM)

3. **CRMs**
    a. When starting off, a well-filled-out Excel sheet works just fine.

b. Pipedrive

c. Hubspot

The other key ingredient is to create a relevant lead list. Companies on the list should fit your ECP criteria, such as industry, number of employees, yearly revenue, etc. It is important to find relevant decision-makers in companies and send the campaign to specific people.

Most internet users have grown to be almost immune to cold pitching without any personalization and added value. It is wise to aim to build trust and goodwill before you go all-in on the sales pitch right from the get-go. Personalization and great targeting are your best allies to do that. What is important to know when you are considering cold outreach as a way to generate demand for your business? Consider the following:

- **Do not simply spray your cold email to 1,000 addresses and pray it works**: It is vital to contact relevant decision-makers with cold outreach. If you simply scrape the web or buy a database, it is very unlikely that you will get great response rates with generic outreach. Instead, it pays off to do some homework. You should target your decision-makers more precisely and invent a pitch that actually makes sense to them. People are bombarded with messages, so it's crucial to stand out.

- **Personalize the message:** Use their first name, last name, company name, job title, common challenges, solutions, etc.

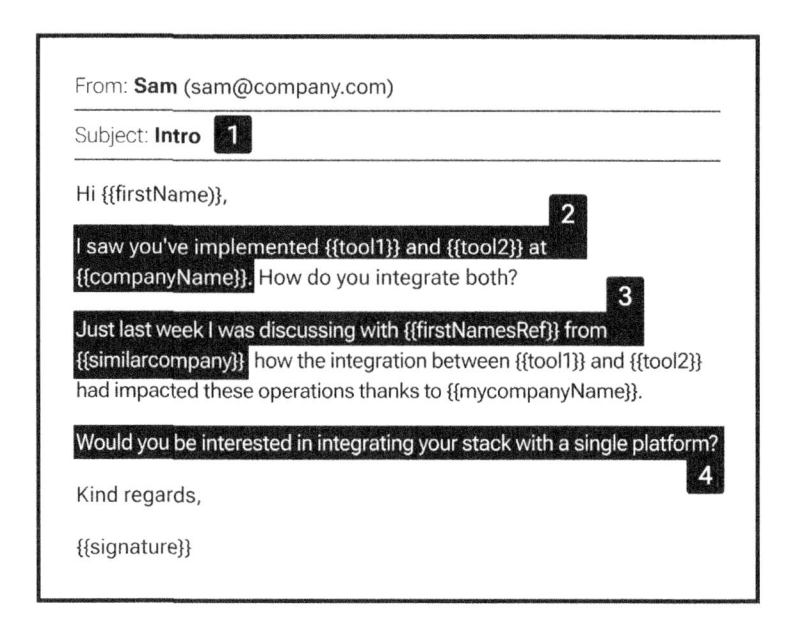

```
From: Sam (sam@company.com)
Subject: Intro  [1]

Hi {{firstName)},

[2] I saw you've implemented {{tool1}} and {{tool2}} at {{companyName}}. How do you integrate both?

[3] Just last week I was discussing with {{firstNamesRef}} from {{similarcompany}} how the integration between {{tool1}} and {{tool2}} had impacted these operations thanks to {{mycompanyName}}.

Would you be interested in integrating your stack with a single platform?
[4]
Kind regards,

{{signature}}
```

- **Provide value:** Share resources such as lists and ebooks/PDFs, or send them a Loom video that goes through their website while providing constructive feedback on how you would solve their challenges.

- **Have a meaningful and contextual sequence based on a contact's behavior**: Someone who has not opened a single email is at a different stage of the customer journey than someone who has been clicking on links in every message you have sent so far. Here's an example:

Day 1: Send a personalized cold email and view their profile on LinkedIn.
Day 3: Send a cold email and a connection request with an added note.
Day 5: Send a personalized cold email and call them.
Day 7: Send another personalized cold email.
Day 10: Send another personalized cold email.
Day 12: Send another personalized cold email.
Day 15: Send another personalized cold email.
Day 17: Send another personalized cold email.

By leveraging cold outreach effectively, businesses can not only win new customers but also establish long-lasting relationships with them. With the right approach and strategy, you can unlock new growth opportunities and expand your customer base quickly, inexpensively, and automate a large proportion of this process. So, if you haven't explored cold outreach as a traction channel yet, give it a go if it fits your business model and the industry.

But, would a CTO, John Smith, at Microsoft consider trying your product if you send him an outreach email? Unlikely. To get to the "Johns of Fortune 500 companies," you will need to develop a relationship first before he would ever give you a shot. And we have a plan for you to do that.

Account-Based Marketing (ABM): Market of One

You might be thinking, "Everything that I have read so far sounds like a lot of work and rather insecure placement of my GTM efforts." And you might be right – 87% of marketers who are measuring the ROI of ABM agreed that ABM outperforms all other channels in B2B in profitability.[80]

ABM engages individual accounts as markets of one rather than targeting a broad audience. Highly personalized and coordinated approaches that focus on resources are the most likely to yield results. ABM starts by narrowing down the market and identifying targets that will be the most valuable to your business. Later on, sales and marketing engage with them using very tailored efforts to close the first deal and later expand the account.[81]

Lead Generation
- Database Selection
- Interest
- Nurture
- Lead Conversion

Account Based Marketing
- Account Selection
- Contact Identification
- Nurturing
- Account Conversion

Source: Patel, N. (n.a.) What is Account-Based Marketing? An Inside Look at How to Get High-Ticket Clients. Niel Patel by NP Diginal https://neilpatel.com/blog/account-based-marketing-inside-look-get-high-ticket-clients/

---

80 O'Neill, S. (2022). Account-Based Marketing: Stats and Trends for 2023 . LXA Hub. https://www.lxahub.com/stories/account-based-marketing-stats-and-trends-for-2023
81 Patel, N. (n.a.) What is Account-Based Marketing? An Inside Look at How to Get High-Ticket Clients. Niel Patel by NP Diginal https://neilpatel.com/blog/account-based-marketing-inside-look-get-high-ticket-clients/

Imagine you are selling a B2B SaaS product that helps companies prepare for their most important industry events. The solution is licensed to clients for $5,000 a month (a $60,000 annual value) and is specifically tailored to hardware companies that exhibit at more than 10 fairs a year. There are merely 400 companies that are a good fit for you.[82] If you hope to get a large company in the space, would you bet it all on inbound and advertising to potentially get their interest, or would you seek a more direct way in?

If your Beachhead Segment, or overall TAM, consists of a limited number of prospects with expected high LTV (+$20,000 to $50,000), you may be better off using ABM than orchestrating a marketing broadway show to see who wants to hop on a sales call with you. Here is a simple calculation of how many customers you really need to capture $1 million in revenue.

LTV of a client	$10K	$100K	$1 million
Estimated win rate	20%	10%	2%
Accounts needed to nurture	500	100	50

If you only have to nurture 50 to 100 accounts to hit your GTM targets, ABM might be the answer. But how to do it? I use ABM myself all the time in my consulting business. It doesn't really make sense to outburst the content and invest in ads to obtain many leads if I can only accumulate up to 100 clients a year. A much better approach is to:

1. **Analyze previous clients that had a high LTV**. These are businesses I'd love to work with again. If you do not have data yet, you can use insights from your research.

2. **Create a lead list of top-fit clients.** After understanding the shared characteristics of your best-performing accounts, you create a dream client list based on company size, industry, country, or whatever other shared characteristic best describes your audience.

---

82 If your business model relies on attracting more customers at lower prices such as ecommerce, apps or B2C products, this section is indirectly useful for you. These principles apply searching for new partners (suppliers, retailers, strategic partners and vendors).

3. **You identify decision-makers in these companies**. Ideally, you could talk to a direct decision-maker about what you are selling. In my case, they are usually founders, CMOs, Head of Products, or Directors of Innovations. Develop a deep understanding of how decisions are being made in these companies and who responds to them. It is best to have some customer discovery calls to learn that. I like to keep my dream clients list short and sweet, up to 20 companies a quarter. You can have a broader list if you can allocate more resources towards ABM.

4. **Nail messaging and positioning**. Why should they care? What value are you bringing to their lives? Everything you have analyzed in the previous chapter comes into play and has to be adjusted to each member of DMU that you get in touch with.

5. **Start with your ABM campaign**. Engineer a plan for each account. Bring sales and marketing together and align their efforts based on jobs to be done for each account. Every touchpoint with DMU should be aligned with the specific decision-maker and coherent with the overall messaging. An ABM campaign should include multiple touchpoints and channels, for example:

    - Personalized LinkedIn invite.
    - A personal LinkedIn post that focuses on the topics of interest for that DMU.
    - Engagement with their posts.
    - Direct message with valuable content.
    - Invite for a webinar.
    - Retargeting campaign.
    - Nurturing with newsletters that serve highly valuable information.
    - Networking at an event or a conference.
    - Client dinner.

6. **Measure success and optimize the approach.** Like all marketing strategies, it's essential to measure the success of ABM campaigns and optimize them over time. Metrics may first include indicators such as engagement at the account level, number of touchpoints, response rates, and conversion rates to meetings. Once you see success in the program,

you should also follow sales metrics such as the revenue generated, deal-to-close time, deal size, etc.

7. **Create new opportunities on existing accounts**. You can also use ABM for expanding accounts and upselling existing clients. A client who has had a positive experience with your organization previously is much more likely to buy from you again.

But as with anything great in business, ABM brings in some new challenges when you undertake it. Here is what you should consider before going all-in on ABM as a channel in your GTM:

- **ABM is resource-intensive**. Creating customized content and campaigns for individual accounts, as well as following up with them and helping them advance on their customer journey, takes significant marketing and sales resources. Before going full-in on ABM, it is smart to test the approach in a smaller client dream list and commit to it for a quarter in GTM. Sales might not happen in that time, but you will see other signals, such as willingness to engage and how far ahead they are in the buying cycle.

- **ABM requires organizational maturity**. If your marketing and sales teams are more of a dog and a cat than allies, implementing ABM could be very challenging. It is best to start on a smaller scale and build a more complex operation once you see some traction. It is definitely a good practice to start with colleagues who are eager to try out the channel and assign a clear line of responsibility and targets for each account.

- **Track the touchpoints.** There are so many touchpoints to track in ABM that it can quickly become messy if more people are doing it. At least you need a CRM or a spreadsheet to track the activities. You will be much better off if you use a CRM or outreach tools so you can actually track all of the activities and learn what works and doesn't work much faster.

Many growth strategists outside enterprise sales often have a blind spot for ABM; it is massively undervalued, but its importance in B2B marketing is increasingly growing. In GTM, it is much better to become "the best salesperson" in the company than to go on a hiring spree before even validating a channel. You can also use similar approaches for developing partnerships, searching for employees, or other fields in business where you need to build and nurture relationships. However, one-on-one relationship management takes time and effort. Can you do it at scale? Good news, sometimes you can.

Community: Build a Tribe of Raving Fans

Building a strong community or becoming a go-to person for what you do in an established community can be pivotal in your GTM. The route there is long and often challenging, but if you can build a tribe of raving fans that endorse you and even "defend" you at times, your GTM route will be much smoother and nicer to walk on.

People are tribal by nature. For millennia, we have formed tribes to increase our chances of thriving in life and work. As a species, we are wired to form relationships and connect with others. It makes us feel happy and fulfilled. Remember Maslow's hierarchy back in high school? Social needs of love and belonging are universal.

No wonder communities continue to thrive. Groups of people with shared interests, experiences, characteristics, or values make us feel safe and sound. In GTM, communities come in many shapes and sizes. You can be a part of mastermind groups where trusted members exchange information, learn from each other, and open opportunities for each other. Or you can lurk in a 15,000-member group to get insights and catch up on the latest business opportunities. You can build your community or join an existing one to add value.

In that case, pay attention to the culture of the community. In great communities, members feel strongly connected, and if you simply go there to post your latest offer, bad things could happen. You might get banned, restricted, outed in comments, or nearly worse – no one will care. It takes time and effort to build a community or become an MVP in an established flourishing community.[83] It is a long game, but worth playing if you are serious about this channel and your audience is "tribal" by nature. BTW – are you team iPhone or Android? Team Linux or Windows?

---

83 MVP refers to the most valuable player, not the minimum viable product in this context

I have several strong opinions about communities because I have been on the admin, as well as the active members side, for as long as I can remember. Personally, I find a lot of value in learning, interacting with others, understanding market needs, and building business bridges in communities. Some of the members of the professional communities I manage have built their careers by only being present and helpful there. I strongly believe that the community was one of the key contributors to the fundraising success we experienced with OriginTrail, where we raised $22.5 million to support development. As a community leader, I have been approached for many partnerships, opportunities, and speaking gigs, which greatly contributed to my career progression.

The benefits are enormous if you do it right. But how do you play the community channel game? Here is a little **Community Playbook** that I put together for you.

	Your Own Community	External Communities
Rule #1: Give before you get	Kicking off and nurturing an engaging community takes work and deviation. At first, you will have to lead by example and commit to creating value for yourself before others follow your lead.	Consider starting with value posting and commenting first. If you simply hit your link to the "community wall," members will feel like you are an intruder in their home. Show that you can add value first before making an ask.
Rule #2: Become obsessed with value and member experience	Make every community governance decision using a prism: Is it good for the user? Does it add value to them? You can no longer only follow your gut. Smart members have entrusted you to curate the content and keep the group alive. People get annoyed and bored more easily than ever these days. Always pay attention to your group's quality and govern it with value-added and inclusivity in mind.	Before any post or comment, think hard about whether it really adds value and how it impacts community experience. Not only what you post but also how you behave and engage with others positions you in a community. As a person, I love to think critically, and I do enjoy a good intellectual clash. But in most communities, it would backfire. As a hothead, I have to keep it down a little to not only the community's rules but also the culture of conversation.

Rule #3: Be tough but fair	Being an admin is one of the most ungrateful but wonderful missions. You have to have rules that govern your community. Members need to know and respect the rules. Even if your friend violated the rules, rules of behavior are the glue of a high-quality community. You can still be nice and explain rules violations helpfully, but without the rules, communities can turn into Wild West desserts.	Learn the rules. When in doubt, it is better to ask admins for permission than forgiveness. While critical thinking and presenting contra-arguments is welcome in most communities (especially when expressed respectfully), you as a member will never become a GOAT if your engagement strategy only consists of "bravo," "good job," and "congrats." Think about relevant problems. Offer your POV, experience, and solutions on how to solve them.
Rule #4: Consistency is the golden key	Community kick-off can be a slow burn. After your buddies have joined and you keep posting, it can get a bit depressing if only the admin is doing the work. Do not give up. Great achievements take time, and you have to earn member's trust and loyalty. Keep the group interesting by inviting other people to participate and make a content calendar to ensure that there are at least 1-2 high-value posts a week.	One value post does not make legends. It may even happen that the initial engagement is disappointing. Most people do not trust strangers. By continuously engaging and adding value, you will build trust in time. The safest engagement strategy for most is to start with value commenting and solving other members' questions. You win a lot of goodwill for your future "solo action" if you provide value in comments before you go solo.
Rule #5: Express gratitude and empower members	Never take for granted that members pay attention to you and your group. They are the heroes of your community's story. Celebrate their success, give them shoutouts for their contribution, and honor shared experiences together. As an admin, you can also organize meetups, webinars, or mentorship programs for the community where members have an opportunity to shine. Be grateful and connect with people.	A kind word can go a really long way. If you found a great piece of advice in the community or a new opportunity, express gratitude for that. Even better, create a post in which you give out shoutouts and share your story for other members to inspire and empower. Community is a team sport, not a pavilion for individual egos. In most communities, there are more "silent members" than active members, and by being helpful and respectful, you will build great karma and open many doors.

Since communities offer a brilliant opportunity to understand, attract, and win early adopters, you now probably want a plan on how to develop yours.

The first mistake I'd like you to avoid is not to start this process by considering the platforms. Communities can live on Facebook, Reddit, Discord, Telegram, LinkedIn, Twitter, etc. The options are limitless. Narrow down this selection by asking yourself:

1. Who is your ideal member?
2. Where do they naturally seek such information?
3. Which social media platforms do they gladly use to interact with others?

One of the toughest areas in community building is retention. Acquisition can be challenging, but if the group is good and you keep adding value, members will invite others to join, and you will not have to actively promote it. It's all about developing habits. It is a safer bet to choose a platform they gladly spend their time on. This can be an email newsletter, an old-school platform like Facebook, or a new and shiny channel such as Discord or Twitch. When selecting a community home, make sure there is a good notification system to communicate with members before you tie the knot with the platform. The other important factors to consider are the rules of engagement and privacy policies of each platform. Ideally, you can communicate with members directly, which means you need their email address or phone number. By definition, community enables and encourages two-sided communication. Building an audience on a social media channel or email list where you communicate one-to-many is an inbound tactic, not a community. The same channels can be considered as a community if the audience actively engages in the conversations and co-creates content.

Now, it's time to understand what's needed to make a great community. Three elements that shape them are:

1. **Identity**: What ties people together? What are their shared beliefs, lifestyle, interests, etc.?
2. **Experience**: What are they getting from the community? What are the rules and interactions that shape their behavior?

3. **Structure**: Which channel is the community hosted? What are the forms of interaction? How do you govern them and continue to add value?

To develop a community strategy, you can use a tool called **Community Canvas**. To walk you through all of the elements of the canvas, I will be using my local Professional Growth Hacking group with over 9,000 members that I founded in 2017 on Facebook and co-admin with a couple of colleagues who have proven to be community GOATs. It is known to be one of the best channels to post jobs, find new business, and promote events in Slovenia, where I am from. Some members even said the only reason they have not deleted the Facebook app from their phones is to read the content in the group. Love appears to be strong there, but how is it structured to continuously deliver value to its members?

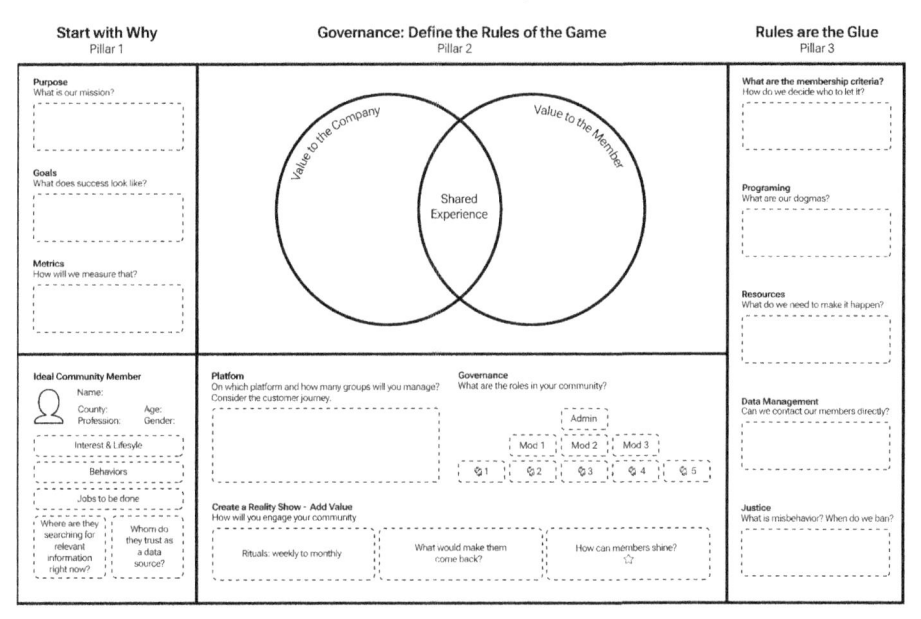

Start with Why Pillar 1	Governance: Define the Rules of the Game Pillar 2	Rules are the Glue Pillar 3
Purpose What is our mission?	*Venn diagram: Value to the Company ∩ Value to the Member = Shared Experience*	**What are the membership criteria?** How do we decide who to let in?
Goals What does success look like?		**Programming** What are our dogmas?
Metrics How will we measure that?		**Resources** What do we need to make it happen?
Ideal Community Member Name: County: Age: Profession: Gender: Interest & Lifestyle Behaviors Jobs to be done Where are they searching for relevant information right now? / Whom do they trust as a data source?	**Platform** On which platform and how many groups will you manage? Consider the customer journey. **Governance** What are the roles in your community? Admin / Mod 1 / Mod 2 / Mod 3 ⭐1 ⭐2 ⭐3 ⭐4 ⭐5 **Create a Reality Show - Add Value** How will you engage your community Rituals: weekly to monthly / What would make them come back? / How can members shine? ⭐	**Data Management** Can we contact our members directly? **Justice** What is misbehavior? When do we ban?

For many legendary companies such as Figma, Airbnb, GitHub, MongoDB, Miro, and Hubspot, the community has been an essential part of their GTM strategy. Community is much more than a "home" for your early adopters. You can get tons of insight and inspiration or even initiate co-creation for the product. Community members will gladly engage in testing, provide valuable feedback, buy from you, and help other members navigate through the challenges they're facing.

However, building a strong community takes a lot of time and effort for most GTM companies. It requires investing time, labor, sometimes funding for events, and a huge deal of persistence and goodwill. If you are not in a position to devote at least six hours a week to this channel and cannot hire a Community Manager at the moment, it's better not to do it for now because the ROI is very uncertain at first, and without a critical mass of efforts, it is a risky bet.

Before going all-in on developing a community, make sure to study and start engaging on the platform of choice. You will learn the rules of the game and get a much better feel if the community is a good channel fit for you.

For our next order of business, let's transition from marketing to sales.

Partners: Together, We Stand Stronger

Generating traction from the ground up is difficult. What about if you piggyback on someone else's audience to get a little boost and borrow the trust they have built with your audience?

Say hello to another undervalued channel in GTM – partnerships. Spoiler alert: They only work well if both parties bring value to the table and share goals and values.

Joanna Bunker, Strategic Partnerships Lead at Wing (an Alphabet Company), defines strategic partnerships as a mutually **beneficial arrangement** between two separate companies that don't directly compete with one another.

But what can you add as a gentle GTM company if you are flirting with the idea of teaming up with an established company? More than you can think of now, probably. Consider these types of partnerships to leverage your GTM strategy. With each type, I provide a real-world example from when I was a CMO at OriginTrail. The team was amazing at building and nurturing partnerships; it was one of the strongest growth levers for the company, which led to numerous speaking opportunities, PR articles, and new leads from partners.

1. **Solution development partnership.** Partners team up and build a new solution together. Each partner brings their best capabilities to the mix. Teams have to work tightly together, and the goals, metrics, and roadmap of the partnership should be made to get the best results.

- At OriginTrail, we partnered with the British Standards Institution (BSI) to create a pilot building management system. This was made according to their standards and later co-promoted through their network, our network, and a PR campaign. OriginTrail brought valuable technology and infrastructure knowledge to the partnership, and BSI excelled at domain knowledge and access to the market.

2. **Promotion partnership**. A company finds a partner with a great reach to their target audience and strong marketing channels to promote their solution. A partner is compensated either with a fee, revenue share, or services in exchange.

    - An important partnership that we built was with GS1, a global organization for standardization. You probably know them best for barcodes; they govern how they are structured. We developed a pilot project together with a commercial partner and presented it at their global summit in Brussels. We got great traction and momentum from this presentation.

3. **Sales partnership.** Partners agree they will join efforts in sales, customer support, and exchange of information, which are relevant for successful sales to happen. A partner who will perform the sales is paid with a revenue or profit share and gets marketing resources and technical support from the solution provider.

    - We joined the Oracle marketplace, obtained their partnership badge, and ensured we could connect with their technology stack. We worked together with a local and global team to identify and implement opportunities for the platform the company was developing.

4. **Purpose-driven partnerships**. A collaboration that demonstrates your mission, values, and ethos. A purpose-driven partnership can help support the outcomes of all other partnerships.

    - In China and elsewhere in the Eastern world, a wine exporter Plantaže, the largest vineyard in Europe located in Monte Negro, was aware of the challenge that European wine is being countrified. To provide safety and restore the trust of customers, we participated in the development of a traceability system by which a customer could check if the item is really authentic.

How to build them successfully is the big untackled question in a GTM partnership. Some professionals are naturally good at them. They can passionately invite the partner to join forces. If you are new to partnership building or it does not click immediately, Jaïr Halevi, a leader in partnership management at Miro, previously at Airbnb, put together a wonderful framework to help you get started.

Jaïr Halevi's Partnership Playbook was slightly adjusted for GTM by yours truly:

1. **Define individual and mutual value**. Every great partnership exploration meeting should start with three questions:

    - What is in it for you?
    - What is in it for the partner?
    - Is there enough incentive on both sides for the partnership to be worthwhile?

2. **Do the cultural due diligence**. Secure that both organizations share common values.

    - What are the shared values and mission?
    - Can both parties work together based on their values, principles, and missions?

3. **Be clear on your timeline and goals**. Time to value in the partnership is important to agree on in advance. Determine goals and commitments that are expected from the partnerships in a given timeframe and help transform them into a more tangible form.

    - What is the timeline?
    - What problems are you trying to solve together (the partnership's mission)?
    - To whom are you solving these problems (audience)?
    - What type of collaboration can you expect from this type of partnership?

- What is the budget?

4. **Define how you will measure success.** Different types of partnerships are valued differently. Here are some metrics to consider for each type:

    - Technology partnership: Time to market, percent of spend vs. return (ROI), customer experience and satisfaction, scalability.
    - Promotion partnerships: Press hits, reach sentiment, engagements, increased followers, and traction measures, such as conversion to users/customers.
    - Sales partnerships: Direct revenue, retention, cannibalization, goodwill, and brand perception, number of new users, number of paid users, user/customer quality score compared to other channels.
    - Purpose partnerships: Community impact, increased awareness, public endorsements, awards and accolades, increased employee engagement scores.

5. **Assess and communicate regularly**: Set up clear processes and lines of responsibility and make sure to check in often with your partner.

    - What are the key milestones?
    - Who is involved? The recommended structure of responsibility is the RASCI matrix.
    - How are you going to communicate (frequency, collaboration tools, project management)?
    - How are we going to iterate on the execution?

But how to start with building partnerships? Can you go ahead and aim high, or should you first focus on more attainable targets? Jair shares his experiences:

"At Miro's Startup Program, if I go and speak to a partner, mentioning that we are working with big companies such as Sequoia or Techstars, we will likely nail the partnership. We have credibility. We delivered for some of the most sophisticated partners in the space. The way I could best describe it is that FOMO, the fear of missing out, happens.

Always focus on the offer. What would be an offer so good that it's practically impossible for the partner to pass? Amazon Web Services (AWS) is giving $100,000 in Cloud Hosting to startups that are part of accelerators such as Y Combinator and Techstars. Suppose you give $100,000 of cloud space to a company. This is an offer that is hard to pass. Remember the defense function of a partnership as well. If they benefit from $100,000 of AWS value, how likely would they suddenly switch from Microsoft to Google? It would be difficult, but there are numerous acceleration and marketplace opportunities available for GTM companies, so you might want to consider them too.

If you are just starting out with partnerships, the other tactic you can do is to go for smaller partnerships first to practice the partnership pitch. Start where you already have access and a relatively sure gate to the company. Get some traction, validate your partnership model, and scale it with more prominent partners. Not many companies can go and pitch to Microsoft or Google from the get-go. Once you have verified the product and your partnership program, it is possible to get as far, and here is some good news. Others are likely to follow as soon as you get one of them to trust you and work with you."

Jaïr firmly believes that partnerships are all about people. Therefore, he is not a fan of automated partnerships, at least not when you are first crafting your partnership programs.

Jaïr explains: "You can reach thousands of potential partners via platforms such as Builtfirst or Proven, but that is a scaling mechanism, not the right mechanism to establish early traction of a partnership program in my experience. I prefer to build some psychological safety and trust. In my opinion, it is important to understand the intentions of my partner and vice versa. If you can attend conferences and meetups, you can meet people in person. You will have a more genuine connection and, therefore, a better partnership with them. You build trust and feel more connected. Research shows that it takes roughly 50 hours of face time to move from mere acquaintances to casual friends.[84] Meet on Zoom instead; that time is likely to be five times higher."

---

[84] Hall, J. A. (2019). How many hours does it take to make a friend? Journal of Social and Personal Relationships, 36(4), 1278–1296. https://doi.org/10.1177/0265407518761225

After going through more human touch-intense channels in the last three sections, let's return to the safe lands of your office. Let's explore the idea that the product could sell itself. Meet a new kid on the block, product-led growth, which is gaining traction and momentum these days.

Product-Led Growth (PLG)

Have you ever used Zoom, Slack, or Netflix for free? Then you are familiar with product-led growth as a user. You get value from the tools before you ever considering paying for them. It's a huge game-changer in the space and reduces the risk of giving a new product a chance.

From as early as the acquisition of customers and onwards, **the product itself is key in your growth.** If it delivers value, you will unlock the holy grail of PLG – virality loops – which is phenomenal continuous referrals, which will be described in the next section.

PLG is not a "shiny new concept" useful for software businesses. In simple terms, it's a "try it before you buy it" strategy, which is what we do for shoes, cars, houses, and perfumes.

In SaaS, the biggest difference between product-led growth and sales-led growth is that you engage users *before* you monetize them.

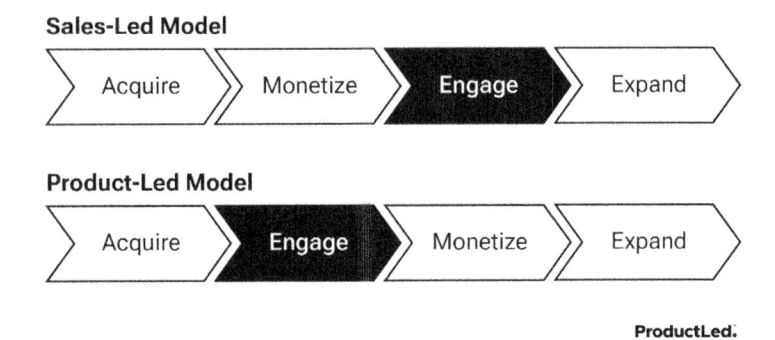

Sales-Led Model

Acquire > Monetize > **Engage** > Expand

Product-Led Model

Acquire > **Engage** > Monetize > Expand

ProductLed.

Now, let's break the biggest myth in PLG: that it's only a free trial. It's not. It's an entire shift in how the organization operates. Every team needs to be aligned around one key element: user success. Wes Bush, founder of the product-led movement and author of *Product-Led Growth: How to Build a Product That Sells Itself*, shares a story of the first failed product-led attempt of the video software Vidyard that offers advanced tools for video sharing and analytics:

"At Vidyard, we were excited to offer a free trial. The nature of software at the time was sales-led. Users had to book a demo with our sales team to experience the product. My team was eager to introduce a "14-day trial" call-to-action on the website, and we got many people to sign up for it, but very few people actually converted to paid customers from it. The challenge was that in 14 days, a user could not fully unlock the product's value. As the product worked, a user would have to record the video, publish it on the website, and use their marketing automation software to deliver it, and only then would they see advanced analytics.

We got very few active signups from this experiment, and sales provided feedback that they weren't closing well. On the other hand, the previous mechanism – sign up for a demo – was working quite well, so we discontinued the motion for the time being. The free trial was still available to users, but only if they had excitedly asked for it. It was not the main call-to-action on the website."[85]

Wes reflects on that experience: "Your users' success will ultimately become your success. After we understood that, the second attempt of Vidyard to become a product-led organization was a success. Instead of offering a free trial, we launched a simple Chrome browser extension plugin that enables easy making and sharing of videos, and the user could actually get to the aha! moment. In one year, the product got 100,000 users from all around the globe, and now there are millions."

The lesson learned here is that a light version of the product gave the aha! moment experience of Vidyard in a manner of minutes. What happens often in software is that 40 to 60% of users who sign up for something never show up again. It might be due to pricing, its complexity, or they were simply not motivated to use the product to begin with. This is why, in product-led growth, you obsess over the user and getting them to value *before* asking them for money. Because the odds of them upgrading after they hit that aha! moment skyrocket.

---

85 Bush, W. (2019). Product-Led Growth: How to Build a Product That Sells Itself.

To decide if PLG is right for your business, Wes offers this decision framework that's based on three factors:

1. How complex, dynamic, or new the problem and/or solution is.
2. How easy it is for your users to set up the product and start seeing results.
3. How you connect with the buyer and user — top-down or bottom-up.[86]

Let's look at them in a bit more detail to help you decide if PLG is the right ally for your GTM strategy.

Is the problem and/or solution difficult to convey or different for each customer?

The first consideration when deciding whether PLG is right for your business is the complexity of the problem you solve and the solution you're providing. If the problem or solution is highly technical or if it changes with every customer, it will be difficult to communicate the value of your product without an in-person conversation.

For example, SAP is a multinational software company that provides accounting, enterprise resource planning, human resources, and supply chain management solutions for enterprises. Each customer they work with has highly intricate, complex use cases, and the solutions SAP provides are customized to each customer. SAP can only share the value of their service by having a salesperson learn about the prospect's needs and then create a custom proposal.

On the other hand, a business like Slack provides the same product for all users and solves a simple problem. Slack has seen great success with PLG because its customers are able to understand how the product solves their problems simply by using it.

How easy is it for your customers to set up the product and start seeing results on their own?

The next question to consider is whether or not your prospective customers have the expertise and bandwidth to set up and begin using your product.

---

[86] Wes Bush, 2022, Is Product-Led Right For You? https://productled.com/blog/saas-go-to-market-strategy

Returning to the Slack example, any professional can easily set up a Slack account, add coworkers, and start sending messages, so a product-led approach is likely the best choice.

On the other hand, migrating to a new payroll and HR system typically requires a lot of configuring on the back end before it's operational. It would be difficult for a company to set up a new payroll software and see the value of it during a free trial, which is why you would need a sales rep to demonstrate its value.

Are you going to take a top-down or bottom-up selling approach?

In B2B sales, where you often have managers making decisions for an entire team about what SaaS products to purchase and adopt, there are generally two selling approaches: top-down or bottom-up.

A top-down selling approach is when you start by attracting the buyer, who then passes the product down to the users. This sales strategy is most effective in situations where it's important for everyone on the team to use the same product, as with CRMs and task management tools.

A bottom-up selling approach starts with attracting the user, who then convinces the higher-ups to invest in the product for the entire team. This approach is most effective when it's possible for different people to use different solutions within the same company.

For example, one employee may start using Loom to record quick explainer videos for their coworkers instead of explaining tasks via email or in person. Then, their coworkers might start recording Loom videos, too. Eventually, if enough people are regularly using Loom and exceeding the limits of its free plan, they may ask managers to provide access to the premium version.

A bottom-up selling approach is usually paired with PLG because most individual users prefer to self-educate rather than meet with a salesperson.

PLG is definitely here to stay. It will not suffocate good old channels such as conferences, billboards, dinners with clients, and mass media, but it does give a fighting chance to GTM teams that might need traction faster. Remember, with channels, it is not "one to rule them all." They evolve, and you can very successfully create synergies together. The art is to find those that work well for your users and can create a predictable inflow of new opportunities. But there is one more secret ingredient for your GTM growth stack that can give you a huge boost. Growth Loops are up next.

Growth Loops

"Compound interest is man's greatest invention."
Albert Einstein

When I started working in growth marketing back in 2010, our go-to framework for understanding how the customer journey translates to business was The Pirate Metrics - AARRR (Acquisition, Activation, Retention, Referral, and Revenue) by entrepreneur and investor Dave McClure.[87] We were enthusiastically drawing funnels on every whiteboard that we could find and tweaked our growth strategies and analytics system to make them measurable.

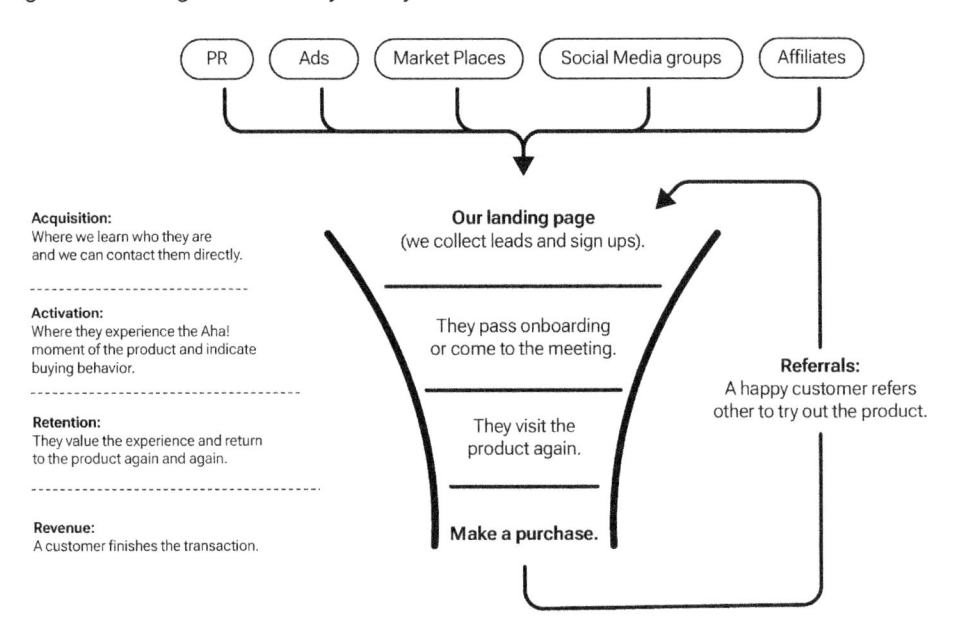

Acquisition: Where we learn who they are and we can contact them directly.

Activation: Where they experience the Aha! moment of the product and indicate buying behavior.

Retention: They value the experience and return to the product again and again.

Revenue: A customer finishes the transaction.

Referrals: A happy customer refers other to try out the product.

Funnel stages: PR, Ads, Market Places, Social Media groups, Affiliates → Our landing page (we collect leads and sign ups). → They pass onboarding or come to the meeting. → They visit the product again. → Make a purchase.

It siloed responsibility and ownership for different stages of the funnel to different departments instead of aligning them towards a single objective.

We needed to find a better solution. It came from Reforge, a career development education platform. They popularized the concept of Growth Loops.[88] The fastest-growing products are better represented as a system of loops, not

---

87 McClure, D. (2007). Startup Metrics for Pirates. https://www.slideshare.net/dmc500hats/startup-metrics-for-pirates-long-version
88 Balfour, B., Kwok, K., Winters, C., & Chen, A. (2018). Growth Loops are the New Funnels. Reforge. https://www.reforge.com/blog/growth-loops

funnels. Loops are closed systems where the inputs, through some process, generate more of an output that can be reinvested in the input. Growth Loops serve different value creation, including new users, returning users, defensibility, or efficiency. For each stage of the loop, you define:

- **What** is the action?
- **Who** performs the action?
- **Why** are they performing the action?

What does a Growth Loop look like in practice? Ben Williams is an experienced growth and Product Management leader and founder of advising practice PLGeek. He provides a useful framework on how to start thinking about Growth Loops with an example from the company Snyk, a cybersecurity company specializing in cloud computing that targets developers, where he previously led growth and developer experience.[89]

Snyk Advisor CGCD Loop

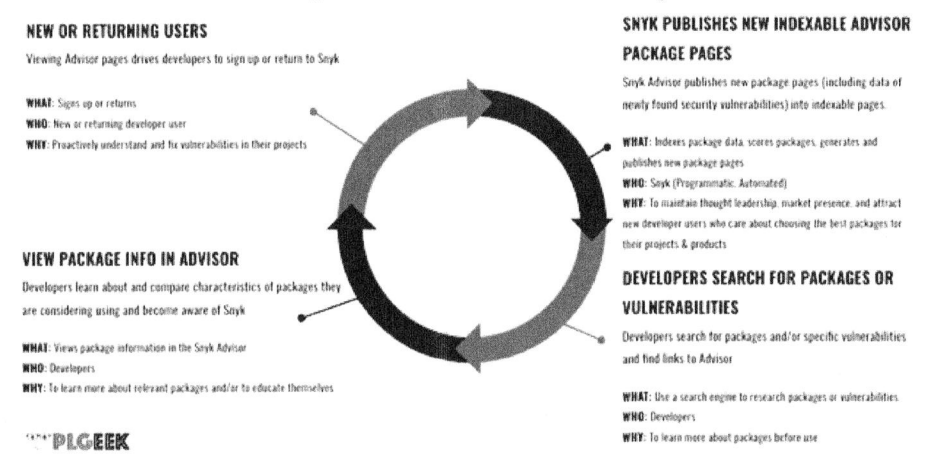

NEW OR RETURNING USERS
Viewing Advisor pages drives developers to sign up or return to Snyk
WHAT: Signs up or returns
WHO: New or returning developer user
WHY: Proactively understand and fix vulnerabilities in their projects

SNYK PUBLISHES NEW INDEXABLE ADVISOR PACKAGE PAGES
Snyk Advisor publishes new package pages (including data of newly found security vulnerabilities) into indexable pages.
WHAT: Indexes package data, scores packages, generates and publishes new package pages
WHO: Snyk (Programmatic, Automated)
WHY: To maintain thought leadership, market presence, and attract new developer users who care about choosing the best packages for their projects & products

VIEW PACKAGE INFO IN ADVISOR
Developers learn about and compare characteristics of packages they are considering using and become aware of Snyk
WHAT: Views package information in the Snyk Advisor
WHO: Developers
WHY: To learn more about relevant packages and/or to educate themselves

DEVELOPERS SEARCH FOR PACKAGES OR VULNERABILITIES
Developers search for packages and/or specific vulnerabilities and find links to Advisor
WHAT: Use a search engine to research packages or vulnerabilities
WHO: Developers
WHY: To learn more about packages before use

PLGEEK

But how to do it for GTM companies before we have a whole bunch of traction to understand how things work? To better understand Growth Loops, I interviewed Ognjen Bošković, previously Head of Growth at CXL Institute and Growth Advisor to tech companies. Ognjen specializes in Growth Loops.

---

89 Williams, B. (20237). Minute Monday 15: The Product-Led Geek Growth Loop Slide Template.. PLG.News.https://www.plg.news/p/minute-monday-15-the-product-led

His answer will amaze you:

> *"Growth Loops are legal Ponzi schemes. You get one user in. They bring more users to you for free."*[90]

Ognjen continues: "A more traditional and technical definition of Growth Loops is that they are a closed system where you put an input through a process to create output, and then output is reinvested into creating more input. The most basic example is a word-of-mouth loop, where a user signs up for your product, uses the product, and then tells others about it or directly invites them to use it. If we compare them to funnels, we can look at funnels as a finite game. Growth Loops are less finite than funnels. There is more continuity to them. Funnels usually work the best in the beginning. If you start a Facebook ads campaign, it performs best at the beginning and after that peak.

It is not a dilemma between making funnels and Growth Loops. You start by building a funnel. If you are building Growth Loops, you will still need funnels to get the initial traction, something to predictably feed the loop. Growth Loops take some time to build up and take off, but if you get them working, they produce compound interests. Due to many factors, like ad fatigue, the growth slows down on your GTM journey, and you can no longer rely only on your funnel to grow.

Essentially, Growth Loops are a way to control, manage, and optimize word-of-mouth. If you can influence it, you can grow it. In the example of an online banking service, Revolut, a user gets a bank card in a beautiful package. They have a great Growth Loop going on, where the user orders a card, receives the beautiful package, and then posts about it on social media. You brag about it, are thrilled about it, and then post about it. It's broadcasted to your friends, connections, and followers."

Sounds great. But word-of-mouth comes in many different shapes and sizes. How do you choose which one is right for you?

---

90 Voje, M. (2022). Growth Loops with Ognjen Bošković [Podcast episode]. Product Led Podcast. Retrieved from https://productled.com/blog/podcast/growth-loops

5 Archetypes of Growth Loops

Growth Loops depend on your product, business model, user preferences, and many other factors. I invited Ognjen to elaborate on different types of Growth Loops that you could consider. Here's what he said:

1. **Usage-Based Growth Loops**: Where users use a product or a certain feature and share it in the product with others.

   Example: When you use Loom, you record a video and send it to someone to watch. It can be a team member, a follower on social media, or a business partner. By sharing the video, you display the value of Loom to others, and if they find it valuable, they can take it for a spin as well.

2. **User-Generated Growth Loops**: Users create and share the content. You provide a platform to enable them to do that.

   Example: Google is the largest search engine and has a user-generated content Growth Loop. Companies create content that's shown to people searching based on queries and set content. The more people create content, the more people will find good answers to their questions on Google. The more people will be using Google, the better the inputs will get, and the cycle goes on
   .

3. **Collaboration Growth Loop**. Through collaboration with other people, you are exposed to the product. Once someone using the product tells you about it, that word-of-mouth motion can be productized into a Growth Loop.

   Example: Figma is a design tool for prototyping. Ognjen never used Figma until a creative agency sent him a Figma file with a design to review. He self-onboarded and grew to like the product a lot and started sharing design prototypes in Figma with others.

4. **Viral Growth Loop**. This Growth Loop will happen if you have a shareable and relatable piece of content. Users feel some emotion connected to using the product.

Example: At the end of every year, Spotify runs a popular campaign summarizing what a user has been listening to on Spotify. It is a custom video for each user sharing their top songs from the year. When they do this campaign, all of the social media platforms are overwhelmed by people sharing their videos.

5. **Distribution Growth Loop**. This one is a self-fulling process of added value exchange. Your business scales as customers scale theirs.

   Examples: Lead generations or opt-in tools such as Privy, OptinMonster, and Drift offer a free way to get started. At first, free users cannot remove the vendor's logo on integrations they have created. When website visitors see the chatbot or an opt-in form, they encounter a branding of the vendor, which could be displayed to millions of people. Another brilliant example is Calendly, a software to schedule online meetings. The more users they have, the more other people will be exposed to the tool. Whenever someone shares their Calendly link to book a meeting with them, more people are exposed to Calendly. It is compound interest building.[91]

When considering Growth Loops, you should play a long-term game. If you aim to build something really big and ambitious or aim to conquer a market segment of an industry, Growth Loops are usually the go-to tool for companies aiming to achieve exponential growth.

Apart from building a Growth Loop, what else do you need to successfully transform your GTM strategy into a well-oiled growth machine? In the next chapter, we will build a GTM system to guide you through the chasm and, ultimately, to the growth stage of a company.

But let's recap the key lessons of this chapter first with your action items.

---

91 Bošković, O. (2021). The Big five growth loop archetypes. Executors. https://www.patreon.com/posts/big-five-growth-69035990

Key Takeaways:

- While it is great to start thinking about scaling, there are times when you have to do stuff that does not scale (i.e., fairs, conferences, personal sales) before you can effectively scale them.

- **The Bullseye Framework** will help you decide which channels to test first. You start by selecting best-fit candidates and run experiments on them to identify two to three channels that actually drive repeatable business.

- **Attribution** refers to a measure of how each of the channels participates in the final goal of the customer journey, whether it be a purchase, download, sign-up, or submitting a contact form. Most companies analyze attribution with vendor analytics tools, but you should consider using self-reported attribution to get realistic feedback from clients about which channel they learned about you from.

- Channels change in time; new channels emerge, some get saturated and no longer work, and others just work and should not be dismissed for the sake of being "too old school" for GTM companies.

- You can either **generate demand** for a product or **capture existing** demand. Your channel selection should be done with regard to that.

- There are **seven different channels** worth considering to be the backbone of your GTM growth model.

    1. **Inbound** content creation with the intent to generate leads.
    2. **Paid digital** media buying to attract the attention of your target audience.
    3. **Community** creating valuable content and comments for members of a community.
    4. **Account-Based Marketing (ABM)** is when the sales and marketing teams work together to target and engage specific high-value accounts with personalized campaigns. The focus is on individual accounts or a select group of accounts rather than a broad audience.
    5. **Outbound** of companies and people that match your target audience

via email, social media, telephone, or even snail mail.
   6. **Partner** agreement with a comparable company to join marketing and sales efforts for mutual benefit.
   7. **Product-led growth (PLG)** is a way a prospect can self-onboard and get value before monetization efforts begin.

- When choosing a channel in GTM, always consider ROI within your GTM lifeline, which in most cases is 3 to 18 months. It is best to reverse-engineer your GTM objectives and choose channels that will most likely get you there.

- **Growth Loops** are closed systems where the inputs generate more of an output that can be reinvested in the input. Growth Loops help to create value, including for new users, returning users, defensibility, or efficiency.

To-Do List:

☐ Present the channels you believe will work well for your GTM using the Bullseye Framework.

☐ Choose your range of GTM channels based on analysis and develop action plans on how to implement them.

☐ Start exploring the possibility of having a Growth Loop using one of the five archetypes.

Find all the worksheets, frameworks, and models mentioned in this chapter at *https://gtmstrategist.com/resources*. They are free and yours to benefit from.

CHAPTER 8

GTM System

"I have never seen a successful company that didn't have a great go-to-market strategy, and the implementation of that strategy is just as important as the strategy itself."

Marc Benioff,
CEO of Salesforce

Finally, we are here. We've confidently made critical GTM decisions, all based on evidence. It's time to bring it together and build teams, processes, and tech stacks to secure resources to execute the plan. We'll go from the strategic phase to the tactics and operations phase to transform your carefully crafted GTM plan into a fierce special ops team set up for success.

We will build you a GTM System that aligns your team with your GTM goals. And we will use a lot of data insights to break department silos and make it work like a well-oiled machine.

At this stage, you'll likely have the same question Jasper had:

To: **Maja Voje** (grow@majavoje.com)

Subject: **How many people do I need to get GTM to life?**

Maja, my GTM friend!

Thanks so much on behalf of me and my team for guiding us through this journey.

We are confident with our choices and cannot wait to bring things to life!

Here is a practical question. Now that we know the channels, I wonder if I roll out a job post, hire an agency, or get one of my developers to do the marketing for now, before we validate our model?

Also – how do you find good GTM partners?

Drop by the office sometime to celebrate our launch. You have been incredible throughout this journey. We have learned so much from you.

Let me know when you need a website for a project. Our treat!

Take care, and surely let me know if you have some recommendations for GTM recruiting or outsourcing.

Cheers

Jasper

Jasper is a technical founder, and he does not necessarily "like marketing." But by now, he understands that somebody must do some level of marketing to get users and customers to the product, and he'd like to outsource it.

At this point, I keep encouraging Jasper to be present at sales calls and meetings, but it's perfectly reasonable that he, as a founder, cannot be solely responsible for traction. There is also a product to maintain, an investment to negotiate, and partnerships to make. And he needs some sleep.

This chapter will equip you with the tools and processes to move from the GTM Strategic Phase to GTM execution. After analyzing hundreds of GTM teams, I realized there are static and dynamic components to a well-oiled GTM machine.

- **Static:** Prepare the grounds and do the fundamentals right. This means building a team, securing a budget, and setting up processes and tools on how you'll be doing this.

- **Dynamic:** Kick off a rapid experimentation process to test and learn fast. Establish a GTM weekly meeting, launch experiments, and tweak your GTM actions towards what you have discovered through experimentation.

You want to keep it realistic and learn to work with what you have. If you are very constrained with a budget and searching for inexpensive solutions, I've got you. If you are part of a larger organization and need to align your GTM with a border business strategy, I'll make it work for you, too. Ideally, GTM is a team sport, but even if you are a solo player, there are plenty of applicable ideas on how to start your GTM engine in this chapter.

GTM values speed and agility over anything else. Tactics will inevitably change over time. If you start procrastinating and wait for all GTM elements to come together, a competitor might beat you and skim the cream from the market, or you may run out of resources. Which means you need to put everything into action.

Let the GTM execution begin!

Prepare the Grounds

"Your go-to-market strategy is your roadmap for success. Without it, you're just guessing."
Mark Cuban, entrepreneur and investor

Every successful GTM execution starts with a clear plan that gets buy-in from all key stakeholders. The other fact is that the plan will change a lot as you gain more insights from the market and respond quickly to new opportunities and insights. A simple plan is easier to update than a complex one with multiple dependencies. Instead of writing a 50-pager or putting together 200 slides to get buy-in for your GTM, consider using a GTM Canvas:

GTM Strategy

Objective:

Market	ECP	Product	Pricing	Positioning	Growth
Identify opportunity	Early Customer Profile	UVPs of the product	Value metric	USPs of the product	Select 2 to 3 channels to test
Core competitors & differentiation		Key metrics to measure Product-Market Fit (PMF)	Minimum Viable Pricing: How much will you charge?	Minimum Viable Branding: What is your idenitity?	Engineer a Growth Loop
Best segments to target					

The ground logic of a winning strategy is to "play on your strengths" and swiftly attack the "enemy weaknesses" and move fast. To move fast, you have to pack light for your GTM journey. Yet, some essentials are mission-critical. Before we dive into GTM essentials, let's look at one additional point.

If you work on a GTM strategy within a larger company, it needs to align with your overall business strategy and mission. Otherwise, you will waste time and energy on internal fights before even going to market, and you're unlikely to move far.

I was working with an enterprise SaaS client who wanted to introduce PLG to their company, but most of the sales came from partners. Implementing PLG would be a huge risk for their main channel. Instead of going head-to-head with other departments, they developed an independent sub-brand and assigned a team to the project. They targeted a different audience at a different price point to not be perceived as a threat to the partner channels. In this case, the downsides of potential backlash outweigh the potential benefits of it.

In such a complex situation, it is essential to establish a shared understanding of risks and benefits and agree on how GTM can be done in a way that does not damage the "core business." But your GTM has to have a fair chance to succeed.

As a GTM strategist, you need to secure resources in advance, agree on what success looks like, define what is off limits, and what is the lifeline of validating your product on the market. Regular reporting on progress and diligently communicating new findings and opportunities can turn your gentle GTM notion from a danger within a larger system to a laboratory where a lot of testing can happen that can provide valuable insights to other departments. It's not politics; it's playing to win. "Move fast and break things" rarely works well in a larger system. Starting small to become big works much better.

The opposite is true for solo executors of a GTM strategy or who work with very scarce resources. There are so many things to do and so little time to do them. Every activity you choose comes with trade-offs. Prioritization will probably become your daily go-to tool. Embrace the mindset of "Is this mission critical?" and remain laser-focused on tasks that will bring in the most impact. While it's a "you against the market," there are many battles to be won. Choose them carefully and recover in between. It is not a sprint. It is a marathon. Your ability to prioritize the actions that will most likely help you succeed will become your next superpower.

Without further ado, let's find out which essentials you should put in your GTM backpack.

What sets you up for successful execution?

Your GTM Execution Backpack: Pack What You Can Carry

Have you ever packed for a mountain hike? You pack light, but make sure all of the necessities are there. You should expect the unexpected and be prepared for some risks, such as an injury or rainfall. It is also more fun, and it is safer to hike as a team. Sounds a bit like GTM, doesn't it? You might not have everything you need, but you must directly negotiate the essentials.

After analyzing hundreds of GTM teams, I've concluded the most successful teams have a clear understanding and at least some maturity in adopting these five GTM execution essentials on their journey:

1. **Timeline**. When will you make it or break it? A timeline usually consists of milestones, roadmaps, and OKRs.

2. **Team.** Either internal, external, or hybrid. GTM requires many competencies and skills that are hard to find in a single person. Interdisciplinary collaboration also creates many synergies and ultimately increases your chances to win.

3. **Organization.** GTM teams meet regularly, measure the progress, adjust tactics, and share insights and progress reports with those "higher-ups." Even for smaller teams, regular meetings make much more sense since they help with accountability and alignment.

4. **Tools.** The ones GTM teams use can be categorized as project management tools, analytics tools, tools to systemize communication and collaboration, and technical tools to actually get the work done. While work can be managed in a spreadsheet, purpose-built tools add value. Keep the stack lean and compatible.

5. **Budget.** Your job as a GTM strategist is to negotiate and secure the budget that includes costs of labor, media buying, tooling, and external services (if needed) and has some contingency because "just in case" always happens.

Let's break each one down and share some best practices to equip you for this journey.

Timeline: When Will You Make it or Break it?

Throughout the book, we vaguely claim that a GTM stage lasts for 3 to 18 months. Now, you need to determine how much time you really have to achieve the objective of your GTM mission. If you are doing the OKRs suggested in the first chapter, you already have the answer, but if you are making this decision now, consider that the timeline closely relates to the lifeline in GTM.

What resources and budget is the company ready to invest in supporting the GTM assets? Sometimes, this is determined based on a "give it everything logic" because the existence of the company might depend on the GTM's success. Other times, especially in larger systems, the logic is more of "invest what we are ready to lose."

Most people work best if the expectations are set up clearly. As a leader, you need to develop a clear answer to:

In _ _(secured time)_ _, we have to achieve _ _(Objective of the GTM mission).

This will become the glue of all the other GTM essentials: team, organization, tools, and budget. GTM leaders often come from product or growth backgrounds. Reverse engineering the overall objective to smaller steps is in their blood. Timelines and roadmaps are a great way to visualize the GTM journey.

Now it's your turn. How much time do you have, or can you negotiate, to achieve your GTM objectives?

Avoid promising big results in a month or less. Most GTM traction takes longer because you are still in an intense learning phase and operating with many unknowns. The minimal acceptable time for reviewing your GTM is three months.

If a "higher up" gives you a Big Audacious Hairy Goal that you don't see happening in that time to the best of your ability, ensure those arguments are addressed.

You can either realign the timeline, change the tactics, or agree on an intermediate milestone target. Often, it is better to underpromise and overdeliver.

Your Special Ops Team

After this is off the table, it is time to announce it to your chosen colleagues. They are a part of your GTM team and are about to embark on an amazing journey. But do not only take your best buds on the path. Recruit them carefully.

What makes a great GTM team?

A successful GTM team is capable of getting the following jobs done:

- Independently execute core tasks and experiments.
- Can make product decisions based on insights and market changes.
- Are data-driven and empowered to make decisions based on data.
- Masters the core growth channel selected.
- Has domain expertise in the area and great customer empathy.
- Shares a mindset of "learning by doing" and "done is better than perfect."
- Are eager to learn and do not let their egos get in the way.
- Moves fast.
- Handles and manages uncertainty well.

Consider recruiting for these skills when planning your GTM team:

- Product management with the power to execute.
- Product marketing.
- Sales enablement expert.
- Data analyst.
- Various channel experts, depending on your selected GTM channels: community managers, social media managers, sales enablement and business development experts, outreach experts, media buyers, PR, and customer support (optional).

"Intelligence"
Data Analyst

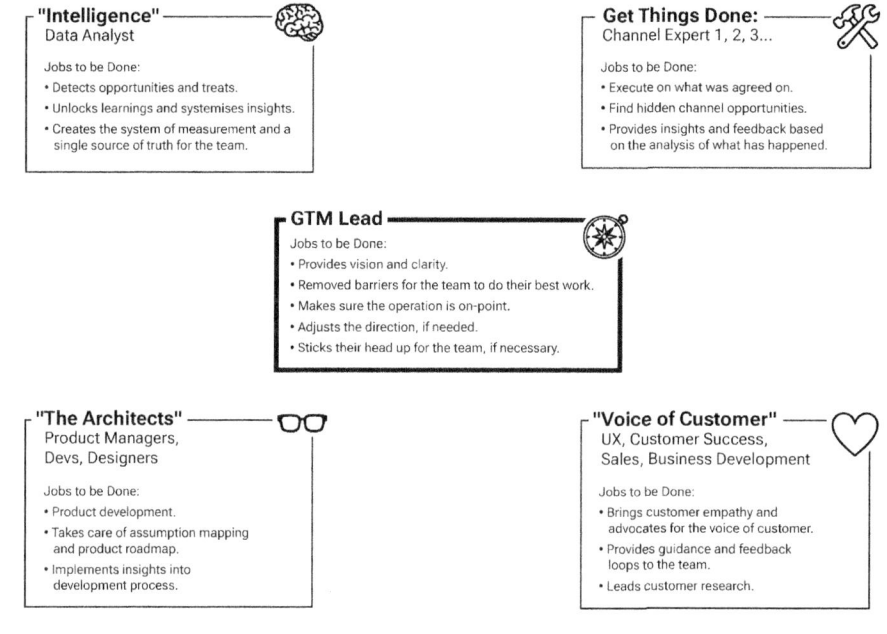

Jobs to be Done:
- Detects opportunities and treats.
- Unlocks learnings and systemises insights.
- Creates the system of measurement and a single source of truth for the team.

Get Things Done:
Channel Expert 1, 2, 3...

Jobs to be Done:
- Execute on what was agreed on.
- Find hidden channel opportunities.
- Provides insights and feedback based on the analysis of what has happened.

GTM Lead

Jobs to be Done:
- Provides vision and clarity.
- Removed barriers for the team to do their best work.
- Makes sure the operation is on-point.
- Adjusts the direction, if needed.
- Sticks their head up for the team, if necessary.

"The Architects"
Product Managers, Devs, Designers

Jobs to be Done:
- Product development.
- Takes care of assumption mapping and product roadmap.
- Implements insights into development process.

"Voice of Customer"
UX, Customer Success, Sales, Business Development

Jobs to be Done:
- Brings customer empathy and advocates for the voice of customer.
- Provides guidance and feedback loops to the team.
- Leads customer research.

The team lead is usually a product manager, the founder (if it's a small company), and/or a product marketer. A GTM team collaborates with other departments or hires external executors, consultants, or field experts for advisory. In many micro to SME companies, the GTM team is run as a special ops – a project within a company and not as a full-time obligation. As you "hire" GTM team members, you can also "fire" them if their field of expertise is no longer needed.

Keep your GTM squad small and purpose-built. It is not a set-it-and-forget-it job. Execution-wise, having two or three people working closely to stay laser-focused on executing the GTM mission is often more effective than having a committee of 15 field experts who struggle to find a slot to book a meeting together.

Successful GTM relies on open knowledge, learning together as a team, making data-based decisions, and playing together towards the same goal. Two traps to avoid here with hybrid GTM teams are:

- If GTM team members are torn between their job obligations' and GTM work, or when multiple external participants are involved, execution can suffer. Set up clear expectations and rethink their personal KPIs. What gets measured gets done.

- When multiple agencies and freelancers work together on the same account, strange things can happen, such as hiding their intellectual property, not communicating with each other, or proving they are better than other vendors, etc. The GTM lead is responsible for negotiating the participation rules and ensuring everybody is on board with them. This establishes an environment of trust and shared interest by including external team members in the conversations and encouraging them to share learnings.

It is time to get the work done after recruiting your colleagues and aligning with the team. Your next job is establishing a GTM process, accountability checks, and workflows to execute your GTM strategy successfully.

Organization: The Way You Work

Funnily enough, after working in GTM for a decade, one of my key findings is that you should become your best "secretary." The other is extreme ownership and accountability. In a hectic GTM environment, your team seeks clarity, deliberate decision-making, and guidance from you as their leader.

Most successful GTM leaders provide clarity, responses, and reliable guidance to their teams. Our most important job is to set our team up for success and create an environment in which everyone can focus on work that actually contributes to the mission.

To set the team up for success, it's smart to build a system that will provide you with real-time oversight of results and workload that is efficient and easy to grasp for everyone and can be scaled easily once you add in more team members. To achieve that, you will need the following:

1. **A single source of truth** creates a consensus regarding key metrics to track and a dashboard where you monitor the team's progress toward your GTM objectives. It is best to consolidate data sources so that everyone is on the same page when it comes to discussing your progress. Lead with clarity and accountability.

2. **Project management** so you can execute fundamental tasks. For example, preparing landing pages, writing content, making presentations and sales decks, and experimenting. It is best to differentiate these types of tasks, so you have a clear view of your learnings. All tasks are best kept on a single platform so team members do not have to switch between tools, and you have a clear overview of the workload and progress.

3. **Only one channel to communicate** to be effective. It is annoying and ineffective if the information is scattered in emails, private messages, texts, and random water cooler discussions. If you see that happening, remember there can be only one. You can also consider the RASCI framework for core communication flows: Responsible, Accountable, Supporting, Consulted, and Informed. If you decide to send emails so everybody is in the loop, clearly communicate what is expected from whom. From the get-go, you will probably have to over-communicate to establish the processes and share all of the information. Later on, over-communication removes gravity from messages, and the team begins to ignore them since not everything is that important. When the team moves to the intense execution phase, you should reduce communication to the "mission-critical" level. Many product managers, developers, and designers complain that each ping on the shoulder, notification, or phone call ruins their focus for approximately half an hour. Attention and focus are your new superpowers.

4. **Documentation and your knowledge base** will come in handy later on once you are onboarding new team members or leading your next GTM operation. It will also become a treasury of knowledge and insights. Written communication is a much more effective way to repeatedly deliver the message than doing one-on-ones with everybody. It can also be reused and updated in time. You will do yourself and your team a favor by recording processes, writing down instructions on how to use each tool, and recording insights. Build a system for knowledge management and sharing. Random links on Slack or Teams stating, "This is an interesting article," annoy most people. Build an easy-to-access knowledge base instead. Start this sooner rather than later so that you are not missing out on insights. It sounds boring, but it really adds value and improves the team members' work experience.

5. **Weekly meetings** are one of the most effective communication tools for alignment and relationship building between team members. Most GTM teams meet once a week for 45 to 60 minutes. Here's a sample agenda:

- First 5 minutes: icebreakers and "Do you see my screen?" questions.
- 10 minutes: key metrics and progress of GTM with commentary.
- 10 minutes: core discoveries, milestones, and opportunities that should be considered.
- 15 to 20 minutes: workflows and task alignment and backlog grooming.
- 10 minutes: potential problems, challenges, and dependencies.

Most GTM teams meet once a week for 45 to 60 minutes:

- Up to five minutes: **Icebreakers and "Do you see my screen?" questions.**
- 10 minutes: **Key metrics and progress of GTM with commentary.**
- 10 minutes: **Core discoveries, milestones, and opportunities that should be considered.**
- 15 to 20 minutes: **Workflows and "up next" task alignment (backlog grooming).**
- 10 minutes: **Potential problems, challenges, and dependencies.**

Inspired by Weekly Growth Meeting Agenda by Sean Ellis

While new ideas occur randomly at meetings, keep in mind that this meeting is operational, and you do not want to waste time of everybody discussing a new website banner for 10 minutes. Some teams decide to do daily stand-up meetings in addition to weekly meetings, and others meet once every two weeks. The point is that meetings make sense when progress has been made. When you are establishing your GTM process, it's recommended to hold these meetings weekly to eliminate the obvious barriers and friction in working together. Later, you can shift to a biweekly cycle if you feel like workflows are nicely aligned and there is not much to talk about every week. For my team, I record weekly video overviews on weekends and meet with them individually each Monday to discuss their workflows for the week. Each briefing starts with defining the "three must-win battles this week" and how to collaborate to win them. Each leader finds their own pace and style. My team really does not like meetings, so I keep them at a bare minimum.

6. **Retrospectives and rituals,** brainstorming, and planning how to move forward together are important, but they don't need to happen during weekly meetings. Create a time and space for them. Many GTM teams organize a retrospective meeting once a month, a quarter, or when important milestones are achieved. The structure can be straightforward, such as listing feedback on what was good and bad, along with what can be improved. You can do more advanced retrospectives, but the job is to achieve alignment, find room for improvements, and appreciate the work that was done. You can also send out periodic progress reports to "higher ups" and include GTM updates in an internal newsletter. All these actions help to create momentum and goodwill for GTM operations inside and outside of the team.

At some point, you will likely encounter silos with knowledge and data sharing between all of your teams. Most silos occur when the processes are not streamlined and there is no single source of truth. You want to avoid this. One proven way to break silos is to empower GTM teams to have a single decision-maker who is empowered to make rapid decisions. If a decision has to be approved by 14 people who sit in five different countries, you are unlikely to move fast enough, and the window of opportunity might close. You want to stay agile and lean.

Tools: A Lean GTM Tech Stack

Now let me answer what is probably your favorite question: which tools should I use in GTM? Instead of thinking about tools, you should first set up processes and then adopt or build tools that support your processes – not vice versa. Tools are here to elevate, systemize, and automate your thinking, not do the thinking for you. Even if you are 100% team Notion, Loom, or Jira, keep an open mind to reconsider if those tools are "mission-critical" or if it could be done with a shared spreadsheet instead.

What you want to do in your GTM is to keep your tool stack lean, not only because of budgeting purposes but also because you aim to create a single source of truth and streamline the work of your team members. Tool onboarding adds unnecessary friction to the processes.

Let's start thinking about tools as their jobs to be done. In this table, I've gathered some popular tools that GTM teams use:

Job to be Done	Recommended GTM tools
Analytics and dashboarding: You need to know what is going on in real time.	Google Analytics, Plausible, Self-hosted analytics such as PostHog, Hotjar, FullStory, Looker, Power BI, Mixpanel, Amplitude, Metabase, Pendo
Project management: You need oversight of your timeline and execution progress.	Jira, Trello, Asana, ClickUp, Monday, Smartsheets, Basecamp, Wrike
Communication: You need all communication to flow to a single platform.	Team: Slack, Teams, Pumble Video: Vidyard, Loom, Synthesia Scheduling: Calendly, Google Cal Scheduler Documentation & knowledge: Google, Microsoft, Notion, Coda, Confluence, Github Conferencing and video calls: Zoom, Google Meet, Microsoft Teams Creative collaboration: Miro, Mural, Figjam
Testing tools for conducting A/B and multivariate testing in experimentation.	Google Optimize VWO Optimizely Omniconvert AB Tasty
AI and Automation tools: Once something works, you would like to scale it.	AI: Jasper, Midjourney, ChatGPT Automation: Zapier, Microsoft Power Automate, Integrately, IFTTT.

Getting the "actual work done."	Design: Figma, Adobe Creative Cloud, InVision

Customer Feedback and Product Management: SurveyMonkey, Typeform, UserVoice, Aha!, Maze, Miro, Intercom, Zendesk, Freshdesk, Tawk.to, Drift, AnnounceKit, as Productboard, ProdPad

Strategy & Strategic Alignment: Jira Product Discovery, Loopedin, Airfocus, ProductBoard, Craft.io, ProductPlan
Feature Flagging: LaunchDarkly, Split.io

Onboarding & Product Adoption: Appcues, UserPilot, Intercom, Userflow, Chameleon.io

Pricing and Billing: Paddle, Stripe

Interactive Demos: Walnut.io, Reprise, Navattic, Demostack

Marketing and Sales (vary largely on the channel)
SEO: SEMRush and Ahrefs
Social Media: Content Studio, Buffer, AgoraPulse
Advertising: AdSpy, TikTok, and Meta Ads library
Outreach: Lemlist, Phantom buster, Zoominfo, LinkedIn Sales Navigator
Scraping: Phantom Buster, Apollo.io, TexAu
Lead Generation: Hunter.io, FindThatLead
Affiliate Marketing: Partnerstack
Email Marketing: ActiveCampaign, Marketo, CRM software Hubspot, Salesforce, Microsoft solutions, Pipedrive |

It is easy to fall in love with the greatest and latest tools. But when you are selecting your GTM lean tool stack, keep in mind that it's best to select tools that are:

- **Easy to onboard**. Tools do not require radical changes in process, and the team "gets them" easily without spending months on learning how to use them.

- **Relatively inexpensive**. With some exceptions, you should keep the budget for tools lean. The cost of tools can escalate pretty quickly. Always consider tools in relation to expected value add. Many GTM tools actually have special pricing for early-stage companies, so always ask about options.

- **Scalable**. Do not always go for the cheapest alternative. Sometimes pricing escalates radically when the usage increases. Check out the "scaling packages" of tools as well and reconsider the value added.

- **Integrable.** Avoid creating data silos in your tech stack. Also, if you are a part of a larger organization, you should make sure each tool is compliant with privacy and security measures at hand. In that case, do not "sneak in" tools because they can end up being a serious security vulnerability.

Before spending time searching and trying out different tools, ask yourself if you could solve the problem with a spreadsheet or a Google Doc before you upgrade to something more advanced.

Now, let's have the money talk.

Budget

There are many different practices in setting up and managing the GTM budget, but the core principles are "expect the unexpected" and "risk as much as you can lose." The rule of thumb in established post-PMF companies is to assign 10 percent of the marketing and growth budget towards experimentation. This percentage in pre-PMF can be much higher. A well-executed GTM strategy can generate significant returns on investment and unlock or contribute to the long-term success of the business.

The exact allocation of the budget for a GTM strategy is company-specific, but make sure to account for the specific needs and goals of the company, as well as the tactics and channels you've decided to focus on. Here are some of the budget areas you should consider regardless of the specific GTM strategic directions you have selected:

1. **Labor (both in-house and outsourced)**: This includes the cost of hiring and compensating the team responsible for executing the GTM strategy, including Marketers, Salespeople, Developers, Copywriters, Designers, and other professionals. The budget allocation for labor will heavily depend on your selected channels and normally range from 30 to 70% of

the GTM budget. Many GTM experts do not account for labor in their CAC and calculate it purely on a media-buying basis.

2. **Marketing/Sales/Growth budget**: Depending on your selected GTM channels, plan these investments ahead so you won't have to go back and forward with the "higher-ups" whenever you would like to do testing. Usually, a minimum budget for solid testing is at least $5,000. Most companies invest more. Remember that paid channels are not just advertising but also fairs, media buying in professional publications, influencer marketing, and fees to present and attend events. In an ever-changing GTM environment, it is smart to include market research and educational budget in your foreseen marketing expenses as well.

3. **Technology and tools**: This includes the cost of any software or tools required for the GTM strategy, such as marketing automation software, analytics platforms, and other digital tools.

4. **Contingency**: New opportunities emerge, competitors do something unexpected, and some costs will be bigger than you budgeted for. A good start is 10% of the overall budget, so you can work fast and not be dependent on other decision-makers.

Here is an example of a simple GTM budget for a five-member team that is working on launching an AI-empowered content creation tool for LinkedIn creators.

		Month 1: MVP development	Month 2: MVP test	Month 3: Launch	Share
Labor	Developer 1 (full time)	$5,000	$5,000	$5,000	The budget allocation for labor will heavily depend on selected channels and could normally range from 30 to 70% of the GTM budget.
	Developer 2 (part time)	$2,500	$0	$2,500	
	Designer (part time)	$2,000	$2,000	$2,000	Many GTM experts do not account for labor in their CAC, and calculate it purely on the media buying basis.
	Product Manager	$6,000	$6,000	$6,000	
	Growth Expert	$5,000	$5,000	$5,000	
Marketing/ Sales/ Growth budget	Google Ads	$0	$300	$2,000	Usually, a minimal budget for solid testing is at least $5,000. Most companies invest more. It depends on the size of the market you aim to cover, and also if you can count on existing demand and PLG, or if you need to consider demand generation which is usually more expensive.
	Meta Ads	$0	$0	$3,000	
	Influencer collaborations	$0	$0	$2,000	
Technology and tools	Jira (4 licences)	$84	$84	$84	Plan up to 10% of the budget for technology stack.
	Other dev & design tools	$200	$200	$200	
	Miro (2 licences)	$30	$30	$30	
	Google Suite (5 licences)	$29	$29	$29	
Contingency		$2,000	$2,000	$2,000	A good start is 10% of the overall budget so you can work fast and not be dependent on other decision-makers.
Per Month		$22,843	$20,643	$29,843	
Total expenses		$73,328			

GTM STRATEGIST

The fundamentals are now set. You can pack even lighter, especially if you are a solo executor of the GTM strategy. Take what is useful and add value to your execution. Deliberate testing and structured learning processes are the best medicine to quickly and effectively cross the chasm.

GTM Experimentation Process

> "Our success at Amazon is a function of how many experiments we do per year, per month, per week, per day."
>
> Jeff Bezos, founder and executive chairman of Amazon

In the uncharted territory of GTM, experimentation plays a vital role in making decisions with confidence. Therefore, it deserves a special place in the book: a pedestal. While some decisions can be taken from past experience and based on a gut feeling, most decision-making benefits from following a scientific method and generating evidence before going all in.

You know this scientific method from primary school: form a hypothesis and test it. The more you test, the more you make any decision with confidence.

Why is the scientific method still so difficult to implement in your business? It's because many assumptions occur. Even though testing is learning, it takes a lot of time and effort, and it can sometimes hit the ego when implemented.

There are certain decisions you need to make in GTM that will have huge consequences and might even make or break the business, such as selecting your ECP, your price point, and your marketing channels. Throughout the book, we developed a notion that when you have a hard time deciding which option to choose, testing comes to the rescue.

In this section, we'll structure the experimentation process to fit your GTM needs. First, you have to agree that statistical significance is not always possible to achieve in GTM due to various reasons such as too small of sample sizes, not enough time/resources to run an experiment long enough to achieve it, and others.[92] But you can still benefit from experimentation.

---

[92] A common threshold for statistical significance is 0.05. In simple words, there is a 95% probability that the test provides reliable results. It is measured by "p", a value associated with a hypothesis test. When "p < 0.05," it indicates that the observed data is unlikely to have occurred if the null hypothesis is true, leading to the rejection of the null hypothesis in favor of the alternative hypothesis. Where "p ≥ 0.05" suggests that the observed data is consistent with the null hypothesis, and there isn't sufficient evidence to reject it. You easily calculate "p" with online calculators and testing tools or make your own calculations.

Experimentation Loop

"We love experimentation. That's where the gold nuggets come from."
Reggie Fils-Aime, businessperson, previously CEO of Nintendo's North American branch

It all starts with deciding what you want to test in the experiment. In a standard experimentation process, there is a phase called **inception**, where you create experiment ideas. This can be a huge trap for some beginner practitioners because of "garbage in, garbage out." You should purposefully develop your experimentation program to bring value to your GTM operation instead of getting hyped up about it and shooting random experiments out.

On each and every growth workshop that I run for companies, I always ask one question up front:

"How many experiments should you run per week?"

While the popular answer is from three to 10 each sprint cycle, taking this number at its face value can lead to bullshit (forgive my French) experimentation.

The fast-growing companies such as Amazon, Booking.com, Airbnb, and Meta run thousands of automated tests each day to stay ahead of the competition and learn what works well for their business. This is outside the reach of most GTM companies.

What is obtainable is to design experimentation programs around your GTM objectives and focus your first experimentation sprints in a single direction, which will generate a critical mass of proof and momentum that experimentation really works well for you.[93] Anecdotally speaking, most teams have more than a 10% success rate. Following this logic, your worst-case scenario is that you launch 10 tests, and one is likely going to be a win. Fair enough? Now, let's move to how to get the experimentation program started.

---

93 Thomke, S.H. (2020). Experimentation Works: The Surprising Power of Business Experiments. Harvard Business Review Press.

For most teams, an interconnected GTM experimentation loop works best since the processes of inception and actual experimentation are closely interconnected. There are two stages of making decisions with confidence in GTM, and they provide different levels of confidence:

- **The Inception Stage** provides initial proof and is closely connected to the assumption mapping process you are already familiar with. It provides you with an idea that something could work but not enough evidence that you would feel confident to do a full-blown execution just yet. This stage can be based on observations, anecdotal, based on previous experiences, expert advice, competitor research, market and data analysis, customer interviews, social media monitoring, and/or surveys.

- **The Experimentation Stage** provides a stronger level of evidence, which is statistically significant. Testing is usually done at the fraction of a product or with a prototype of the solution you are investigating. Experimentation consists of five sequential steps:

    1. Hypothesis creation: what do you believe will happen? What needs to happen to find the experiment successful?
    2. Setting up the experiment and launching it.
    3. Collecting data and analysis.
    4. Gathering and mapping insights from the data.

If successful, implement the changes and transfer the learnings into the knowledge base you have created. Even if the experiment is not successful, you can still generate learnings from it that continue to serve the Inception Phase. This is how the experimentation loop closes and creates an ongoing process of learning, progress, and growth, which nurtures the competitive edge of the company.

Best-in-class companies view experimentation as an ongoing strategic commitment that produces a competitive edge, new insights for business improvements, and impacts the business results favorably.

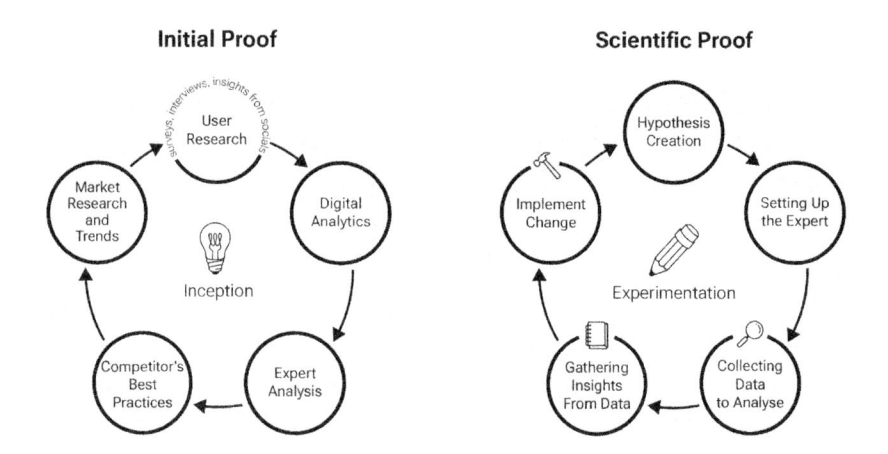

Initial Proof

Inception
- Market Research and Trends
- User Research (surveys, interviews, insights from socials)
- Digital Analytics
- Expert Analysis
- Competitor's Best Practices

Scientific Proof

Experimentation
- Hypothesis Creation
- Setting Up the Expert
- Collecting Data to Analyse
- Gathering Insights From Data
- Implement Change

Before spinning the experimentation wheel, remember that you have to set your operation for success. Do not do experimentation just for the sake of experimentation. Center it around your GTM objectives and choose the battlefield where you are most likely to win.

Do not scatter experiments too broadly (e.g., optimizing landing pages, testing price points, testing value propositions in ads, testing new promising channels, etc.), as you are unlikely to generate a critical mass of success on each front or even achieve statistical significance within the limited resources you have at your disposal.

Most teams know what to do and are great at generating ideas, but the critical difference is how much experimentation can really be done and learned from. The theory, "the faster you experiment and learn, the faster you will grow," holds true. In reality, it breaks when GTM teams start launching scrappy experiments that produce inconclusive results because they optimize around launching a specific number of tests per week rather than what will make an impact.

Focus on experimentation towards a limited number of objectives (1 to 5) that will make the most impact on your GTM operations. Your first wins should comfortably present and defend the value of experimentation. A Growth Ideation Workshop, which I co-developed with growth expert Anuj Adhiya, can help you generate ideas for the experimentation process in 90 minutes.

Once you've determined your objective for experimentation sprints, it's time to learn how to execute them.

Experimentation in Practice

"If you know the answer, it's not an experiment."
Jeff Bezos, founder and executive chairman of Amazon

Many companies aim to make data-driven decisions and want to establish an experimentation process. Running a single experiment or a set of experiments, as we showed in the ECP chapter, is a good start. Ultimately, most organizations aim towards a process of continuous experimentation and learning to navigate the wild waters of GTM, speed up their growth, and secure their chances to cross the chasm.

Some companies want to commit to running a certain number of experiments per day/week/month, and they push hard to achieve this benchmark. But this can be a trap of faux experimentation. You don't want to experiment for the sake of doing experiments that sadly produce little-to-no added value. Your resources could be better used elsewhere.

To learn how to differentiate between faux and purposeful experimentation, let's play a game — is it an experiment or not?

Question: Is writing a blog post an experiment?
Nope.

Question: Is an A/B test of a newsletter opt-in form on a high-traffic blog post an experiment?
More so.

Harvard professor Stefan H. Thomke studies the fastest-growing companies that conduct millions of experiments to grow their business by creating unfair advantages based on their proprietary insights. He provides the following guidance on thinking about what is or could be an experiment and what is off the table to test. Here are the questions to consider:

- Does the experiment idea have a testable hypothesis?
- Is this decision a done deal, or will the experiment influence it? (If it is a done deal, just put it in your work backlog and experiment with it after

you see the results.)
- Can the company do the experiment (they have the resources, infrastructure to measure, budget, etc.)?
- How can you ensure the results of the experiment are reliable?
- Do you understand cause and effect?
- Can you create business value with the experiment?
- Are you ready, as a company, to make decisions based on the results of experiments?

If the answer to all of the above is yes, then congratulations! You have an experiment idea.

But is it worth executing? There are multiple activities and trade-offs associated with executing an experiment. And there are always more ideas than we could realistically execute. In GTM, you must be laser-focused on what battles are worth fighting since you have scarce resources. This is why prioritization becomes your best friend. How do you select the experiments that will most likely move the needle in your business?

If you are just starting out and working towards a single objection with your experimentation efforts, you can use a simple prioritization framework such as Impact and Ease. We present this matrix in the Growth Ideation Workshop, and it works perfectly well when you select the low-hanging fruits for a mission-critical single-objective experimentation program.

How about if you work in more complex organizations where GTM is only one of the strategic business areas and there are multiple dependencies within the organization?

Prioritization gets more complex. I asked Jeremy Epperson, who spent 16 years consulting and advising for the fastest-growing startups in Silicon Valley, to share his CRO Prioritization framework, which was developed on a meta-analysis of more than 5,400 experiments that he ran with his team.

		Experiment 1 Name Description	Experiment 2 Name Description
Business Allignment	Does this improve our 90 day KPI?	- - - -	- - - -
	Can you support this with specific evidence?	- - - -	- - - -
	Does this improve user experience?	- - - -	- - - -
Relevancy	Is this at the bottom of the funnel?	- - - -	- - - -
	Is this test visible to most users?	- - - -	- - - -
Impact	Does this target 100% of users?	- - - -	- - - -
	Can this get above a 7% lift?	- - - -	- - - -
Dependencies	No high Level of Effort of Design?	- - - -	- - - -
	No high Level of Effort of Dev?	- - - -	- - - -
Statistical Significance	Enter visitors per week	- - - -	- - - -
	Enter baseline CVR?	- - - -	- - - -
	Outcome Description		
	Priority - Total	- - - -	- - - -

This visual is the courtesy of Jeremy Epperson

Keeping and nurturing an experimentation backlog is the spine of your experimentation knowledge and a treasury of learning for your organizations. New ideas always occur. Make sure to capture them in a single shared space. An Experimentation Backlog Spreadsheet does the job, but some teams prefer using software such as Notion, Miro, Trello, Jira, etc., as their experiment idea banks.

Yet, the best practice is to filter the half-baked, non-actionable ideas sooner rather than later. Keeping half-baked experiment ideas without hypotheses and well-developed measures creates clutter and confusion in your experimentation backlog. Develop an understanding that only well-presented ideas can reside in your backlog. Just the act of thinking about how to write an experiment card brings clarity and purpose to the experimentation process.

Finally, it's time to spin the experimentation wheel. After deciding on which experiments to do in the next sprint, assign the ownership and keep a clear record of their status throughout the sprint. Especially at the beginning of the experimentation process, there will be friction, and the process of developing, launching, and analyzing experiments will have to be sequentially improved. It might take several to get it right, but it's worth doing it.

Experimentation provides systematic proprietary findings that drive the business forward and signal it's moving on the right track. It's a path to the goal of the GTM journey. Experimentation makes us better professionals and people. Less ego, more stamina, increased collaboration, learning by doing, and ultimately calling the right shots – it is wonderful.

Your Turn to Go-to-Market

"From overwhelmed to hyper-focused."

(I have no idea who said that, but I love it)

Congratulations, you have reached the end of this book. Thank you so much for picking it up and following along on our rocky boat in the wild waters of GTM.

My One Metric That Matters for this book is the number of insights per page, so I will happily hear your feedback on how well I delivered. Before I wish you good luck on your GTM journey, I have one final gift for you.

By now, you know that GTM is so much more than launching new solutions. It starts much sooner and provides guidance after the launch as well. Nurturing GTM strategic competence gives you a competitive edge and significantly contributes to your sustainable business success.

That's why I'm sending you off with a fully-fledged 90-day Go-To-Market Plan.

					Common nominator
Month 1: Mission Critical = Doing the Research & Setting up fundamentals	Week 1	Agree on the objectives and what does success of your GTM look like	Meet the team - do at least 3 internal interviews	Review their historic data	Focus on the inside - team & company
	Week 2	Conduct a solid market analysis	Review the competition	Have hypothesis of beachhead segment ready	Focus on the outside - market
	Week 3	Run at least 12 interviews or a survey to learn more about your beachhead segment	Refine your understanding of the Beachhead Segment with these insights	Understand what channels are they using and what offers are attractive to them	Focus on the customers
	Week 4	Run a WTP - willingness to pay research	Revise if the offers are coherent with what your beachhead segment needs	Make sure that the business model is sustainable by running projections	Focus on the offer
	Week 5	Map customer journey	Select critical metrics to track and implement event tracking plan	Prepare the dashboard	Focus on measuring what is going on
Month 2: Mission Critical = Run the first experiments and empirically test your assumptions	Week 6	Do the positioning exercise	Refine branding and messaging from your findings	Run experiments if your ECP reacts well to the messaging - measure traffic with marketing tests	Focus on presentation
	Week 7	Refine your offer to what you have learned so far	Get feedback on your offers with usability testings	Run experiments such as waitlist or presale to validate that ECP would pay for the offer as presented	Focus on testing the offer
	Week 8	Dive deep into the channels - what are the "natural channels" for your ICP	Test different channels and compare how the conversion behaves	Get some additional fuel in by creating a Growth Loop	Focus on growth fundamentals
	Week 9	Craft your customer journey	Select 2 to 3 channels that you bet on and leave some space for experimentation	Secure that you can repeatedly attract, convert, retain and engage customers to refer you	Focus on building a repeatable growth system
Month 2: Mission critical = Run the first experiments and empirically test your assumptions	Week 10	Prepare a simple GTM plan for your endeavour, which is easy to communicate and understand	Secure your GTM budget	Communicate internally your GTM system and get and nurture the buy in and support for your ops	Focus on internal buy-in
	Week 11	Formalise your GTM team	Organize weekly or bi-weekly sprints	Introduce your meeting agenda	Focus on aligning the team
	Week 12	Formalize the research and customer discovery process	Formalize the experimentation process	Prepare your backlog to capture findings	Focus on spinning on the experimentation loop
	Week 13	Analyze thoroughly of what has been learned so far	Make adjustments to the GTM strategy if needed	Stay open to opportunities and nurture agile and pragmatic mindset to seize them	Focus on interaction and learnings

Smaller teams and individuals can follow it almost to a tee, but larger teams in more complex organizations will be better off setting it up and adjusting it in their project management software. However you apply it, make sure to assign reasonable due dates and assign task owners according to their superpowers and availability.

You can make good adjustments to the plan by:

1. **Revisiting past launches and GTM activities** of your company or organization. Check if there is a written plan, a project management board, or a spreadsheet that could provide guidance.

2. **Co-create the plan with your colleagues**. Ask for collaboration and include many experts from your company or outside experts in bringing your GTM strategy to life. Involve the team in your planning process early on and learn from their expertise and shared experience to develop your best plan. The best GTM plans are proprietary. Find your X-factor to increase your chances to win.

3. **Look for inspiration from your competitors and role model companies**. Check how they manage their GTM and see if someone from those companies could mentor you. Are there any podcasts, social media posts, blogs, or conference talks in which they discuss their GTM strategies? You cannot do a full-blown Apple launch event if you have $2,000 to invest in getting traction, but you can still be inspired by it.

4. **Start with verified GTM templates.** You get more specific plans (for ecommerce, SaaS, sales-driven organizations, etc.) online. When deciding whom to trust for such guidance, my bets are always on practitioners who have walked the talk. Use plans that are similar to your company's size and business model.

With tested GTM plans, you can start developing GTM Standard Operating Procedures (SOPs) that will help you do the planning in a much more structured and effective way. It is also a fail-safe way to ensure that the GTM strategy will be developed and executed according to your best practices. Creating a well-documented GTM plan may seem tedious and time-consuming, but it's a worthwhile investment in the long run.

Finally, I wish to say farewell by emphasizing that mindset is very important to grow as you are growing your business. It will be tough. There will be roadblocks. But no great company was ever built as "easy as a breeze." So hold on, stay resilient, adapt quickly, done is better than perfect, and failing equals learning in GTM.

GTM journeys might feel solitary at times. Not everyone shares this intense experience. But you can surround yourself with other GTM-curious minds who share your passion for the field and offer helpful guidance based on their expertise. Join fellow GTM strategists at www.gtmstrategiest.com.

No one went to school to study GTM. It is a skill we develop by doing it. Share your insights, best practices, and learnings with others to make their lives and our field better. There are many ways to do it; you do not have to become a LinkedIn influencer, a podcaster, or a public speaker. Doing an event, sharing some of your templates, mentoring others – everything helps greatly in improving the GTM discipline.

With the right mindset and a commitment to continuous learning and improvement, you will succeed and possibly even create one of the stellar cases and careers in GTM history.

Be bold, take risks, and keep pushing forward.

I am cheering for you!

Maja Voje

Key Takeaways:

- GTM values speed and agility over anything else. Tactics will inevitably change over time. Do not wait for your GTM plan to be perfect; learn how to improve it by starting to execute it.

- There are static and dynamic components to well-oiled GTM machines.

- Static: Prepare the grounds and do the fundamentals right. That means building a team, securing budget and other resources, and setting up processes and tools on how you will be doing this.

- Dynamic: Kick-off rapid experimentation process to test and learn fast and make it happen. Establish a GTM weekly meeting, launch experiments, and tweak your GTM actions towards what you have discovered through experimentation.

• The essentials in your GTM execution backpack should be:

1. **Timeline**. This usually consists of milestones, roadmaps, and OKRs.

2. **Teams.** GTM requires many competencies and skills that are hard to find in a single person. Interdisciplinary collaboration also creates many synergies and ultimately increases your chances to win.

3. **Organization.** GTM teams meet regularly, measure the progress, adjust tactics, and share insights and progress reports with the "higher-ups." Even for smaller teams, regular meetings make a lot of sense since they help with accountability and alignment.

4. **Tools.** GTM teams can be categorized as project management tools, analytics tools, tools to systemize communication and collaboration, and technical tools to actually get the work done. While work can be managed in a spreadsheet, purpose-built tools add value. Keep the stack lean and compatible.

5. **Budget**. Your job as a GTM strategist is to negotiate and secure the budget that includes costs of labor, media buying, tooling, and external services (if needed) and has some contingency because "just in case" always happens in GTM.

• Spin the wheel of experimentation to make decisions with confidence based on empirical proof. Experimentation should be ongoing and centered on key GTM objectives. Each growth idea should have a testable hypothesis.

- Most teams have more than a 10% success rate with their experiments.

- When preparing your GTM experimentation plan, score experiment ideas and first prioritize those with the highest score.

- Each winning GTM plan includes proprietary elements, those that are specific to you. Do not only copy-paste other company's plans. Develop a plan that will create unfair advantages for your company.

- There will be roadblocks. Hold on, stay resilient, adapt fast, done is better than perfect, and failing is learning in GTM.

- Document your GTM path, share learnings, and become a decorated GTM team member yourself by helping others make their GTM route a bit smoother. Best GTM knowledge is not shared in schools; it is acquired by brave practitioners who are walking the talk.

To-Do List:

☐ Present your GTM plan in a clear framework such as the GTM Canvas.

☐ Optional: Do the Growth Ideation workshop by Anuj Adhiya and Maja Voje https://miro.com/miroverse/growth-hacking-ideation-workshop/

☐ Set up your experimentation process and score the ideas.

☐ Create a 90-day GTM plan.

☐ Find help, inspiration, and encouragement during your GTM journey in our community, and continue the conversation at www.gtmstrategist.com.

Find all the worksheets, frameworks, and models mentioned in this chapter at *https://gtmstrategist.com/resources*. They are free and yours to benefit from.

Glossary

Big 4 - Big 4 refers to the four largest professional services firms by revenue: Deloitte, KPMG, PwC, and EY.

CAGR - The compound annual growth rate (CAGR) is the annualized average rate of revenue growth between two given years, assuming growth takes place at an exponentially compounded rate.

The CAGR between given years X and Z, where Z - X = N, is the number of years between the two given years, is calculated as follows: CAGR, year X to year Z = [(value in year Z/value in year X) ^ (1/N)-1]

Customer churn rate - The percentage of customers who cancel their subscription or stop using a company's product/service during a given period. A high churn rate indicates that a company needs to improve its product or service offerings to retain customers.

> **Formula**: *Number of customers lost during a given period / total number of customers at the beginning of the period x 100.*
>
> **Example**: If a company starts with 1,000 customers and loses 100 customers over a year, the churn rate is 10%. The rate at which customers stop doing business with your company.
>
> The best SaaS solution gets a 1.5 to 3% churn rate. With 25% monthly churn, the average customers last for four months (100/25 = 4). If the churn is 5%, the average customer lasts for 20 months (100/5 = 20), and if the curb is 2%, the average customer lasts for 50 months (100/2=50).

Customer Acquisition Costs (CAC) - The amount you spend to acquire a new customer. The cost of acquiring a new customer is a critical metric that every business should track. When time passes, it is important to ensure that the cost of acquiring a new customer is less than the amount of revenue that the customer will generate for the company.

Formula: *Total cost of sales and marketing / number of new customers acquired.*

Example: If a company spends $50,000 on sales and marketing and acquires 100 new customers, the CAC is $500.

It is recommended in SaaS that the CAC should be under ⅓ LTV. If you have a lifespan of a user for 20 months and charge $30 per month per customer, it means that your LTV is $600 per customer, and you can invest ⅓ of that, so $200 to acquire it.

Customer retention rate - The percentage of customers who continue to use a company's product/service during a given period. A high retention rate indicates that a company has loyal customers and is providing value to them.

Formula: *(Number of customers at the end of the period - number of new customers acquired during the period) / number of customers at the beginning of the period x 100.*

Example: If a company starts with 1,000 customers, acquires 200 new customers, and ends with 900 customers, the retention rate is 90%. Most businesses use Daily Active users (DAU), Monthly Active Users (MAU), and retention cohorts to measure retention.

Economic moat - According to Warren Buffett, an economic moat refers to the sustainable competitive advantage that a company possesses over its competitors. It represents the unique factors that protect a company's market position and allow it to earn above-average profits over the long term.

Economies of scale - This refers to the cost advantages that companies gain as production becomes more efficient, allowing them to spread costs over a larger quantity of goods.

Event Tracking Plans - Event tracking in analytics refers to monitoring and recording user interactions or actions on a digital platform, providing valuable insights for understanding user behavior and optimizing user experience. You can find guidance and templates on how to create an event-tracking plan here: *https://amplitude.com/blog/create-tracking-plan.*

FAANG - Refers to the five epic Silicon Valley companies: Facebook (now Meta), Amazon, Apple, Netflix and Google (now Alphabet).

Gross Margin - Gross margin gives a good indication of "how much does it cost you to do business vs. how much you make from doing business." While it does not include all costs and revenues into consideration, it is a good indication for GTM because it can be easily presented just for the mission you are on and isolate your GTM operation from other things in business that are not directly connected to your GTM.

> **Gross margin** = [(Revenue - Cost of goods sold) / Revenue] x 100.
>
> Successful SaaS businesses typically achieve 70 to 80%, according to OpenView's yearly survey that includes hundreds of SaaS businesses in their sample. Compared to products, which is a much higher number, gross margins go from 20 to 50% for most products, which heavily depends on the category.

Level of effort (LOE) - The framework stands for the support that needs to be provided from other areas or departments to execute the experiment.

Lifetime value - The total amount of revenue a customer will generate for a company during their lifetime. This metric is important for understanding the long-term value of a customer and can help companies make informed decisions about how much they should spend to acquire new customers.

> **Formula:** *(Average Order Value * Number of Repeat Transactions * Average Customer Lifespan).*
>
> **Example**: If a company has an average order value of $100, and a customer makes three repeat transactions and has an average lifespan of 2 years, the CLV is $600.

Metrics that signal GTM success

Other metrics that can signal your GTM success in the revenue stage are:

Monthly Recurring Revenue (MRR): MRR is a key metric for subscription-based businesses that helps measure the predictable revenue stream over a certain period. It represents the total amount of revenue generated by all active subscribers in a given month. The amount of recurring revenue generated each month by your business.

> **Formula:** *MRR = (Number of paying customers x Average revenue per customer) / Number of months in the period.*
>
> **Example:** A company has 100 active subscribers who pay $50 per month for its services. The MRR for one month would be: MRR = 100 x $50, MRR = $5,000

Website conversion rate: This metric measures the percentage of website visitors who take a desired action, such as making a purchase or filling out a form. A high conversion rate indicates the website is effectively engaging visitors and turning them into customers.

> **Formula:** *Conversion Rate = (Number of Conversions / Number of Website Visitors) * 100*
>
> **Example:** If a website had 1,000 visitors and 100 of them made a purchase, the conversion rate would be: Conversion Rate = (100 / 1,000) * 100 = 10%, which is rather good. In ecommerce, the conversion rates are normally between 0.5 to 3%.

Sales Conversion Rate: The sales conversion rate in B2B is the percentage of leads that convert into paying customers. A high conversion rate indicates that a company has an effective sales process.

> **Formula:** *Number of paying customers / number of leads x 100*
>
> **Example:** If a company generates 500 leads and converts 100 of them into paying customers, the conversion rate is 20%.

Opportunity Win Rate (OWR): This measures the percentage of opportunities a company successfully converts into deals. This metric helps evaluate the effectiveness of the sales team and identify areas of improvement in the sales process.

Formula: *OWR = (Number of won opportunities / Total number of opportunities) x 100*

Example: If a company had 50 opportunities in a given period and won 20 of them, the OWR would be: OWR = (20/50) x 100, OWR = 40%.

Net Promoter Score (NPS) - NPS is a measure of customer satisfaction and loyalty. It's determined by asking customers to rate their likelihood of recommending your solution. It is calculated based on the percentage of answers users provide when answering the question: "How likely would you recommend this product?" on a scale from 0 to 10. The responses are then grouped into three categories: detractors (0-6), passives (7-8), and promoters (9-10).

Formula: *NPS = (% of Promoters - % of Detractors) x 100.*

Example:
- 78% of users gave 9-10 marks (promoters)
- 15% scored 7-8 (passives)
- 7% of users answered 6 or less (detractors)

In this case, NPS is 78-7 = 71, which is a fairly good score for any industry.

Price elasticity of demand - The ratio of the percentage change in quantity demanded of a product to the percentage change in price. Different goods have different price elasticities.

Think about this from an extreme perspective when you would double your price. If 50% or more of your customers would keep buying from you and you could still make more profit, this is an inelastic good. Such examples would be gasoline, prescription drugs, luxury goods, and life essentials. Customers are unlikely to churn in the short run but would be encouraged to actively seek alternatives in the mid-term. Oppositely, if you doubled the price of a relatively generic good with multiple alternatives and low necessity, such as a white-label chocolate bar or a plastic fork, the demand is likely to drop by more than 50% since there is too high of price sensitivity that you could justify this action and remain profitable. This is an elastic good, and buyers are price-sensitive.

RASCI Matrix - The RASCI matrix helps to clarify the roles and responsibilities of different team members who work together on a project. RASCI stands for Responsible, Accountable, Supporting, Consulted, and Informed.

Sprint cycle - A sprint is a short, focused period of time during which a team works intensively on a specific project, task, or goal.

Statistical significance - Statistical significance, often denoted by the p-value, assesses whether observed differences or effects in data are likely to be real or due to chance.

A small p-value (usually < 0.05) indicates high statistical significance, while a larger p-value suggests that observed results may not be meaningful and could be attributed to random variation.

In simple words, you would like to be 95% confident that the result is valid, if you have p=0.05. Most survey and split testing tools calculate the statistical significance for you.

Unicorn - A unicorn company is a privately held startup that has reached a valuation of $1 billion or more.

Viral Coefficient (K) - A metric that signifies if the product has a referral or even viral potential to expend on.

>**Formula:** *Viral Coefficient (K) = i (number of invites sent) * conv (conversion % of accepted invites).*
>
>**Example**: 2,000 customers sent out 5,000 invites on your site (invitation rate is 2.5). For every 10 invitations received, one gets clicked (acceptance rate is 0.1). The coral coefficient for the solution is 25%.

GTM STRATEGIST

Whenever K>1, you have some virality going on that could lead to exponential growth. Whenever you do not, you should reconsider the validity of your viral loop for the product.

Word-of-Mouth (WOM) - Some referrals happen naturally outside your product analytics. Word-of-mouth is the oldest and still relevant in today's world. In service businesses, up to 70% of new business can come from referrals. You can measure it by surveying the customers and calculating the share of WOM referrals and recommendations.

Acknowledgments

People say it takes a village to raise a child. And this was definitely true for this book. In the year it took to create it, more than 1,500 pages were written, verified, and critically thought out by wonderful field experts who helped me on this journey.

But first and foremost, I need to thank my husband of more than a decade, Anže Voje, for being supportive, patient, incredibly kind, and very encouraging on this journey. Without you, I do not think I would have had the courage and stamina to go here. I love and appreciate you to the moon.

Next, I'd love to give a shoutout to my family, Sabina, Brane, Jure, and Simona Knehtl, and all of my other relatives. My uncle Drago, who is a retired major of the French Foreign Legion, gave me a quote I posted on a wall and read every single day.

"We finish what we have started.
Despite all the obstacles on the way and the loss of enthusiasm.
With our natural pride."

It became my anchor for getting the job done and it's a principle to live by.

It was a lonely and challenging year of maker-mode. But thank you so much for encouraging me on this journey and understanding that I have a GTM science to write.

Third, kudos to my GTM special ops! Our editor Laura Kluz stoically tolerated me to make changes as I was learning and evolving, and guided me on the journey. Also, to my designer/developer/brand manager/cousin Domen Klinc for making such a wonderful brand that makes this book look fantastic. Nejc Jamšček and Ognjen Bošković for being the generals and muscles of our content engine, helping me to focus on the quality of the book in its final stages, and to Ula Stepančič for helping us enable the Amazon sales and Matej Aleksov for taking up to 14 of my phone calls a day and executing mission-critical assignments with me.

You are one hell of a team; without you, this launch would not be as successful. Teamwork is dream work!

Last but not least, a GIANT kudos to all of the contributors to this book who challenged me, provided me with your knowledge and experience, and helped me create this masterpiece that it is today!

Thanks to you all:

Amplitude – for pitching in with analytics and dashboards.
Paddle – for working together on the Pricing chapter.
Miro – for co-creating and hosting our GTM frameworks in Miroverse.

Sean Ellis	Romina Kavčič
Wes Bush	Matic Batagelj
Rishi Chowdhury	Ishita Jariwala
Eugene Segal	Tadej Udovič
Dr. Else van der Berg	Dr. Blaž Zupan
Sara Stojanovski	Emilia Korczynska
Jim Huffman	Tjaša Saje
Leah Tharin	Tim Berce
Robert Kaminski	Ognjen Bošković
Anthony Pierri	Patrik Bogataj
Jeremy Epperson	Vuk Vukosavljević
Dr. Maja Konečnik Ruzzier	Ignas Gee
Jesus Raquena	Ben Williams
Andrej Peršolja	Jaïr Halevi
Matic Moličnik	Joanna Bunker
Jaka Berdnik	Tania Kefs
Simon Belak	Anuj Adhiya
Rok Hrastnik	

My brain works like a hive. I play my best game if I continue to bounce ideas, rethink concepts, and build on others' inceptions based on my own findings. We were buzzing and creating wonderful science together.

To my test readers and experts who brainstormed with me – you will forever have my gratitude, and I am happy to return the goodwill anytime.

We are in it to win it.

Let's go and connect with experts in this amazing GTM community.

Knowledge is power.

Network is leverage.

One final thought: if you enjoyed this book and – even better – if this advice already helped you go-to-market, it would mean the world to me if you review this book on Amazon. Spreading the word will help even more GTM strategists find the book and help our community thrive. Thank you!

Your friend Maja

Printed in Great Britain
by Amazon